Alsager in the Great Wa

*Dedicated to the Royal British Legion and its work*

Every effort has been made to acknowledge copyright for photographs and references in this book.

The author is grateful for the individuals, archives and libraries who have given permission to reproduce pictures and documents.

All proceeds from this book go to the Royal British Legion Poppy Appeal.

The Royal British Legion, Alsager Branch, would like to thank the following sponsors of this publication:

Rotary Club of Alsager

Alsager Town Council

Alsager Lions

Alsager Town Council

William Gwilt

Joseph Edwards & Sons

Lynton Exports (Alsager)

Manor House Hotel (Alsager)

Mr H. & Mrs E. Pinkney

Rotary International

Steve Wallace Photography

Mrs K Knight

Anonymous sponsor

*Cover: Walter Hollinshead (seated left) and his friend, F. Holland, (centre rear) with whom he established Holland & Hollinshead Motors in Alsager after the Great War.*

# Contents

# Alsager in the Great War

## Preface

Since 1922 the Alsager Branch of the Royal British Legion (RBL) has maintained its proud tradition of remembering and honouring the service and sacrifice of those killed and injured in wars, especially those listed on the town War Memorial. Since the War Memorials Act (1923) Alsager Urban District Council and Congleton Borough Council were enabled "under certain circumstances to maintain, repair and protect war memorials vested in them". Both local authorities used public money for these purposes when requested. This practice continued until 2009 when the new unitary authority was created. As the 100th Anniversary of the outbreak of the First World War neared, the restoration of the memorial became an urgent priority. Damage to the stone statue became more obvious and a professional restoration was needed.

Jim Sutton and I suggested that a Trust be established to raise funds to restore the Alsager War Memorial in time for the 100th Anniversary of the Declaration of War which would occur on 4th August 2014. The Alsager War Memorial Restoration Trust was formally established on 5th September 2012. By May 2014, the Trust had raised £8,220 in grants and awards from Alsager Town Council and War Memorials Trust and in donations from groups and individuals in the town. The first stage of the restoration could begin.

In preparing for the Rededication of the War Memorial, the Trust produced a brief resume of each of those named on the memorial. Much of this initial research was carried out by Mrs Cynthia Ankers and it became clear that service records for some of the men could not be found or verified. There were others who had been buried locally but were not commemorated on the memorial; the reasons were not known at the time.

After the Rededication Service held on 3rd August 2014, the Alsager Branch (RBL) agreed to honour all the servicemen with ceremonies to be held at the War Memorial on the hundredth anniversary of each of their deaths. The first of these was held on Thursday, 13th August 2015, when wreaths were laid by representatives of Alsager Town Council, the B'HOYS of Alsager and Alsager RBL. The ceremonies will continue until all the servicemen who did not return have been so commemorated.

At this point a fuller research of the lives and service of the "Fallen" was undertaken by Rob Blaney (Alsager RBL). He produced accurate biographies of each so that these could be read out at the relevant anniversary ceremony. Following this research, Rob proposed that a book be produced about all of Alsager's "Fallen" and that any proceeds from its sale be donated to the RBL's Poppy Appeal. Alsager RBL agreed that this was a worthwhile venture and gave its support to the project.

The present volume is the result of many months of painstaking research carried out by Rob with zeal and a great care for accurate reporting. It fills a major gap in our knowledge and extends our appreciation of those who went to war, of their families and of a community which would be changed by the conflict and its aftermath. Those who did not come home had tales to tell. This book provides a significant part of that missing information. A picture of a small village at the start of the twentieth century emerges, using reports and pictures from the newspapers to supplement the servicemen's records. The ever-increasing casualty lists confronted the whole community with the effects of a brutal war. Rob also pays tribute to the sense of duty and the sacrifice of Alsager's "Fallen" in the service of their country.

So the next time you read the names on the Alsager War Memorial or when you stand there "in Remembrance" on November 11th, you will be able to answer the question: "Who were they?" And we will all be able to honour more appropriately those who did not return and so give them due recognition.

> *"We are the dead. Short days ago*
>
> *We lived, felt dawn, saw sunset glow,*
>
> *Loved and were loved, and now we lie*
>
> *In Flanders fields."*

Excerpt from "In Flanders Fields" by John McCrae

Les Bickerton

President

Alsager Branch

The Royal British Legion

1 June 2016

# Introduction

This book is the story of the men and women who served in the Great War of 1914-18 and of the community of Alsager during that period.

In his poem 'Anzac Cove and After', Anglican Curate of Alsager, Harold Augustine Thomas wrote from Gallipoli from personal experience of the horrors of war and anticipated how future generations might treat the conflict like 'tourists'. He writes of his dead comrades;

*'Surely their fame shall live immortally,*

*With light of age-long glory overshed,*

*Who here gave all for Country King and God.*

*No! Some sleek tourist in the days to be*

*Shall name these stones empurpled with our blood*

*"A lonely cairn of the forgotten dead" '.*

His ironic prediction has partly come true; war is glorified, battle sites have become stopping points for holidaymakers, and many of the soldiers killed have been forgotten. Alsager is proud of its heritage. This book helps to perpetuate the memory of those who fought and gives background information about Alsager between 1914 and 1920, putting it into historical context.

For the purpose of those who are not from Alsager, it is a town in South Cheshire two miles from the Staffordshire border. The surrounding settlements of Betchton, Thurlwood and Linley are included in this book because some of the men commemorated on the Alsager War Memorial came from those smaller communities.

How did Alsager react to the commencement of hostilities and gear itself up to support the war effort? As the war dragged on for over five years how did it sustain this support? This book tries to answer these questions and describes how the town coped with the stress of nearly five years of war. It gives details of the men commemorated on Alsager War Memorial and tells the stories of others with an Alsager connection who were killed, but whose names were not included on the Memorial. There are also many biographical details of the servicemen and women who served and survived. Finally, there are chapters on the planning and construction of the War Memorial, its history to the present day, and of the work of the British Legion.

# Alsager before the Great War

In 1912, Mr Ecclestone, addressing the annual dinner of the B'hoys, a men's social club in Alsager, said the town was one *'of the best residential areas he knew'*. It had the *'advantages of a town without the disadvantages' … and it was 'sociable'*. The B'hoys epitomised the social make-up of a thriving and prosperous community. The B'hoys were formed in 1911 and included many of the well-to-do men of the town: manufacturers, managers and professionals who had moved to the village to enjoy its rural charms and attractive housing away from the pollution of the Potteries. By 1912 Alsager was a prosperous and pleasant community with no slum housing, and little crime. It was a semi-rural settlement which celebrated its gala days, harvest festivals, and parades.

In 1973 Mrs Mabel Wilson, in her 'Jottings of Alsager', described Alsager in Christmas 1913 as an almost idyllic place. It was a *'lovely wooded village where nearly all the people knew one another …The nights in our village were silent except when the carollers went out in the cold night air. On the crisp sunny Christmas days, when the mere was still frozen, then it would become crowded with revellers. The curlers curled, the skaters waltzed and the learners laughed and tumbled…With its many trees, frosted and silhouetted against a blue sky its few main roads lined with cottages, the larger residences approached by wooded drives in isolated spots, the local taxi or cabby man Mr Band perched high in the seat or a mirror liked polished coach…The motor car then had not invaded Crewe Road, therefore the main road almost belonged to the village children, large skipping ropes stretched across from one pavement to the other…'*

*Curlers on the Mere. Photo: Sentinel Newspaper*

Within one year of this innocent description, Alsager's men were enlisting in the armed forces, its people were involved in raising money and making clothes for war effort, and the town sank into five years of great stress and misery. Children said goodbye to their fathers, and employees on the farms and the railway sheds were asked to work harder and make sacrifices.

Alsager's development had been rapid during the second part of the nineteenth century. Until the eighteen fifties it was just a small farming settlement. The open heath or common land had been enclosed in 1821 and parcels of land sold to buyers. The Alsager lake, the Mere, was unencumbered by housing, development was sparse, and roads were poor. Alsager was not on a major route way, the main road to Knutsford being north of the village at Lawton. In 1841 Alsager had a population of 446 and 87 houses. Most people worked in agriculture. The coming of the railway in October 1848 improved communications with the Potteries and this encouraged new residents to settle in the village. Villagers could find work in Stoke and commute to and from work each day. Alsager's economy developed and diversified.

In 1891 the Alsager Locomotive Sheds were built as a facility to provide accommodation and repair for railway engines. Although Agriculture was still important (Alsager farms won several of the prizes in the South Cheshire Agricultural Society competitions in the 1890s), the township was becoming important for its railway network. The railway sheds accommodated up to 15 engines and up to 100 men were employed there in 1914. In addition marshalling yards for 14 sidings were established. The yard loaded trains with coal from local collieries which were marshalled forward to various destinations. The engine sheds employed drivers, firemen, platelayers, and labourers. Alsager had its own Station Master and staff of porters and signalmen. The increase in railway employment boosted the town population and encouraged new housing.

*Alsager on the 1911 Ordnance Survey map. Alsager grew from 400 people in 1841 to 2,700 in 1914. Housing was built along the main roads, and land around the Mere during the 19th century*

By 1914 Alsager had a total population of 2,733 with an adult population of approximately 2,100. The civil parish and urban district was made up of 2,229 acres (902.7 hectares). Many of the working class families lived along Crewe Road, Audley Road, Shady Grove, Wesley Street and Talke Road, the wealthy in their new villas.

Apart from the railways and traditional agricultural industries, employment in local shops was important. Other local employment took the form of shoe repairing, tailoring, or gardening for the large houses. Many young women worked as domestic servants. According to Urban District Council reports Alsager was a healthy place with mortality rates below the national average. The national average of infant mortality was 10% whereas Alsager's was near 4%. The town did not have a high incidence of premature mortality. There was little overcrowding and low incidence of disease. Alsager Urban District Council's Medical Officer, Dr Kington, reported there were 42 deaths in the town in 1914 (15.3 per 1000 population) with six infant mortalities under the age of one. There were five cases of tuberculosis in 1914, three of which were fatal. All teachers were instructed by Dr Kington to prevent diphtheria and other viruses by insisting children saw a *medical assistant if they came to school with a temperature*. Population growth was greater because families moved into Alsager rather than because of the birth rate. Only 23 boys and 29 girls were born in Alsager in 1914.

In 1914 the town still had no mains electricity; it was only installed in 1928. A reliable water supply had only just been secured and water shortages had been a regular problem. The early 20th century brought a steady increase in the number of shops. For a small population the town had a wide range of commercial premises. The 1914 Kelly's Directory lists them: butchers, confectioners, jewellers, two saddlers, cycle shops, tailors, ironmongers, and several grocers including Bickerton's, Hancock's at Shady Grove corner and the Butt Lane Industrial Co-operative Society. Thomas Smith operated a family butcher from the Railway Stores, and E.J. Dean ran a hairdresser's business at Wesley Place. In the early part of the century Cooke and Gould Ltd opened the first garage, *'automobile engineers'*, as it was called, at their Falcon Motor Works. It concentrated on car repairs and hiring of Sunbeams and Fords. They also sold cycles and were agents for the Gramophone Company. William Ashmore, who later gave his name to Ashmore's Lane, (formerly called Sandy Lane) was a florist and seedsman with a nursery in The Fields (Road) and a shop in Sandbach Road.

From an analysis of the 1911 census there were very few households without work in Alsager and as the town grew a wide range of recreational clubs and societies flourished to entertain them. Eight out of ten residents who were registered as *'head of household'* in the 1911 census were born outside Alsager. Most of these households contained children or adult children who were born in Alsager. Out of a population of 2,743, 1,547 were thirty or younger. In total 789 individuals were born in Alsager, mostly young people. 633 people in Alsager were born in Staffordshire. Over 9% of households in Alsager employed servants who lived in their employer's house. In 1911 Rev. Arnold had four servants and a governess. 6% of households were headed by wealthy factory owners; 10% by professionals or managers; 33% by skilled workers, tradesmen or clerks; 10% by shopkeepers or publicans; 7% by farmers; 25% by unskilled industrial or agricultural workers, and 9% by servants.

Alsager had its own library in the form of the Alsager Club and Reading Room. The Alsager Institute was built in 1908. The town had a telephone exchange, a Fire Station and two banks; the Manchester & Liverpool District Bank, and Parr's Bank. It had a post office with its own public telephone facility.

Alsager was very self-sufficient; it was governed by its own Urban District Council employing a Medical Officer of Health, a Surveyor, a Sanitary Inspector, and a Rate and Tax Collector. Alsager County Police Station in Crewe Road employed a sergeant and six constables. There were a wide range of societies, organisations, and sports clubs. There were two tennis clubs, a golf club, and cricket, football and bowls clubs thrived. Men's clubs and societies were popular and well attended. They included men's social clubs such as The Druids and the B'hoys, the Ancient Order of Foresters, and The Primrose League. The Primrose League was a society set up to promote '*conservative values*', included both men and women. Alsager Institute built in 1898 provided a central venue for organisations to meet and it was to become an important meeting place during the Great War. In 1914 the town had two schools, the National School adjacent to Christ Church, built in 1885, and the St Mary's Church of England School, which opened in 1900. It is now the primary school annexe next to Alsager Highfields Primary School (2016.)

If you lived in 1914 you could expect a delivery of post at 7am, 1pm, and 5.15 pm, and have your letters dispatched at 11am and 8.30 pm. There was even a Sunday post service, with letters despatched at 7.15 pm.

In 1914 Alsager was very much a town rooted in the 19th century. Mabel Wilson in 'Jottings of Alsager' remembered living in a cottage at the bottom of Hall Drive. She considered it a great privilege to open the big iron gate for her father to drive the landau through. He drove for the Settle family who lived in The Hall. Although the wealthy in Alsager predominantly came from the new industrial class they employed servants, chauffeurs and maids. Divisions between rich and poor were considerable.

The social divisions even extended to the churches. Rich families even owned their own pews in Christ Church. The Alsager Methodist churches were predominantly but not exclusively supported by the working class.

With the outbreak of hostilities all the local churches and organisations came to the fore to help the war effort. Their resourcefulness was crucial to meet the challenge of supporting the troops and the community.

# Alsager -August 1914

## Background: War in Europe - the British Military and Alsager's response

Why did Britain go to war in 1914? The immediate cause was the assassination of Franz Ferdinand, the Archduke of the Austro-Hungarian Empire in July 1914. His death at the hands of Gavrilo Princip - a Serbian nationalist with ties to the secretive military group known as the *Black Hand* - drove the major European military powers towards war. The gradual emergence of a group of alliances between major powers was partly to blame for the descent into hostilities. By 1914, those alliances resulted in the six major powers of Europe uniting into two broad groups: Britain, France and Russia formed the Triple Entente, while Germany, Austro-Hungary and Italy comprised the Triple Alliance. The German Government sent an ultimatum to Belgium demanding passage through Belgian territory so it could attack France. German troops crossed the Belgian frontier and attacked Liège on August 4th 1914. Britain declared war against Germany because of its alliance with France and Russia and to support Belgian neutrality. The British Army mobilized and the first British troops arrived in France on 7th August.

In 1914 the British Army was made up of regular Battalions. For example, the important local Regular units were the1st & 2nd Cheshire Regiments, and 1st & 2nd North Staffordshire Regiments. Each battalion had up to a thousand soldiers. These Regulars were the first troops to fight in France. In addition to the Regular army the nation's Reserve Army were the men who had left the army but who were retained and were called up to bring the army up to full strength. The third strand in the military forces available to fight was the Territorial Force (TF), a force of part time soldiers. The TF were designated to serve at home but in late 1914 over 90% of these troops elected to serve overseas. Both the Cheshire and North Staffs Regiments had their own TF battalions.

The fourth element in the military capacity to fight the war came when in August 1914 Field Marshall Earl Kitchener, Secretary of State for War, formed the 'New Armies', new battalions to boost fighting strength. The Regular, Reserve, and Territorial Battalions were not large enough to fight a war against Germany and her allies. By 21st August Kitchener's recruitment campaign had enlisted 100,000 new soldiers. By September over 33,000 men were joining the new battalions daily. In addition to the army the Royal Navy had its own part time force, the Royal Naval Volunteer Reserve, founded in 1903. The Royal Air Force was not constituted until 1918. In 1914 the fledgling air force was called the Royal Flying Corps and the Royal Naval Air Service.

## Alsager's response to the declaration of war

After the declaration of war on the 4th of August 1914 influential Alsager women quickly set up a working party to support the British Red Cross, the leading charity with the function of providing medical and welfare support to the British Army. Alsager proved to have a large number of resourceful citizens to raise funds and materials for the Red Cross.

Alsager Parish Magazine, which catered for the congregations of St Mary's and Christ Church, published monthly, gives a record of the events between 1914 and the end of the war. No church magazines still exist for the Methodist or Congregational churches in Alsager in the Great War. The Parish Magazine made no reference to the threat of war in its August 1914 edition. The war seemed to *'come from nowhere'*, as the Rev. Alfred Waller wrote in September 1914. He encouraged parishioners to participate in the war work spiritually and practically. Waller, who had been away from Alsager in August, returned to find his parishioners had already started to organise themselves. Waller wrote that he was grateful the town had quickly contributed men for the forces and money to the National Relief Fund, a government scheme to assist needy families.

*Rev Arthur Hamilton Waller, Vicar of Alsager during the Great War*

Waller organised intercessions for prayer and encouraged contributions to the Alsager Red Cross Working Party which had been set up on 10th August only six days after the declaration of hostilities. On the outbreak of the First World War, the Red Cross was practically the only organisation ready to collect and distribute resources. Working Parties were formed across the country, organised on county and then district lines. Though not strictly under the control of the Red Cross, they organised the supply of clothing including socks, shirts, blankets and belts for soldiers. Working parties also made essential hospital equipment such as bandages, splints, swabs and clothing. The parish magazine reported that vast quantities of wool for socks, calico, cotton, tape, and mufflers had already been garnered for the Red Cross. In addition, by September 1914 the Alsager Working Party provided the Belgium Relief Fund with *'56 bandages, 24 pillowcases, 56 nightshirts, 7 pairs of bed socks, 48 mufflers, 35 shirts, 24 pairs of socks, 30 bed jackets, 24 hot water bottle covers, and 2 pairs of sheets'*. Armies of women volunteered to join the Working Party. It included many of the prominent ladies of the town such as Mrs Maddock (wife of the Chairman of the Council), Mrs Pidduck, Mrs Palfreyman, Mrs Dudson, and Mrs Huntbach. Also in the group was Mrs Corfield, wife of the headmaster at the National School, and Edith Goss, daughter of Councillor Adolphus Goss. Sewing meetings were set up in the St Mary's Schoolhouse on Monday afternoons between 2.30 to 6 pm to make the clothes. The first sewing meeting was held on 17th August in the schoolhouse. By the end of August the Working Party had already raised by public appeal £21. 0s. 3d and had purchased £2. 7s. 8d worth of materials. (One pound in 1914 was approximately equivalent to £63 in 2016).

Alsager had proved it could quickly organize itself by the fundraising efforts during those first weeks of the war but the Parish Magazine gave no indication of the potential financial hardship which might be suffered by the wives and families of local servicemen with the onset of war. The focus was all on supporting the troops not their families left behind.

The Nantwich Guardian reported in October 1914 that an Alsager Belgian Relief Committee, a local organisation set up to assist Belgian refugees had been formed. The organisation was in communication with Mrs J. C. Cotton, who said her empty house in Station Road could be made available for Belgian refugees. A body of workers were making the house ready for occupation and furniture had been lent or given by sympathetic Alsager people. The Committee agreed to lodge several families in Alsager and to cover their expenses.

**Introduction of the Defence of the Realm Act**

Alsager like all other towns became subject to national security legislation hurried through parliament called the Defence of the Realm Act. Alsager citizens' freedoms were curtailed. For example:

*It became illegal to photograph military bases or try and get information from military personnel.*

*It was illegal to own or use equipment relating to phones or telegraph without a government permit.*

*People needed a permit to keep homing pigeons.*

*Flagpoles or any other equipment that could be used for signalling were banned.*

*There were strict controls on firearms, chemicals and even film for moving pictures or photography.*

*The military could take over any piece of land without the agreement of the owner.*

*Local councils could take over land that was not being used for food production and grow crops on it.*

*The sale of drugs and alcohol was strictly controlled.*

*Shops had to close at 8 pm.*

*Lights had to be put out or kept to a minimum.*

If Alsager people read the Staffordshire Sentinel, or any other newspaper, or letters from the front, they would be aware articles were censored; the government wanted the people to hear mostly positive things about the war, though casualty lists were exempted from censorship.

**Formation of the Volunteer Training Corps**

By October there was great anxiety throughout Britain. The British Expeditionary Force had been forced to retreat from Mons and only a good response at the battle of the Marne saved the army from disaster. As trench warfare began local communities started to organise their own defence forces. Invasion was a distinct possibility. On 29th October 1914 a crowded public meeting was held in the Alsager Urban District Council chamber to arrange for the formation of an Alsager and District Training Corps for men who were ineligible to enlist in Kitchener's Army because they were younger than 18 or older than 41 or were in an *'essential'* occupation such as mining, but who wished to train as reservists. Nationally the force came to be called *'Volunteer Training Corps'*. The corps formed and met in St Mary's Schoolroom on Tuesdays and Saturdays. Drilling took place on *'the infants' yard'*. On alternate weeks the Primitive Methodist schoolroom was used, (this schoolroom was demolished in the 1960s to be replaced by Chapel Mews). Mr G. Palmer was appointed the drill instructor. George Palmer was the Captain of Alsager Fire Brigade. Over £13. 0s. 0d in subscriptions was collected towards expenses and a shooting range proposed, sites for which were being investigated. Dr Kington was elected Medical Officer, and Rev. H.A. Thomas, Assistant Curate of St Mary's, became its Chaplain.

As the war extended into its fourth month more local patriotic events were encouraged in Alsager. Rev. Waller wrote in the December 1914 edition of the Parish Magazine that a muffled peal of bells was tolled at Christ Church following the death of Earl Roberts, the former Commander of the (British) Forces, who died of pneumonia visiting Indian troops in St Omer France on 14th November. The Death March was played after morning service. In December the Vicar celebrated the positive response of the people of Alsager assisting the needs of refugees and servicemen, but he deplored the *'callousness and selfishness of others … shown by the continued round of pleasure seeking and utter indifference to the needs of the country at this time'*. He could have been referring to the continued popularity of pubs in the town. There were five pubs; The Railway, The Alsager Arms, The Lodge, The Mere, and The Plough. They continued to be popular though licensing laws had been introduced for the first time. Claims that war production was being hampered by drunkenness led to pub opening times being shortened and alcohol strength reduced. Under the Defence of the Realm Act 1914 the *'No treating order'* also made it an offence to buy drinks for others. Pubs could only open for two hours at lunchtime and three hours in the evening. Beer was watered down. The government also introduced controls over the use of opium and cocaine. The freedoms enjoyed by Alsager people and the enjoyment of its many clubs and societies was significantly diminished by December 1914. The new ethic was hard work, austerity, and service for the nation.

## Alsager Men Enlist

Over 400 men were between 18 and 40 years of age in Alsager at the outbreak of war and potential soldiers. At least 78 local men enlisted or were already serving in the Forces between August and December 1914. There was no compulsory military service until 1916 but in December 1914 the Alsager Parish Magazine listed the men who had enlisted in the forces including several sets of brothers: Goss, Settle, Ellis, Davies, and Greenwood. A few were already serving regular soldiers: two of the Ellis brothers, and Harry Johnson, who was a Lieutenant Colonel (Alsager's highest ranking soldier during the Great War). Other men had been called up because they served in the Territorial Force, men such as Robert Hall and Robert Ellis.

*Robert Ellis in the Territorial Regiment Artists' Rifles a year before the war*

Most new recruits volunteered into the New Armies or were called up by being in the Territorials. They included a significant proportion of men working in the professions. Dr George William Lloyd, from Crewe Road, joined the Royal Army Medical Corps. He later became a Captain on HMS Hospital Ship Oxfordshire. Working miners such as Maurice Clowes and William James Pincher enlisted, and several railwaymen, such as Christopher Mitford joined the army. 29 Alsager men enlisted in the new battalions formed with the North Staffordshire Regiment. It indicated Alsager's close employment links with North Staffordshire and only two men were serving with the Cheshire Regiment, including George Jacobs, from the reserve of officers, who was to become a prisoner of war for nearly five years. Seven men enlisted in the Royal Navy, and four in the Royal Marines. The nearest permanent recruiting centres to Alsager were in Kidsgrove and Crewe but some Alsager men enlisted further afield in London or Manchester. It was a simple interview, a form filled, a medical, and a promise to serve for the duration of the war. There was no check to make sure recruits were under 18 years of age.

Of the above list of men who enlisted or were already in the ranks before December 1914, here reproduced from the Alsager Parish Magazine, only two were still serving in 1918, the remainder were dead, retired, transferred to the reserve or were prisoners of war. 14 of the original 78 men were to perish in the war. These first 78 men constituted approximately 10% of the men aged between 18 and 40 years eligible to join the services. (Eligible men were between 19 and 30 years).

New recruits embarked to training camps for six months basic training and were commanded by regular soldiers. The Territorial Force regiments and New Armies prepared for war but most Territorial Regiments did not fight abroad until 1915.

As well as men joining the forces many enlisted to serve in the Red Cross at home and abroad. Some of these became stretcher bearers on the front line.

*St John's Ambulance workers photographed by Alsager Junction Signal Box (Preparing to go to France as Stretcher Bearers.) In 1914, the Order of St. John Ambulance joined forces with the British Red Cross Society to create the Joint War Committee to assist in providing medical care overseas during the First World War.*

By late September 1914 some of the Alsager men were already in the thick of it. Francis Rupert Walker, a Sick Berth Attendant in the Naval Brigade, was sent into Antwerp to assist the Belgian army and was nearly trapped by the invading German army. He told of informers and spies trying to lead the beleaguered British troops to the enemy. Nearly betrayed by two Belgian nurses passing messages to the enemy he was witness to their immediate execution. The Nantwich Guardian, which reported his story, managed to circumvent censorship. That the British troops were summarily executing women spies would normally have been censored. Walker managed to escape from Belgium on 8th October just before the city fell to the enemy. The realities of brutal warfare and stories of executions were far removed from the relative calm of the home front.

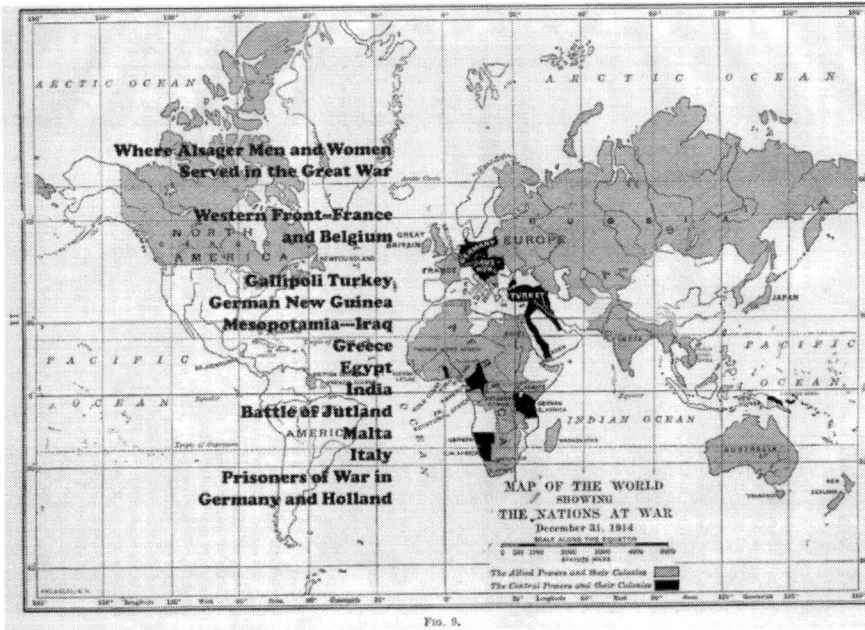

The map contains labels: "Where Alsager Men and Women Served in the Great War", "Western Front—France and Belgium", "Gallipoli Turkey", "German New Guinea", "Mesopotamia—Iraq", "Greece", "Egypt", "India", "Battle of Jutland", "Malta", "Italy", "Prisoners of War in Germany and Holland". Bottom title: "MAP OF THE WORLD SHOWING THE NATIONS AT WAR December 31, 1914".

*Map: Where Alsager men served 1914-19. Women from the Voluntary Aid Detachment and Women's Auxiliary Army Corps served at home and in France.*

## Late 1914: Alsager people rally to bolster the war effort.

To honour the recruits and support the war effort, the Parish Magazine announced in December 1914 that Union Flags were to be displayed at Christ Church and St Mary's and the National Anthem should be sung after services. The Vicar wrote, *'We could not have withstood the German armies unless the God of battles had been with us'*. The B'hoys of Alsager, depleted in ranks due to men enlisting, gave £2. 2s. to the *War Relief Fund*, £1. 1s. to the Belgian Relief Fund, and 10s 6d to the local Red Cross Society. Their prominent members were busy councillors and officials and club meetings were sparsely attended. The Alsager branch of the Church of England Men's Society attended patriotic lectures organised by the Daily Mail, and the Alsager Branch of the National Children's Union, (N.C.U) ran a tobacco stall in their 'At Home', with proceeds towards men fighting in France. The Miss Settles also sold patriotic buttonholes and the tea room did a brisk trade. On 9th December 1914 a play was performed in Alsager called 'The War of the Fairies', with actors representing soldiers from countries including a 'truculent Kaiser', and 'our treasured Tommy Adkins'. The play included a 'stirring' rendition of 'Your King and Country Wants You', sung by Misses Edwards, Beswick, and Tyrer. £10. 10s. 0d. (£10.50) was raised for the Relief of Belgian Orphans campaign (This was equivalent to £630.00 in 2016)

The war had not ended by Christmas. Men were leaving the town to enlist in greater numbers. Employers could not recruit replacements. Young women from rich families began to enlist as Red Cross helpers and nurses. Prospects for the New Year were uncertain.

# Alsager in 1915

The New Year began with a patriotic occasion to boost civic morale. On 3rd January 1915 a well-attended service was held in St Mary's for National Intercession Sunday involving Councillors, the B'hoys of Alsager, Boy Scouts, the Ambulance service, and Fire Brigade. The service was bolstered by the presence of 'a considerable number of men in khaki'. The principal councillors were Gilbert Parsons (Chairman of the Council), Mr Maddock, Mr Adams, Mr Proctor, and Mr Goss. Mr Lynam was the Council Surveyor, and J.J. Nelson was the Council Secretary. The Council had the role of not only keeping up morale but being responsible for enforcement of the Defence of the Realm Act. A collection of £17 was raised for the Red Cross Sick and Wounded Fund at the service.

On 7th January children at St Mary's Sunday School performed a play entitled 'Britannia's Reception'. The play was repeated three times that week and donations from the Friday performance were sent to the North Staffordshire Regiment.

*Britannia's Reception. Photo: Sentinel newspaper.*

On 13th January at the annual Parish Tea repeated the patriotic tableau performed at the N.C.U in December, and also put on a children's play, 'The War of Fairies'. Rev. F.T. Anderson, a chaplain at the front, wrote to the Alsager N.C.U. to thank them for their gifts of pipes, mittens, socks, scarves and gloves donated by the Working Group. In February an 'American Tea' arranged by The Ladies' Patriotic Working Party raised £20.15s. (£20.75) towards the war effort out of a total collection of £34 that month. It was held in the St Mary's Schoolroom. The American Tea included sketches, songs, and *an excellent tea*. Part of the performance, called the *'Darkies'*, included the Christ Church choir with blacked faces and costumes who sang minstrel songs to *'shrieks of laughter'* from the audience. This was seen as acceptable at the time.

By January 1915 seventeen Belgian refugees had been welcomed to Alsager and given accommodation. Mr H.V Lynam, Secretary of the Belgian Refugee Committee in Alsager was in contact with the Belgian Consul in Amsterdam in neutral Holland to arrange passage of refugees to Alsager. The Nantwich Guardian reported that some of the Belgian children were attending Alsager schools, and 'making remarkable progress with their English studies.' Their fathers had secured employment locally, and their mothers were engaged in knitting clothes for servicemen at the front. 'These people are very thrifty and are putting by their earnings until such time they can return to their own country.'

The majority of the Alsager Working Party funds went to help the troops at the front. Between August 1914 and January 1915 the following items were made or donated to the war effort: 74 day shirts to the Red Cross and 208 day shirts to individual men at the front; 69 Bandages and 30 pillow slips to the Red Cross; 129 mufflers to the Red Cross, and 371 to individual men at the front; 70 pairs of socks to the Red Cross and 346 socks to men at the front; 97 belts and 54 helmets to individual servicemen; 12 pairs of bed socks to the Red Cross and 12 pairs to the North Staffs Infirmary; 67 bed jackets to the Red Cross and 8 to the Infirmary; 24 hot water bottles to the Red Cross and 2 to the Infirmary. Comforts from the sewing party were sent to Corporal Harrison, Privates Mitford, Mitchell, Holmes, Hopwood, Hollinshead, Morris, Smith, Watson, and to Bombardier Roberts.

**The Volunteers**

On 22nd January 1915 thirty two members of the Alsager Training Corps (soon to be renamed the Alsager Volunteers) paraded under the instruction of Mr Palmer. They marched through Day Green, Hassall, and Wheelock to Haslington. They returned via Oakhanger. The Nantwich Guardian reported they had now acquired rifles and a shooting range. They were now affiliated to the county national battalions of volunteers. In June it was reported their shooting range in fields near Alsager Hall had been damaged by persons unknown. The canvas round the targets had been punctured. A reward was offered for information. Later, in April there was a recruitment drive for the Volunteers held in the Primitive Methodist schoolroom and a patriotic address given by Mr Disbrowe from Stockport. Thirty three more men enrolled bringing the total number serving in the Corps up to seventy five.

## Alsager Urban District Council

With the war the legal responsibilities of Alsager Urban District Council increased. In 1915/16 £6 was even paid out by the parish for 'aircraft insurance' in case of bombing, and Alsager introduced gas street lighting restrictions in case of Zeppelin attack. The Council had been criticised for introducing lighting restrictions and were asked to reconsider the decision. Councillor Adolphus Goss wrote to the Sentinel on the subject suggesting the council would reintroduce some street lighting. In the end three lamps were illuminated and the Kidsgrove Gas Company gave a rebate to Alsager for the reduction in use of street gas lighting from March 1915. The Clerk of the Council said to laughter from Councillors, *'We are not likely to have a raid (in Alsager)'*. Others disagreed; Alsager was near to Crewe and its railway works and munitions factories. It could have been a target for Zeppelins returning from air raids in Liverpool.

### DARKEST ALSAGER.

(To the Editor of the Staffordshire Sentinel.")

Sir,—Will you permit me to state, in reply to the worthy chairman of the Alsager Council, that I have the utmost confidence in the intelligence of the Council, and that I am sure that that intelligence will be eventually manifested. But perhaps it is sometimes a bit slow in action. It requires a little gentle stimulus from public opinion to make it work nicely. According to Mr. Parsons' letter, the municipal intellect is only just beginning to grasp the idea that it may be possible to light a few lamps at important points. This is a great advance from total darkness, and we will patiently hope that when that intellect gets fairly to work, it will be able to solve the problem of giving light to the village, while complying loyally with the military order. Crewe is most brilliantly lighted, not only the town, but the railways for a long distance out. Again expressing my admiration for the intelligence of the Alsager Council, yours, &c.,

ADOLPHUS GOSS.

Alsager, March 9th, 1915.

*The letter from Councillor Adolphus Goss to the Sentinel*

To illustrate the financial hardship imposed on Alsager the Council was forced to postpone the much needed water improvement scheme in the town from April 1915 because of curtailment of borrowing powers by the Local Government Board.

## 'The Slackers and the Shirkers'

There was ill feeling against the men who did not enlist in the services. In March 1915 a soldier from Alsager serving with the 5th North Staffordshire Regiment wrote to the Sentinel; his name was not published.

*'It is shocking out here to every man who is freely giving his all serving King and country to see pictures in the home papers of the very man needed so badly, dressed in flannels and still wasting precious moments in sport when their energies should be devoted to the more serious game of playing a manly part in the greatest event of this world's history. They don't seem to realise that their attitude means the unnecessary sacrifice of life owing to the thinness of the line. There is only one remedy —take them by force and do it at once. Delay is only courting disaster.'*

The soldier called young men who did not enlist as the *'slackers and the shirkers'.* He quoted the famous recruiting poster poem;

*'How will you fare sonny, how will you fare in that far off winter night,*

*When you sit by the fire in the old man's chair,*

*And your neighbours talk of the fight,*

*Will you slink from the room as t'were a blow,*

*Your old head grey and bent.*

*Or will you say, "I was not with the first to go,*

*But I went, thank God I went." '*

The North Staffordshire Regiment received copies of the Sentinel in France. Troops like the Alsager man did not enjoy seeing pictures and reading stories of frivolous games played by those men of fighting age back in Cheshire and Staffordshire.

## Poverty

A newspaper story from the Nantwich Guardian illustrates the fact that there were some Alsager people living in poverty. In March 1915 Mr Henry Morris of Shady Grove was found lying across a footpath in Lawton Road by the police. He was intoxicated and the case sent to Sandbach Petty Sessions. At court Superintendent Sutton did not press for a penalty and revealed Morris was elderly, his wife nearly dead, and they were living in a poverty stricken circumstances. Henry Morris was a retired blacksmith aged 73 in 1915.

## The Curate enlists

In June 1915 the Parish Magazine reported that the Curate, Mr Harold Augustine Thomas had joined the Army and was serving in the Royal Army Medical Corps. He left Alsager on Whit Monday to travel to Peterborough to begin his training. Mr Thomas wrote to the magazine giving details of the privations of army life – sleeping in a barn infested with rats with one hundred and twenty other soldiers, poor rations, bad language, and the derision he suffered when he prayed. Later, in October, serving in Gallipoli, he was sleeping in the field and stretcher bearers were having to scramble to dressing stations near the front line to bring the wounded back to the field hospital. His memoirs describe how close he came to death. The Parish Magazine spared the subscribers the following gory details which were included in Thomas's war memoirs:

*'I heard a loud smack on the shoulder of the man next to me. At first I thought the man behind had thumped him...He fell over in a heap with a groan ... Two of us ripped open his tunic and found a ragged hole from which blood was flowing just behind the shoulder blade. We fixed his 'first field dressing' on and asked an officer for a stretcher ...Next came a flurry of bullets fizzing over.'* He carried the stretcher to the dressing station with a *'whine of bullets around the ears'.* There was *'not an inch of cover.'* It went dark and *'we searched for a long time in darkness and found the casualty clearing station'.*

Thomas did try to be humorous in his letters. He sent the recipe for Gallipoli Pudding. *'Pound some army biscuits with a shell case, make dough with water, put it in a bag and boil it in a mess tin. Add jam or marmalade and there you are.'*

Far removed from the battle Alsager people could only imagine the horror of war Thomas described in his letters and memoirs.

**National Registration**

In July 1915 Alsager Urban District Council began to send out National Registration forms to all households in the town. The National Registration scheme was designed to assess how many men might enlist in the services before conscription and to evaluate the potential workforce to fill their shoes. On 15 July 1915 the National Registration Act 1915 had been passed. This Act required all men and women, between the ages of 15 and 65 years of age, to register at their residential location. The council took on extra people to collect in the forms and chase up forms which had not been completed.

In the summer the Alsager Working Party continued with their welfare duties. They took to the North Staffordshire Infirmary: 6 cushions, 24 night shirts, 54 bandages, 100 pairs of socks, and 50 day shirts for wounded soldiers. In the thirteen months between August 1914 and August 1915 the Alsager Working Party raised over £170 towards the provision of clothing and comforts for men at the front. (Equivalent to over £17,000 today).

**Rates Arrears and poverty caused by the war**

In November 1915 the Urban District Council caused consternation amongst the soldiers' wives of Alsager by sending out summons for non-payment of district general rates. The Council summoned defaulters to appear before the next Council meeting. The Vicar, Rev. Alfred Waller, asked the Council to be reasonable in its deliberations. There was no further council report and it must be assumed there was later a change of heart, a compromise, by the Council on this issue. The Chester Chronicle reported Alsager contributed £123 to the County Relief Fund towards the *'alleviation of distress'*. £8. 12s. 6d of these funds had been given out in the Alsager area by the end of 1914. This is an extremely small amount of money. It would have been direct help to the families suffering financially when their sons or husbands enlisted.

The war undoubtedly caused hardship to working families. Servicemen's pay was much less than even the lowest working men's wage. A private soldier's wages were 8s. 2d a week (41p) in 1914. The lowest wages for agricultural workers in 1914 were 16s 9d a week (84p). A miner might earn £1. 10s. a week (£1.50). A clerk would have earned £4. 10s. a week in 1914. A solicitor earned £26 a week, but if he was commissioned in the army his wages would have fallen considerably. Pay for a Lieutenant in an infantry regiment was nearly £3 a week. Wives with families received a 'separation allowance' which was uprated in March 1915, but the allowance barely covered the basic costs of keeping hearth and home together. It was the first directly-paid form of what we call 'benefit' today ever made to women. One letter writer to The Times most certainly did not approve of the allowance.

*'If we are going to give a pound a week separation allowances to wives, and a pound a week pension to widows, as some people propose, we shall not be able to keep a single maidservant in my particular district.'*

American newspapers (Chicago Tribune) reported in June 1915 that food prices in Britain had risen by 43% since the beginning of the war and the price of bread had doubled. The British press, which was censored, would not have given this information to the public

The Hanley Branch of the Soldiers, Sailors and Families Association reported to the Sentinel newspaper in June 1915 that the separation allowance of 12s. 5d. a week was insufficient to support families. No figures for Alsager exist but the Hanley Association reported they were receiving a hundred new appeals for help a week. They were helping one hundred and fifty four women without children top up their separation allowance. They were paying out two hundred and fifty eight grants of 4s. 8d. (24p) a week to mothers with sons in the army, and grants of 1s. 1d. (6p) to 1,121 wives to help them pay their rent. Between August 1914 and May 1915 over £8,406 was paid out to help families in need in Hanley.

Part of the problem of financial hardship was that separation allowances were not being paid on time to claimants which led to financial hardship.

*Poster: Separation Allowances*

The National Relief Fund, set up by the Prince of Wales in August 1914, designed to help citizens in distress, was severely criticised after the war. In 1923 the Earl of Dartmouth complained in the House of Lords that Staffordshire contributed £35,000 but only received back £1,100 to give to the needy. Other counties such as Cheshire suffered the same problem. Local churches did contribute to the National Relief Fund. Christ Church contributed £13. 10s. 3d up to Easter 1915. Yet the Alsager Parish Magazine made no direct reference to the financial hardships suffered by parishioners, concentrating its efforts through the Working Party on direct assistance to soldiers at the front or to local hospitals. This may have been for reasons of confidentiality, but most of the members of the Alsager Working Party were wealthy members of the community who were not suffering financial hardship themselves. There were also health issues for Dr Kington to address. Although Alsager remained a healthy place to live in late September 1915 all schools were closed as a precaution for two weeks because of an outbreak of measles.

## Church Funding

Despite the war the united parish of St Mary Magdalene and Christ Church in Alsager continued to bring in the same level subscriptions to pay for their Curates' Fund. This was a fund to pay for the wages and expenses of the Curates employed by the parish. This amounted to £ 116. 4s. 0d in 1915. Local wealthy families continued their financial support to their churches. Total Church of England parish collection receipts in 1915 were £283. 12s. 5d, similar to the previous year. Despite hardships suffered by ordinary families the church managed to maintain its levels of income mainly through the donations made by Alsager's leading families. The parish did hold an annual parish 'treat' for the elderly in the form of a 'substantial meal' for one hundred and fifty people. This this was a long standing event in the town but giving to the Church's 'Poor Fund' amounted to less than 10 shillings a week in 1915.

## The war effort, concerts, and keeping up morale

Propaganda was an important part of encouraging men to enlist and invest. In late 1915 in Alsager war films were shown in the St Mary's schoolroom under the auspices of the War Savings Committee to encourage Alsager residents to buy war bonds. They included films showing the work of minesweepers, and films of troops fighting in Mesopotamia and Palestine. On 10th November 1915 St Mary's held its second 'American Tea' to raise funds for troops' comforts and wounded soldiers. A balance of £76. 17s. 3d was made from the concert. Part of the finale was a tableau featuring Miss Gwen Maddock as a nurse and Mr A. Hammersley as a wounded soldier. The Miss

Bowers performed 'fancy exquisite dances' and Miss Lightfoot gave a recitation of 'The Lifeboat'. '*A constant gale of merriment surrounded the original bargain stall, run energetically by Miss Kingston, Mr & Mrs Lea and Miss Goss. Among the side shows were an interesting collection of war and African curios held by Miss Bennett and a bran pie managed by Miss D Hammersley and Miss E Maddock, a fortune telling doll, who in Miss N. Waller's small hands became a fortune collecting doll …*' Christ Church had a special collection for the Mersey Mission to Seamen in November 1915 which raised £5. 18s. (£5.90) toward the charity.

In November Harold Tivey, whose family lived in the Avenue, Alsager, returned from Germany where he had been a prisoner of war for thirteen months having being trapped in Germany at the outbreak of the war when working as a translator.

*Harold Tivey: Family Archive*

He had been released in a prisoner exchange. He later gave a lecture in St Mary's schoolroom to tell the people of Alsager of his experiences in Ruhleben prisoner of war camp. He explained he had been given one meal of poor quality a day, and 300 prisoners had to share four enamel bowls to wash in. The camp's numbers grew to 4000 people including British soldiers who had become prisoners of war after the retreat from Mons. Some prisoners had no bed to sleep in and accommodation in part consisted of horse boxes with lofts above. The International Red Cross, who inspected the camp, were only allowed to see the better part of the camp where there were better facilities. Harold's two brothers, Reginald Tivey, and Tom Brown Tivey were on active service in France. Harold was never called up for military service after his ordeals in Germany. His lecture would have been one of the personal first-hand accounts about the war heard in Alsager. With conscription legislation in the offing many Alsager men opted to enlist in December 1915. The Council opened its offices on 3rd December as a recruiting office. Forms were completed then men proceeded to Dr Kington's surgery for a medical examination. Numbers were few until the Saturday evening when ninety enlisted in two hours. It was decided to keep the Recruiting Office open all Sunday where a further score of men were attested. Altogether two hundred men were attested in Alsager that weekend. The Nantwich Guardian reported that many of them were 'married' and were 'agricultural workers'.

In December 1915 parcels were sent to Alsager 78 servicemen as a Christmas treat. Each parcel included socks, cigarettes and chocolate. It was also decided to start a fund to give all Alsager children with fathers serving in the Forces a treat. Councillor Parsons organized the initiative along with Mr H.V Lynam, Council Surveyor. The committee also hoped to provide Christmas gifts to wounded soldiers in hospitals.

# Deaths of Alsager Servicemen in 1915

Until the summer of 1915 the war must have seemed a long way from Alsager, but the town was to suffer its first fatalities due to the conflict. What follows is a brief biography of each serviceman killed in 1915. The biographies are in chronological order of the date of their death.

*(Where the serviceman is commemorated on the Alsager War Memorial it with will be denoted by the symbol of the poppy cross)*

## Date of death: 4th June 1915

### Sub Lieutenant John Eric Davies: Royal Naval Volunteer Reserve, Collingwood Battalion.

*(A serviceman not on the Alsager War Memorial but with an Alsager connection)*

*Photo: De Ruvigny's Roll of Honour, 1914-1919*

John Eric Davies was born on 31st August 1893, in Glansychan, Aberychan, Monmouthshire, the fifth son of William Henry Davies JP, who moved to Alsager and became the General Manager of the Shelton Iron Company in Stoke-on-Trent. His mother was Sarah Elizabeth (née Richards) Davies, of Glansychan. In Alsager the family lived at The Gables, a large house. The site of this house and grounds are now a small housing estate. The Davies family moved out of the Gables after William Henry Davies' sudden death in 1907. John joined the mercantile marine and travelled the world. After the outbreak of war John enlisted in the Royal Navy Volunteer Reserve, service number Z/377, and was granted a temporary commission as Sub Lieutenant and appointed to the Collingwood Battalion at Blandford in Dorset in late January 1915. He died at Gallipoli on 4th June 1915 fighting against Turkish forces, missing presumed dead. The 'Next of Kin' details on John Davies' service card were his sister, Mrs. Canning-Cooke, of 'Orinston', Olive Crescent, Penarth, Glamorgan; later of Glanmor, Fields Park Road, Newport, and Monmouth. Bizarrely a photograph of John, with his name written on the back of the picture, was found on the battlefield in France hundreds of miles from where he died. It was returned to his sister in Wales. The photograph may have belonged to one of his brothers who were fighting in France. John is not recorded on the Aberychan or Alsager War Memorial but is commemorated on the Commonwealth War Grave, Gallipoli, Helles Memorial, Turkey, on panel 8-12. John was the first of the three Davies brothers who were killed in 1915. John was posthumously awarded the 1914/15 Star, The British War Medal, and the Victory Medal.

# Date of death: 18<sup>th</sup> July 1915

## Private William Robinson: Duke of Wellington's (West Riding Regiment)

*Photo: Staffordshire Sentinel 1915*

On 18<sup>th</sup> July1915 William Robinson was the first Alsager born man to be killed in action. Until the summer of 1915, apart from news of men being wounded or held as prisoners of war, there had been no deaths arising from the conflict. It is impossible to convey the feeling of private grief which came out of the news of the death of local servicemen.

William Robinson was born in in 1895 in Betchton, near Alsager. His parents were Ellen and William Robinson. The family lived in Mistletoe Cottage, Hassall Green, Alsager, and his father was an agricultural labourer. He was the youngest child of the family. His brothers and sisters were Ethel, born 1881, Rachel (1885), Phyllis (1896), Francis (1888), and Ernest (1891). By the age of sixteen William had left home and was living and working on Thorley's Farm, Day Green, Sandbach, where he looked after a herd of cattle. Before the outbreak of war he changed jobs and became a '*Smith Striker*', or blacksmith. Members of his family had been involved in forge work for several decades in South Cheshire. At the outbreak of war William was working in Messrs. Settle Speakman, coal merchants, in Alsager. He enlisted in the army on 28<sup>th</sup> December 1914 in Tunstall, Staffordshire, and was assigned to the 3<sup>rd</sup> North Staffordshire Regiment, service number 16154. He joined the regiment for basic training on 8<sup>th</sup> January 1915. His service records state he was five feet five inches tall and his home address was given as The Fields, Alsager. Following training William was transferred to the 3<sup>rd</sup> Battalion of the West Riding Regiment, service number 16232, but he was immediately posted to the 2nd Battalion, West Riding Regiment, and he was sent to France with them on 3<sup>rd</sup> May 1915. He was drafted to take part in the action to defend Hill 60 near Ypres. German attacks on the hill in early May included the use of gas shells and the Germans recovered the ground at the second attempt on 5<sup>th</sup> May. William Robinson was killed in action on 18<sup>th</sup> July 1915 having only been in active service for six weeks. He was killed fighting on the Ypres Salient defending positions near the town of Ypres. His friend, Private Dale, who fought in another platoon of the Duke of Wellington's, wrote to his parents about William's death. *'He was hit by a bullet through the left lung on Saturday while out digging about midnight. He died about half an hour later. He had just had a parcel and one or two letters.'* In his final letter home Robinson described his experiences in the trenches, *'On the second day we were with our sappers and came across a German mine which they blew up. We were all informed it was going to happen so we were ready for it. It shook the trenches I can tell you. The last day we were in (Saturday) we blew about two hundred yards of the German trenches up, also a big mound and some houses. Our trench rocked like a cradle. I shall never forget that Saturday as long as I live.'*

Family grief was overwhelming. William's father died soon after the news of his son's death, aged sixty six. For sixteen years William senior had been an attendant at Alsager Sewage Works. On 10th August 1915 Alsager Urban District Council gave a vote of condolence on William's father's death, saying he was *'One of the Council's workmen'*.

Alsager Parish Magazine gave a short eulogy for Private William Robinson in September 1915 and described his death. He was *'shot through the lungs while engaged in trench digging at night, and only lived about half an hour'*.

William was buried at the 13th Infantry Brigade Burial Ground at Voormezeele, Enclosure no.3. He is buried in grave reference V C 2. The cemetery is four kilometres south of Ypres and was designed by Sir Edwin Lutyens. William's personal effects were sent home on 15th November 1915. In 1921 he was posthumously granted the 1914/15 Star, The British War Medal, and The Victory Medal.

On 21st August 1915 a service of remembrance was held at St Mary Magdalene Church for William Robinson, which was attended by representatives of Messrs. Settle Speakman, Alsager, and William's family. The choir sang *'Nearer to God than me'* and *'Oh God Our Help in Ages Past.'*

# Date of death: 13th August 1915

**Second Lieutenant Raymond Goss: North Staffordshire Regiment**

*Photo from Staffordshire Sentinel*

Raymond George Frederick Goss was born on 5th June 1892 in Alsager to Sarah Ellen Goss, (nee Dale), and Adolphus Goss. His father was a prominent ceramic artist, designer and local politician. His family were manufacturers of Goss porcelain in Stoke-on-Trent. Raymond's siblings were: Ethel M. Goss born in 1886, Vernon Clarence Goss (1888) Clarence Richard Goss (1890) Hubert John Goss (1891) and Dorothy Goss (1894.) The family lived at The Old Villa, Sandbach Road, Alsager, which is close to where the Alsager War Memorial is located today.

*Raymond pictured at Alsager School (a schoolhouse adjacent to Christ Church) in 1904. He is in the second row from the top, third left. His brother Hubert is 4th from left on the same row. Dorothy Goss is on the 3rd row down on the extreme right. (Photo: from Willian Henry Goss by Lynda & Nicholas Pyne)*

After attending Alsager School Raymond attended Newcastle School, Staffordshire, and during his time there he joined the school cadet force, becoming a sergeant, and went on manoeuvres on Cannock Chase. After leaving school he became a mining engineer at Birchenwood Colliery near Kidsgrove.

*The Goss Family in 1913 at the Old Villa, Alsager. Left to Right: Hubert, Dorothy, Adolphus, Clarence, Raymond (standing) Front Vernon Nellie and Ethel (sitting) (Photo: from Willian Henry Goss by Lynda & Nicholas Pyne)*

Raymond Goss enlisted in the North Staffordshire Regiment, 2$^{nd}$ Territorial Battalion, in August 1914 and transferred to the 1/5$^{th}$ North Staffordshire Regiment and was promoted Lance Corporal. He was commissioned 2$^{nd}$ Lieutenant on 17$^{th}$ February 1915 and embarked to France with his regiment on 3$^{rd}$ May 1915, later than the rest of his regiment as he had to complete officer military training before taking up his commission. Raymond and his brother Richard (Dick) were defending positions a mile north of Hill 60 near Ypres on the day of Raymond's death at six o'clock in the evening. They were together in a railway dugout with their captain, Captain Ridgeway, when a German shell landed, dropping between them. Raymond was killed instantly and his brother, Dick, was wounded in the shoulder. Captain Ridgeway escaped with minor wounds. (Ridgeway was killed in action a few weeks later). Dick Goss said of his brother's death, *'Raymond died as he lived, in happiness, and knew nothing of his end'*.

Raymond is buried near Ypres, Belgium, in the Railway Dugout Ground Cemetery, Plot 1 Row D Grave 7. In 1915 Raymond had sent home a brass shell case to his father. After Raymond's death his family inscribed the following words on the shell: *'French 75 shell sent home by Sec Lt Raymond Goss 1/5 N. Staffs Regiment. (Killed near Hill 60 in Flanders, August 1915)'*

In a letter from Raymond's commanding officer to Adolphus Goss Captain Banks wrote; *'On behalf of the officers, NCO's ( Non Commissioned Officers) and men of 'C' company I wish to offer you and Mrs Goss our sincere sympathy in the great loss you have sustained by the death of your son, Raymond. I know how great your grief must be and no words can lessen it, but I would like you to know that in my opinion he died without knowing of the meaning of the word, 'fear.' In fact his spirits used to rise in the presence of danger. I had the highest confidence in him and he will be sadly missed by his company who were well aware of his cool courage.'*

A service of remembrance for Pte. W. Robinson and Lt. R. Goss was held in St Mary's Church, Alsager, on 21st August 1915. Family, representatives from the community and Birchenwood Colliery, (Raymond Goss' employers) and Messrs Settle, (William's employers) were present. Raymond was posthumously awarded the 1914/15 Star, the Victory Medal, and the British War Medal.

At the 1927 opening of the Goss Memorial window in St Mary Magdalene Church, Alsager, the following was said of Raymond Goss. *'Raymond lives in the memory as outwardly a contrast to the gravity of his brother (Hubert). Raymond, radiating sunshine wherever he goes, Raymond the life and soul of every gathering he joined; Raymond with a capacity for many friendships. He was ambitious – not through motives of personal vanity, but from a delight in achievement for achievement's sake; and with bright prospects before him. Do not be mistaken by that apparent light heartedness, for it seemed that was his working and practical philosophy –even when the smile of his was not as spontaneous as it seemed.'*

*Commemoration stone for Raymond Goss, Christ Church, Alsager.*

# Date of death: 30th September 1915

## Lance Corporal Bertram Ellis Barlow: Royal Engineers.

*(A serviceman not on the Alsager War Memorial but with an Alsager connection)*

*Photograph: Sentinel newspaper*

Bertram Ellis Barlow was born in Odd Rode, Cheshire, in October 1892 to Minerva and John Barlow. John was a village blacksmith in Mount Pleasant. Before 1915 the family moved to The Firs, Sunnyside, Alsager. Ellis, as he preferred to be called, joined the Royal Engineers in 1911, (service number 20997) and trained at Gibraltar Barracks, Aldershot, as a Sapper.

The Weekly Sentinel reported that for the six months prior to the outbreak of war Ellis had been in the army reserve and working at Messrs. Tabley and Sons, Kidsgrove, Staffordshire, and living with his parents in Scholar Green. He was one of the first troops sent to France.

He embarked with 59th Field Company to France on 18th August 1914 amongst the first troops to fight. He later joined 26th Field Company, Royal Engineers, part of the First Division, and saw action in the battle of Mons and the subsequent retreat and The Battle of the Marne (September). He also took part in the First Battle of Ypres (October-November 1914).

The 26 Field Company War Diary for 27th August 1915 states that Barlow was promoted Lance Corporal on that day.

The company marched to the outskirts of Loos at 9pm on 28th September. On 29th September three sections were employed erecting barbed wire. On the 30th one section completed it. *'Two sections wired in front of the Eastern Salient. The Germans had left in Loos a quantity of engineering materials including a novel pattern of barbed wire entanglement. Some seven hundred yards of this was erected during these two nights in Loos.'* Ellis Barlow was killed on 30th September 1915 during this work. His commanding officer wrote to Ellis's family saying he died *'nobly doing his duty for King and Country'*. He is buried in Zouve Valley Cemetery, Souchez, Belgium. Ellis Barlow's family moved to Cheltenham after the outbreak of the Great War. Bertram is remembered on the War Memorial at Mow Cop.

He was posthumously awarded The 1914/15 Star, The British War Medal, and the Victory Medal.

*Grave of L/Corporal B.E Barlow. Photo: Commonwealth War Graves Commission*

# October 13ᵗʰ 1915

Six men from Alsager, five who were members of the North Staffordshire Regiment, were killed on October 13ᵗʰ, or died shortly afterwards because of wounds, during the attack on the Hohenzollern Redoubt. Two of these men are not commemorated on the Alsager War Memorial.

The action was part of the battle of Loos. The Hohenzollern Redoubt was a defensive strongpoint of the German 6ᵗʰ Army on the Western Front at Auchy-les-Mines near Loos-en-Gohelle in the Nord-Pas-de-Calais, France The battle around the Hohenzollern Redoubt took place between 13ᵗʰ and 19ᵗʰ October 1915, towards the end and immediately after the Battle of Loos (25ᵗʰ September to 15ᵗʰ October 1915). The British 9ᵗʰ Division captured this strongpoint and then lost it to a German counter-attack. The final British assault on 13ᵗʰ October failed and resulted in the loss of 180 officers and 3,583 men within ten minutes and achieved nothing. In the official history of the attack, J. E. Edmonds wrote, *'The fighting [from 13ᵗʰ –14ᵗʰ October] had not improved the general situation in any way and had brought nothing but useless slaughter of infantry.'* Of the 700 from the 5ᵗʰ Battalion who began the attack only 138 survived to answer the roll call.

# Date of death: 13th October 1915

## Lance Corporal Arthur Ellis: North Staffordshire Regiment

*Photo: Ellis Family*

Arthur Ellis was born in Wolstanton, Staffordshire, to Arthur and Eleanor Ellis in 1888. His father was a solicitor with a firm based in Burslem. Arthur's brothers and sisters were, Frances born 1881, Agnes (1881), Phillip (1882), Robert (1889), and Henry (1891). Arthur attended Newcastle School and afterwards he was a student farmer and in 1911 trained at Northleach, Gloucester on the farm of Mr Organ. In 1914 the Ellis family were living at 'Fairfield House', Crewe Road, Alsager. Arthur joined the North Staffordshire Regiment in December 1914, service number 2870. He went to France on March 4th 1915. According to Arthur's niece, Lucy Edwards, Arthur was recommended for a commission in 1915 but did not take it up before his death.

He took part in the relief at Neuve Chapelle, and also fought in the Hill 60 engagements. On 13th October 1915 his battalion took part in a disastrous attack on the German lines on the 'Hohenzollern Redoubt' in the battle of Loos. He died in the action and his body was never found.

*'We deeply regret to say there is every reason to fear the death in action of Lance Corporal Arthur Ellis, the son of Mr and Mrs Arthur Ellis of Fairfield, Alsager, during the charge of the 1ˢᵗ 5ᵗʰ North Stafford's. Lance Corporal Ellis was one of the bomb throwers of the 1ˢᵗ 5ᵗʰ who went so gallantly in advance to clear the way for the infantry. Various letters received from wounded soldiers and others close to these brave fellows said they faced heavy fire and very few of this band of heroes escaped. It appears Lance Corporal Ellis was wounded in the hand almost immediately but rushed on with his comrades and was lost to sight. No official notification of his death has yet been received and no evidence of identification has so far been recovered but it is likely he is one of the fallen heroes of that tragic day. Lance Corporal Ellis was twenty seven. Profound sympathy is felt for Mr and Mrs Ellis on the loss of their beloved son —one of the band of four soldier brothers. Lance Corporal Ellis was educated at Newcastle High School and in recent years was studying farming. He enlisted with the 1ˢᵗ 5ᵗʰ North Stafford's on 2ⁿᵈ September going like most of his school fellows straight into the ranks. He trained with the 2ⁿᵈ Battalion at Butterton Hall and went to France on 4ᵗʰ March with the 1ˢᵗ 5ᵗʰ North Stafford's. He wrote home to his mother regularly and on the eve of his last battle in the full knowledge of the dangers which awaited him the following day, and possibly with some premonition he might not win through he addressed a special letter to his father. Since then the rest is silence.'* In a previous letter to his parents, as reported in the Nantwich Guardian, in good humour he reported a German in a trench opposite was heard to shout, *'Hello 5ᵗʰ North Staffordshires. Who won that last football match at Stoke?'* The Sentinel reported: *'Lance Corporal Ellis was one of a most happy and affectionate family circle —bright and fun loving with merry eyes and a kind smile. He had a goodness of disposition, which though quiet and retiring in manner, it gained him the affection of not only humans but four footed friends on the farm. People and animals alike loved and trusted him. His loss leaves a great sorrow in the hearts of his relatives and friends and is another example of the heart wrenching levy of war on our bravest and best.'* Arthur Ellis was awarded the 1914/15 Star, the Victory Medal and the British War Medal. He is commemorated on the Loos Memorial, Pas de Calais, Panel 103 to 105.

# Date of death: 13ᵗʰ October 1915

### Private Robert Hall:  North Staffs Regiment

Robert Frederick George Hall was born in Hanley, Stoke on Trent, Staffordshire, in 1890 to Mary Ann (nee Howkie) and Richard Hall, (a surgeon dentist). His sister Alice was born in 1884, and Beatrice in 1888. He was baptised on 3ʳᵈ December 1890 at Holy Trinity Church, Hanley. The family lived at 75 Lichfield Street in Hanley, but after the death of their mother the family moved in 1901 to Bower Cottage, Shelton, Hanley. The family moved to Alsager before the Great War and lived at Lynwood, Church Road.

Robert appears in the Electoral Register as a lodger in his father's house paying his father £1 a week for his room. Robert enlisted as a private soldier in the 2nd Battalion, Leicestershire Regiment, and served in Madras, India, based at Fort St George. He is described as 'single' on the 1911 Army census return. His service record states he was 5 feet 7 inches tall with a 38 inch chest and weighed 146 lbs. According to his record he left the army in 1913, but joined the Territorial Force, North

Staffordshire Regiment, a condition of resigning from the army. After being called up to re-join the army on 27th August 1914 he declared his home address as 'Lynwood', Church Road, Alsager, and gave his father, Richard, as his next of kin. He described his own profession as a 'student teacher.'

Private Hall entered France on 5th March 1915 with the North Staffs Regiment. (Soldier no 2686) Frederick, as he preferred to be called, was killed in action (missing presumed dead) whilst serving with 'B' Company, 7th Platoon, the 1/5th Battalion, North Staffordshire Regiment, in Loos, Nord-Pas-de-Calais, during the attack on the Hohenzollern Redoubt. He was posthumously awarded the 1915 Star, British War Medal, and the Victory Medal. He is commemorated on the Loos Memorial - Loos Memorial, Loos, Nord, Pas-de-Calais, France and is remembered on panels 103 to 105. His father was paid £4 war gratuity and £4.19s.10d back pay from the army in 1916.

*Loos Memorial*

35

# Date of death: 13th October 1915

## Lt Frank Bertram Mayer: 1/5th North Staffordshire Regiment

*Photo: Staffordshire Sentinel*

Frank was born in Alsager in 1883 to his parents Francis Creed Mayer, a solicitor, and Hannah Mayer. His father, who died before his son's war service, was also Clerk to Alsager Urban District Council. In the early 1900s Frank lived with his parents and brothers and sisters, Ida, John, Gladys, Tom, and Basil, in The Gables, Church Road, the same house as previously occupied by the Davies brothers. Frank attended Richmond High School, Shelton, Stoke-on-Trent, and Clifton College, Bristol, where he was a Cadet Serjeant in the Officer Training Corps. (578 ex-pupils from Clifton School died in the First World War; and in that war, Clifton provided not only the Commander-In-Chief (Douglas Haig) and an Army Commander (William Birdwood), but also twenty three Major-Generals and fifty two Brigadier-Generals).

After school Frank Mayer went on to qualify with honours as a solicitor in 1906 and in January 1907 was admitted to the firm of Mayer and Nelson, Burslem, as a Member in the business. He bought a house in Sandbach Road, Alsager, where he lived alone, the rest of his family having moved to north Cheshire after the death of Francis Creed Mayer. In 1912 Frank was Deputy Clerk to Alsager Urban District Council. He was also a keen, if not successful, amateur golfer who competed in the Trentham Whitsuntide Meeting in June 1912. He was runner up in the Barthomley Norton Vase Cup in May 1914. He was also a good tennis player and cricketer for Alsager Cricket Club. He was

36

also a member of the 'Alsager Constitutional Association,' and the B'hoys club. On June 19th 1912 Frank attended the big society wedding in St Mary's Alsager, the marriage of Gwendoline Settle and T. Stanley Pidduck, (both families which were to suffer losses in the Great War.) No less than seven leading Alsager families attending the wedding had family members were who killed in the Great War. Frank was known to be a good singer at B'hoys events at its meeting in the Alsager Arms pub. He sang at the 1912 annual dinner. In 1914 he was Junior Warden of the Gordon Masonic Lodge, Stoke-on-Trent.

On 11th September 1914 Frank enlisted as a private soldier with the North Staffordshire Regiment with the 1/5th Battalion, service number 8838. On 11th November 1914 he was commissioned 2nd Lieutenant, and in April 1915 promoted Lieutenant. Following training he was posted to France on 11th August 1915. Frank was killed in action while leading 4 Platoon, 'B' Company, 1/5th North Staffordshire Regiment in the first wave of attack on the Hohenzollern Redoubt during the battle of Loos. After leading his men in the attack Frank was wounded in the leg. He crawled over to another wounded man to give him a drink of water but was shot in the head still clutching the water bottle. Frank's death was reported in the Sentinel Newspaper on 20th October 1915. Alsager Urban District Council gave a vote of condolence on the death of Lt. Mayer at its meeting on 11th November 1915. He had been looking forward to two happy events on his next leave scheduled for October. He was to have been married and installed as Chair of Gordon Masonic Lodge. In 1922 his family were awarded his medals; the 1914/15 Star, the British War Medal, and the Victory Medal. As well as being remembered on the Alsager War Memorial, Frank is commemorated on the plinth of the family grave at Christ Church, Alsager. He left over £1,100 in his will to his brother Basil Mayer. He is also commemorated on panels 103-105 of the Loos Memorial, Loos, Nord Pas-de-Calais, France. Frank was one of the founding members of the B'hoys and is commemorated in their annual act of Remembrance.

*Frank Mayer's memorial on the family grave, Christ Church, Alsager. Photo: The author*

# Date of death: 13th October 1915

## Private Christopher Mitford: North Staffordshire Regiment

*Photo: Staffordshire Sentinel*

Christopher Mitford was born in Rode Heath, Cheshire, to Rosa Mitford, nee Critchley, and Christopher Mitford. He was baptised at Odd Rode Church on 14th November 1893. His father was a joiner and died in 1913. His brother and sisters were: Herbert born in 1891, Rosa (1892), Charles (1896), and Nina, (1900). His family later moved from Rode Heath to Yew Cottage, Lawton Road, Alsager before 1901 to live with Christopher's grandfather. Christopher attended the National School, by Christ Church. He was a member of St Mary's Sunday school and was awarded medals for good attendance. After leaving he became a gardener, and later a railway worker.

He was a porter on Alsager Station as shown in the National Union of Railway records from 1914.

NATIONAL UNION OF RAILWAYMEN.
GENERAL REGISTER OF MEMBERS.

*Photo: National Union of Railwaymen Archive.*

Christopher enlisted in the North Staffordshire Regiment in September 1914 in Hanley. He was posted to the 5th Battalion, service number 3251, as a private soldier. He went to France with his regiment on 3rd March 1915. On 13th October 1915 he was involved in the attack on the Hohenzollern Redoubt at Loos and was killed in action. His body lies buried unmarked somewhere on between Cambtin and Hulluch. His death was reported in the Sentinel on 26th November 1915. He was posthumously awarded the Victory Medal, British War Medal, and 1914/15 Star. He is commemorated on the Loos Memorial panel 103 to 105.

Christopher Mitford is included in De Ruvigny's Roll of Honour, 1914-1919 with the following details:

**MITFORD, CHRISTOPHER,** Private. No. 3152, 1/5th Battn. The Prince of Wales's (North Staffordshire Regt.) (T.F.), 2nd *s.* of Christopher Mitford, by his wife, Rosa (Lawton Road, Alsager, Stoke-on-Trent), dau. of Charles Cratchley; *b.* Rode Heath, Stoke-on-Trent, 14 Nov. 1893; educ. Alsager National School; was in Railway employ; volunteered and enlisted Sept. 1914; went to France 4 March, 1915; killed in action 13 Oct. 1915, in the attack on the Hohenzollern Redoubt, France. Buried near Fosse, No. 8 de Bethune, between Cambrin and Hulluch; *unm.*

*Loos Memorial photo: Commonwealth War Graves Commission*

# Date of death: 13th October 1915

### 2nd Lieutenant Henry 'Harry' Davies: North Staffs Regiment

*(A serviceman not on the Alsager War Memorial but with an Alsager connection)*

Henry 'Harry' Robert Griffith Davies was born in Glansychan, Aberychan, Monmouth, in 1887 to Sarah Elizabeth Davies nee Richards and William Henry Davies. His father died in 1907 and is buried in Christ Church, Alsager. Harry was educated at Monmouth School. (Old Boys of the School have been awarded 32 Military Crosses, 11 Distinguished Service Orders, 8 Flying medals (DFC, AFC and DFM) and one Victoria Cross) Harry was a member of the Combined Cadet Force at the school in 1904.

*Monmouth School Combined Cadet Force 1906. Photo Monmouth School*

*(Note their 'slouch' hats unchanged from the Boer War)*

Harry was the second of the three Davies brothers who were killed in 1915.

On moving to Alsager with his family Harry took the position as mining surveyor at Deep Pit Shelton, Stoke on Trent. His father was the General Manager of the Shelton Iron, Steel, and Coal Company. In 1901 he lived at 'The Gables' Alsager and 'Harry', as he preferred to be called, was a prominent number of the B'hoys in the town. He attended their dinner on the first anniversary of the B'hoys in 1912 at the Lodge Inn.

Harry Davies volunteered at the outbreak of war and enlisted in August 1914 with the 5th Battalion of the North Staffordshire Regiment. He was awarded a commission as 2nd Lieutenant on 9th February 1915. He was reported missing on 13th October 1915 during the battle of Loos, and presumed dead. Harry is commemorated in the B'hoys of Alsager annual act of Remembrance. He was posthumously awarded the 1914/15 Star, The British War Medal, and the Victory Medal.

# Date of death: 27th October 1915

### 2/Lt. Arthur Cyril Richards Davies: 5th North Staffordshire Regiment.

*(A serviceman not on the Alsager War Memorial but with an Alsager connection)*

The third of the Davies brothers to be killed in 1915, Arthur, was born in Pontypool in 1885 on 13th October. He was educated at Monmouth Grammar School and moved to live in the Gables in Alsager with his family and became Assistant Engineer at the Shelton Iron and Steel Company

where his father was General Manager.

*A rare photograph of the Gables taken in 1966 before it was demolished in 1971 indicating what a grand house the Davies family lived in. Photo South Cheshire Archives*

In 1911 he moved with his widowed mother to live in Alma Grove, Basford, Stoke-on-Trent. He joined as a private soldier at the outbreak of hostilities, service number 2728. He was commissioned Second Lieutenant in the British Army, 5th North Staffordshire Regiment on the same day as his brother Harry, on 9th February 1915. He entered France on 4th March 1915 with the Regiment and saw active service at Loos where his brother was killed. He was wounded on his birthday. He returned to hospital in England. Arthur died of appendicitis on 27th October 1915 in Kidderminster Infirmary, Worcestershire. His permanent address in his probate record was given as Temple Street, Basford, Stoke-on-Trent. A.C.R. Davies was posthumously awarded the 1914/15 Star, The British War Medal, and the Victory Medal.

# Alsager in 1916

On 2nd January 1916 the first church service of the year in Alsager was a united event concerned with the theme of *'humiliation and prayer'*. There was a collection of £15. 19s. 3d. for the Serbian Relief Fund. St Mary's church was overcrowded as clergy from other churches had encouraged their congregations to attend this service. The service was also attended by Councillors, staff fom the Alsager Fire Brigade, and members of the Alsager Volunteers. Three hundred children were present from surrounding areas at the event. Services such as this had the purpose of motivating the people and boosting morale.

A few days later Rev Arthur Waller presented George Cartwight a copy of the New Testament bound in khaki on him enlisting in the army. George was Secretary of Christ Church Sunday School and had been called up under the Lord Derby scheme. George also received other gifts from Sunday School Scholars. He served as a Sapper in the Royal Engineers, surviving the war. His brother Tom was killed in 1918.

## Women's Work

The main feature in the parish magazine in January 1916 was a long feature on women's war work encouraging every female to come forward to take up jobs vacated by men. The Vicar wrote: *'Women should equally do their duty by volunteering for such work as they can do or for which they can be trained'.* The Vicar was particularly keen to see women work for schemes introduced by the County Agricultural Committee and engage in work such a milking and crop production. He encouraged women to find 10 shillings ( 50p) a week out of their own resources to pay for their own agricultural training. In February 1916 the Chester Chronicle reported that between 400 and 500 local women were registered through the Labour Exchange in south Cheshire for farm and horticultural work. The local Board of Agriculture feared that with conscription there would not be enough men to do farm work. Women were provided with special farm uniforms from February. In August 1916 the Chester Chronicle reported no agricultural workers were employed in 'local' munitions factories and that if farm workers tried to change their employment to work in munitions work they would be discharged and asked to return to their farms. The Rural Tribunals were also keen to stop this practice. The government set up an agricultural training college for women in Holmes Chapel but closed it in 1917 at short notice. It does not seem there was a need for advanced training. Most training was on the job at local farms. It is not known how many local women applied for farm work through the Labour Exchange. British Summer Time had been introduced for the first time in the Defence of the Realm legislation. Food production was crucial to survival but most middle class Alsager women opted for nursing work. The Goss sisters and Miss Palfreyman chose to take up nursing through the Voluntary Aid Detachments rather than do farming work. Crewe was a centre for the munitions industry. It is not known how many Alsager people worked in the Crewe munitions factories but at least one tried to apply for exemption from military service because he was a munitions worker.

## Shocks and Tremors

On January 21st 1916 the Nantwich Guardian reported there had been tremors felt in Alsager over a wide part of the town. People in Audley Road complained of ornaments rattling on the mantlepeice. It is thought the tremors were caused by mine workings in North Staffordshire but at the time people must have been worried the tremors were war related.

## Alsager Military Tribunal

Many Alsager men had enlisted in late 1915 in anticipation of national conscription into the army in 1916. Amongst them was Moses Corfield aged 37, headteacher at the National School, Alsager, who despite his job, would not be exempted from military service. He lived with George Edwards, his father in law, at 'Woodside', Alsager, with his wife Helena and young family. He joined the Royal Army Medical Corps and would not be demobilised until 1918. He was posted to a field ambulance unit in Albert, France. Conscription accelerated the number of men called up into the services. The Alsager Military Tribunal was created to to hear applications for exemption from conscription into the services. Councillor Adolphus Goss was made its Chairman and J.J. Nelson the Secretary. Goss, who by March 1916 had lost one son in the war, and was a local magistrate and churchman would have been seen as an unbiased Chairman. The Tribunal was made up of local councilors and a military representative. Appeals could be made to the County Appeals Tribunal. Appellants had the right to be represented at hearings. No names were reported in newspaper accounts. The first meeting of the Alsager Military Appeals Tribunal was held in March 1916 in the council offices. Fourteen appeals were considered. Four farm labourers were given total exemption from conscription because cultivation on their farms depended on them. A chemist was given total exemption, but a miller, a garage manager, a baker, a sand pit proprietor were exempted for only three months. A bricklayer was exempted for one month, an agricultural labourer for six weeks. The appeal of a clerk was refused outright. He had to enlist immediately.

The tribunals often aroused heated debate between the miltary representative and other members. In June 1916, the military representative appealed for a second time against granting a cowman an extension until October. The military representative's appeal was defeated. The Alsager Tribunal tended to err on the side of appellants and their employers. In June an Alsager farmer's horseman was given exemption for two months to enable his employer to find a replacement. A chauffeur-gardener aged 36, married with one child, was granted conditional exemption on taking up farming work satisfactory to the Tribunal. A wheelwright aged 34 with seven children under eight was given conditional exemption.

11 Tribunal appeals were heard in June with no cases forcing appellants to enlist immediately. At the next meeting more farmers were given conditional exemption but only one month's exemption was granted for a wagon repairer. The claim of a married farm labourer aged 27, a man who worked in a different county but lived in Alsager, was dismissed. He was a householder in Cheshire and his protest failed. In October 1916 Adolphus Goss, Tribunal Chairman, complained to the Chester Appeals committee because two Alsager men had travelled all the way to Chester for medical examinations for a County appeal but had not been seen by the doctor. They even had to pay their own railway fares to and from Chester. In November 1916 thirteen appeals were considered. The case of a chauffeur aged 37 married with one child, a boot repairer, aged 38, with two children, and another chauffeur were rejected. Other cases were given three month exemptions. The exemption certificate of a smallholder, aged 35, was withdrawn. Several cases could not be heard because medical examiners had neglected to forward medical classification cards. By the end of 1916 the trend was to take a tougher stand on exemption from military conscription.

**The Volunteers**

On March 3rd 1916 a parade of newly attested soldiers took place in Alsager. The men, all wearing the regulation arm bands, were led by the Alsager contingent of the Cheshire Volunteers into St Mary's church for a service. The Volunteers also took part in several training activities around Alsager. On the new shooting range in fields near Alsager Hall there was a shooting competition between them company and Shelton Iron Company on 25th August. To the Volunteers' embarrassment they were comprehensively beaten by the Shelton marksmen.

**Deception by a Bogus Soldier and crime in Alsager**

The Defence of the Realm Act provisions had introduced restrictions of movement throughout Britain. People were forbidden to loiter near bridges and tunnels or to light bonfires. Private correspondence was also censored. Military censors examined 300,000 private telegrams in 1916 alone. The police in Alsager were active in protecting the town. On the same day as the shooting competition between the Volunteers and Shelton Iron Company, a youth, Cyril Day, was charged with obtaining food and lodgings by deception. He pretended to be a soldier who had been discharged from the army because of his wounds. He had claimed he was from Colchester and the son of a Wesleyan Minister. The local Wesleyan church had believed the man's story and looked after Day who claimed he had fought with the London Scottish Regiment. People became suspicious and when Day was asked to produce his discharge papers he was unable to do so. He confessed to his crime after being locked in Alsager police cells overnight. At his trial on 1st September it was said he had enjoyed the support of the Wesleyan community between the 9th and 20th August. At Sandbach Magistrates Court he was bound over for three years and given probation. In his defence his father said Cyril was *'simple minded'*. Day's undoing came because from August 16th 1916 the police had new powers to stop unbadged men and demand to see their exemption cards from military duty. The problem with the new power was that individuals could use false addresses and use another man's exemption card to bluff their way during an interview by the police.

There was very little crime in Alsager in 1916 to worry the police. On 10th October, Gordon Kerry aged 12 was seen to throw stones at ceramic insulators on telegraph poles on the drive up to Alsager Hall. Four insulators were broken. Acting Sergeant Penny tried to arrest Kerry but he ran away. He was arrested later in Crewe Road. At Sandbach Magistrates he was bound over and his parents made to pay the costs. Reports of crime like this were rare.

## Keeping up public morale

In April 1916 there was a 'Primrose Flag Day' held in Alsager arranged by the Alsager and Lawton Habitation of the Primrose League in aid of a permanent holiday home in Lowestoft, Suffolk, for disabled servicemen. The event was organised by Miss Wilbraham and Miss Goss along with 60 helpers. 2,552 pennies were collected which weighed 50lbs. The flag and primrose decorations were made by crippled children. The Nantwich Guardian reported, Everyone was kind and helpful and the working people supported the movement generously. £25 17s 8d was collected.

Other fundraising continued in 1916 and £60 was raised at an 'At Home', for the National Children's Union and £34 was donated to sick children of the parish. £56 was collected for the Red Cross Working Party in January. On 6th May 1916 there was a street collection in Alsager for the war effort organised by the Council which raised £12. 12s. 6d., but after paying for flags the sum raised was reduced to £11. 2s. 4d. The council appeal was unsuccessful compared to the voluntary efforts.

Also in May 1916 there was a special collection of eggs from Alsager farms for wounded soldiers; 626 eggs from the Day School and 212 from Christ Church Sunday School were delivered to hospitals. The council took a lead in keeping up public morale. Morale was low after the devastating news of 20,000 casualties on the first day of the Battle of the Somme in July 1916. On 8th August 1916 on the second anniversary of the start of the war, a public meeting was held in the grounds of Milton House, the home of Sir Ernest Crag M.P.. Before the meeting there was a procession through Alsager of councillors, the Fire Brigade, and the town detachment of the Cheshire Volunteers, behind the Crewe Carriage Works Band. A resolution read out by Mr Nelson, Secretary to the Council:

*'This meeting of the citizens of Alsager records its unflinching determination to continue to a victorious end the struggle in maintenance of these ideas of liberty and justice which are the common cause of the allies.'*

The resolution was greeted with loud cheers. Public shows of patriotism were popular. In private some families of wounded or dead servicemen must have hated such shows of jingoism.

In May 1916 an unamed Royal Fusilier from Alsager wrote his parents who passed the letter to the Nantwich Guardian to print. He complained about the attitude of strikers in the Clyde shipyards in Glasgow.

*'The word strike makes me sick. I cannot imagine how any Britisher can be party to a strike in these grave times; it is a pity for some things that the war does not touch the homeland more closely, so these wretched people can see what their conduct amounts to. Their greedy grabbing for money is ghastly; they are selling the lives of their fellows, who without reservation are giving their all for their country's need.'*

Advertisements started appearing in a number of newspapers in 1916 asking for female domestic servants to work in Alsager middle class homes. These advertisements appeared in the Liverpool Echo and the Chester Chronicle. This indicates it was becoming more difficult to recruit women domestic servants when they could receive higher wages in manufacturing work, especially in the Crewe munitions factories. The work of the Working Party continued but collections dropped to only £36 in August, and £22 in December compared to £69 in March, which may have been due to war-weariness and the news of more deaths of local servicemen. The number of participants making clothes for servicemen decreased to three in August, but the number of worshippers at Christ Church and St Marys remained high. Nearly two hundred worshipers were communicants in the Anglican churches in Alsager in November 1916.

One of Alsager's busiest men was Arthur Percival Tiley of 'Hazelmere', Alsager. Over forty years of age at the start of the war, Arthur, a 'Chemical Shopkeeper' worked for the Red Cross as a driver delivering supplies to hospitals. He started his work in January 1915 and continued until December 1917. He covered most of the Staffordshire hospitals and drove hundreds of miles to and from hospitals. The principles of public duty and service were expected and largely accepted.

Meanwhile local men continued to enlist and fight but because no proof of age was required by recruiting sergeants, occasionally an Alsager youth would enlist underage by running away from home. On 9th May 1916, Gunner Jack Howarth was brought home to Alsager by his parents from Woolwich barracks. He had enlisted when he was just 16 years old and served undetected for a hundred and twenty six days.

On 31st May 1916 the largest sea battle of the Great War, the Battle of Jutland took place. Two man with an Alsager connection served in the conlict; Joseph Simcox served aboard the hospital ship *Plessy* bringing wounded sailors back to Britain from the North Sea near Denmark. Ernest Dale served on *HMS Thunderer*.

Alsager women took up nursing and continued to work for the Red Cross. For some of the women this proved to be difficult but they persevered. In October 1916 Bella Skerratt, of 'Hazeldine', Alsager, enlisted at Rode Hall. She undertook 'Morning Duty' as a nurse and afterwards 'Sewing Duty' for the Working Party. Her Red Cross record stated: *'Miss Skerratt is a cripple, & comes three miles on her bicycle to duty'*. Some nurses worked at more than one establishment. Ethel Snell, from the Avenue, Alsager, undertook morning duty at Rode Hall Hospital on alternate weeks with Southport Military Hospital.

In the the summer of 1916 a framed list of men who had joined the services was displayed in St Mary's porch. Unfortunately this list has been lost. There was also a procession by the church through the town stopping at various places for prayer for the parish mission. A special memorial service for those who had fallen in the war was held at St Mary's on 29th October 1916.

# Deaths of Alsager Servicemen in 1916

## Date of death: 12th January 1916

### Private Harold Marfleet: North Staffordshire Regiment

*Photo: Sentinel Newspaper*

Harold Marfleet was born in Hartshill, Stoke on Trent to John Marfleet and Clara Marfleet. Harold's father died when Harold was only a year old and the family, Clara his mother, and Brenda his sister, moved to Alsager to live with Clara's family, the Capeys, in Crewe Road. Harold's grandfather, Thomas Capey, had a butcher's shop at 53 Crewe Road and Harold lived there until he enlisted in the army. In 1914 he was working as a draper's assistant at Timmis Drapers in Tunstall, Stoke-on-Trent. Harold enlisted in the 7th Battalion North Staffordshire Regiment, service number 14719, in 1915 in Burslem. He underwent training before embarking with the regiment to Turkey. The Battalion sailed from Avonmouth in June 1915 and landed on Gallipoli the following month. After arriving in Gallipoli the Battalion landed at Mudros on the 4th July. Between the 6th and 16th July the infantry of the Division crossed to Helles and relieved the 29th Division on the left of the line. The infantry returned to Mudros at the end of the month, and from the 3rd to 5th August the 7th Battalion landed at Anzac Cove. Harold was involved in action in the battle for Suvla in August 1915, then in action on the 8th December 1915 at Cape Helles where the Turks attacked British positions. The Battalion's Commanding officer, Lt. Col. Walker, was killed during the action along with thirty four other ranks. Eighty four soldiers were wounded. Harold Marfleet was wounded on the on the last attack on the peninsula before the evacuation from Cape Helles on 8th December. His left arm was badly injured and the doctors on board ship were unable to save him. The Battalion had moved by sea on the 22nd December on HMS Scotian to Port Said in Egypt. Harold Marfleet died of wounds on 12th January 1916 and was buried at sea between Mudros and Malta.

**The 7th Battalion, North Staffordshire Regiment: dates of Battalion movements**

On 29th Aug 1914 it formed at Lichfield and was attached to the 39th brigade, 13th division, on Salisbury Plain

Jan. 1915 -Basingstoke

Feb. 1915 - Blackdown, Aldershot

June 1915 - sailed from Avonmouth

July 1915 - landed at Gallipoli

Jan 1916 - landed in Egypt

Harold Marfleet is commemorated on the Helles Memorial in Turkey, panel 170 and 171. He was posthumously awarded the 1914/15 Star, Victory Medal, and British Medal

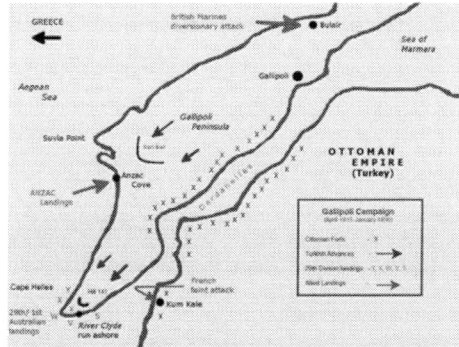

*The Helles Memorial, Gallipoli, Turkey. Photo: Commonwealth War Graves Commission*

# Date of death: 26th February 1916

**George Henry Chadwick Royal Marines: 3rd Field Ambulance Royal Navy Medical Unit**

*An Alsager St John Ambulance Volunteer who died in Greece*

*(A serviceman not on the Alsager War Memorial but with Alsager connection)*

George Henry Chadwick was born in Talke O' the Hill, Staffordshire in 1890 to Ann and Henry Chadwick. He lived with his family at Linley Cottage, Talke, just over the Staffordshire border from Cheshire. In 1911 he was single and working as a 'moulder' in an iron foundry. Before the Great War he joined Alsager St John Ambulance as a volunteer. Alsager had its own Division with St John Ambulance and they met and trained weekly in the town.

George enlisted in the Royal Marines 3rd Royal Navy Field Ambulance on 23rd March 1915, and on 9th May he joined the British Expeditionary Force draft for Gallipoli, where he served from 29th May to 31st October 1915. His service record states he was 5 feet 4 inches tall, of a fresh complexion, and with brown hair. His service number was Deal/3576 (S).

Developing Pyrexia (a fever of unknown origin), he was taken to the Royal Navy Hospital, Malta for medical attention. He joined Base Depot, Alexandra, Egypt on 26th January 1916 before returning to his unit at Mudros, Greece, (now the Royal Navy 2nd Field Ambulance) on 8th February 1916. He developed what was thought to be influenza and was taken aboard Hospital Ship 'Somali', on which he died on 26th February 1916. He was found to have contracted meningitis. His body was taken ashore and buried at Portianos Cemetery. West Mudros, Lemnos, Aegean Sea. He is buried in grave 111. B. 315. It is now a Commonwealth War Grave. George was posthumously awarded the 1914/15 Star, the British War Medal, and the Victory Medal. After the war he was included on the National Roll of the St John Ambulance

*Part of the National Roll of St John Ambulance.*

49

# Date of death: 26th March 1916

## Lieutenant John Wesley Davies: Royal Welsh Fusiliers

*Personal Assistant to Alsager's MP Sir E. Craig*

*Photo: Llangollen Advertiser.*

**Lieut. J. W. DAVIES.**
**Royal Welsh Fusiliers.**

John Wesley Davies was born in Leeswood, Flintshire, in 1885 to Margaret and John Davies. His father was a coal miner. His sister Sarah Anne Davies was born in 1877, sister Victoria in 1880, brother Christopher Davies in 1881, brother Matthew in 1886, brother Armerius in 1888, and sister Gwendoline Davies in 1890. In the 1901 census John is given as living at his parent's address, Granfield Terrace, Gwersyllt, Wrexham. In 1901 he was employed as a Solicitor's Clerk. In 1911 John was still living at home and working as a clerk in a colliery. Although his father is described as a 'coalminer', his children had remarkably good jobs despite coming from a mining family. Christopher was a certificated schoolmaster, Mathew a lecturer in Greek and Latin at the University of North Wales. Armerius Davies was a fitter, and Gwendoline was a school teacher. The family lived at 1 Victoria Terrace, Greenfield, Rhosddu, Wrexham.

Prior to the war John Wesley Davies became personal assistant to Mr Ernest Craig MP for Crewe, who lived in Alsager at Milton House. John Wesley Davies lodged with Ernest Baddeley in Station Road, Alsager, while he was worked for Ernest Craig. He appears on the Electoral Register for 1915.

In 1914 John Wesley enlisted as a private soldier in the Royal Welsh Fusiliers, 8th Battalion, in Rhyl in October 1914, service number 60674. He was commissioned 2nd Lieutenant on 1st December 1915 In 1915 he married Kate Emily Griffiths from Wrexham, and the couple's home was in Stansfield, Mold Road, Wrexham. He was posted to France on 2nd December 1915. In March 1916 John Wesley gained a commission as Lieutenant and was posted to the 16th Battalion of the Royal Welsh Fusiliers. He was killed in action on March 26th 1916. He was accompanying a general on reconnaissance when he was killed by a shrapnel shell. The death is not reported in the War Diary of the 16th Battalion of the Royal Welsh Fusiliers. A short report of John's death appears in the Liverpool Echo on 7th April 1916.

## THE ROLL OF HONOUR.

### OFFICERS.

#### KILLED.

Davies, Lieut. J. T., Royal Welsh Fusiliers.
Son of Mr John Davies, Greenfield, Rhosddu,
Wrexham, Lieut. Davies was one of the earliest
to join the R.W.F. at Rhyl in October, 1914, as a
private, and he obtained his commission in a
few weeks. His brother, Lieut. M. H. Davies
(who before the war was assistant lecturer in
Greek and Latin at the University College of
North Wales), is also in the Royal Welsh Fusiliers, though not in the same battalion. Lieut.
Davies was at one time private secretary to Mr.
Ernest Craig, M.P., and married last October
the eldest daughter of Mr. T. P. Griffiths, Stansfield, Wrexham.

### KILLED BY GENERAL'S SIDE.

Particulars received by his parents show
that Lieut. J. W. Davies (Royal Welsh Fusiliers) was killed by a shhrapnel shell whilst
accompanying a general on reconnaissance
duty. Prior to the war the officer was private
secretary to Mr. Ernest Craig, member for the
Alsager Division, Cheshire, and married a
daughter of Mr. Thomas Griffiths Stansfield,
Wrexham.

In messages to the widow, Brigadier-
General Price Davies refer to Lieut. Davies
as a fine man and a good officer.

*Newspaper reports of J.W Davies' death.*

John's daughter, Joan Wesley Davies was born in Wrexham on 14th August 1916. John Wesley Davies is buried in Le Touret Military Cemetery, Richebourg-L'avoue, Pas de Calais. He is buried in grave 3 E 18. Apart from being commemorated on Alsager War Memorial John Wesley is remembered on Gwersyllt War Memorial near Wrexham.

*The grave of J.W Davies. Photo: Commonwealth War Graves Commission.*

*John Wesley Davies' brother, Captain Matthew Henry Davies, Royal Welsh Fusiliers, Intelligence Corps, and later in the RAF, survived the war. His medals are pictured*

John Wesley Davies was a member of Wesley Place Methodist Church and is commemorated on their Great War Memorial plaque.

# Date of death: 16<sup>th</sup> April 1916

## Lance Corporal Samuel Whittaker: Royal Fusiliers (London Regiment)

Samuel Whittaker was born in Alsager in 1891 to Sarah and Samuel Whittaker.                     His father was an agricultural labourer who died while Samuel was still young. In 1901 the family lived in Lawton Road, Alsager. Sarah, Samuel's mother, was a dressmaker. His sister, Elizabeth Whittaker, was born 1880. His brother Frank was born in 1881 and George in 1883. His younger sister Myra, was born in 1889, and Mary in 1894.

In 1911 Samuel was working as a commercial clerk for an agricultural fruit company, Elder & Tyffe, Hanley, and his sister Myra was a teaching assistant. In 1912 he played in Alsager Cricket Team against St Paul's, Crewe.

Samuel appears on the electoral register as a lodger in his mother's house paying five shillings (25p) a week board.

Following the outbreak of war Samuel enlisted in the 17<sup>th</sup> Battalion of Royal Fusiliers (The London Regiment) in Stoke-on-Trent, and then transferred to the 12<sup>th</sup> Battalion of the same regiment. He was posted to France on 6<sup>th</sup> October 1915 and promoted Lance Corporal.

In mid-April 1916 the 12<sup>th</sup> Battalion were in trenches 132 to 135 near 'Hill 63', in the vicinity of Ploegsteert. All leave had been cancelled because of enemy attacks. The War Diary states on 15<sup>th</sup> April the enemy were very active shelling trench 132. 'Winter Trench' was damaged and 'Borossa Farm,' completely destroyed. Seven private soldiers were wounded. It is likely Samuel was one of these men. In April 1916 Captain Charles K. Masters wrote to Samuel's mother describing her son's death. He had been wounded in his side by a shell falling in to his trench at noon. Because the trench was exposed to enemy fire it was impossible to move Samuel until nightfall. He died of wounds on 16<sup>th</sup> April 1916 at the First Canadian Casualty Clearing Station, Flanders, soon after arriving there. Captain Masters wrote, *'he gave his life bravely and nobly for his country'.*

*1<sup>st</sup> Canadian Casualty Clearing Station Reception. Photo: Wikipedia*

He is buried at the Bailleul Communal Cemetery Extension in France, fourteen miles south of Belgium where he was wounded. He is buried in grave number 2. D. 191. His mother put the following words on his gravestone. *'Grant unto him Eternal Rest O Lord'*

Samuel was posthumously awarded the 1914/15 Star, the British War Medal and the Victory Medal. At the time of Samuel's death his mother and sisters were living at Grove Villas in Alsager. The army paid his back pay of £4. 9s. 8d and a £7 war gratuity to his mother in 1916. In his will Samuel left £329. 16s. 11d to his mother. On Alsager War Memorial he is recorded as Corporal Samuel Whittaker but his medal card and Commonwealth War Graves records give his rank as Lance Corporal.

In 1913 Sam wrote in a friend's album.

*'Life, I know that thou and I must part,*

*And when and where and how we met I own*

*To remain a secret yet.'*

Below Samuel's signature are the words written by his friend,

*'3 years later: Killed in action 16.4.1916 2493 Corporal S Whittaker, Royal Fusiliers.'*

*'Soundly he'll sleep in the grave where they laid him,*

*His last bivouac, peace: admonish strife, to fall in again*

*When the Captain who gave him shall sound the Reveille recalling to life.'*

# Date of death: 24th April 1916

## William Wood:  7th Battalion North Staffs Regiment

*William Wood, right 2nd row, Alsager Football team, 1913/14.*

*Photo South Cheshire Archives, Crewe*

William Wood was born in Alsager, Cheshire, in 1890 to Mary Jane and William Wood. His father was a publican, a butcher, and later a grocer. William's brother, Frank Wood was born 1887. Arthur Wood was born in 1892, sister, Myrtle Annie Wood, was born 1894, Helen Jane was born 1898. Sister, Jennie Wood, was born in 1904. The family lived in Crewe Road at their father's butcher's shop.

William worked as a butcher's assistant for his father and later worked at Settle Speakman Ltd. On 31st August 1914 William enlisted with the 4th Battalion, North Staffs Regiment.

William's service record states he was 5 feet 6 inches tall with a 34 inch waist. He had brown hair with blue eyes with a sallow complexion. On 28th November 1914 William was posted to the 11th Battalion, North Staffordshire Regiment, which was stationed in Alderney, Channel Islands, for training. William suffered an attack of scabies in May 1915 and spent six days in hospital. On 26th October 1915 he was posted to the 7th Battalion, North Staffordshire Regiment, service number 8758, and embarked with the Mediterranean Expeditionary Force to Turkey. By early December

54

1915 William's battalion was engaged in cleaning out trenches in Sulakik, Gallipoli, which had been flooded by heavy rains. A heavy frost followed. In No Man's Land the regiment repaired barbed wire and sent patrols every night to test the enemy's defences. Following heavy losses preparations were made to evacuate the British Army from Gallipoli. Firing on the enemy was discouraged to lessen chance of being attacked but the Turks continued to shell the British trenches. William's regiment was finally evacuated on 19th December to Imbros by the Royal Navy. On 24th December it reached Mudros and on 28th Cape Helles on the Gallipoli peninsular. The regiment finally left Turkey by ship on 28th December 1915 and reached Port Said in Egypt. The Regiment held forward posts in the Suez Canal defences. On the 12th of February 1916 the 7th Battalion moved to Mesopotamia (modern Iraq), to join the force being assembled near Sheikh Sa'ad for the relief of the besieged garrison at Kut al Amara. They joined the Tigris Corps on the 27th of March and were in action in the unsuccessful attempts to relieve Kut, which had been captured by the enemy.

*Picture: Weekly Sentinel photo 20th May 1916*

On 24thApril 1916, Easter Monday, William died of wounds aboard the transport hospital ship Blosse Lynch and was taken ashore and buried in Amara on the left bank of the Tigris in the military cemetery. This cemetery was destroyed in Iraq in the First Gulf War. Amara had originally been occupied by the Mesopotamian Expeditionary Force on 3rd June 1915 and it immediately became a hospital centre. The accommodation for medical units on both banks of the Tigris was greatly increased during 1916 and by April 1917 seven general hospitals and some smaller units were stationed there. William parents, having been informed of their son's death by the Army, reported his death to the Sentinel Newspaper on 15th May 1916. The report mentions William had worked for Messrs Settle Speakman, prior to enlistment. Another Sentinel report, on 20th June 1920, included William Wood in the men commemorated by the 7th Battalion of the North Staffordshire Regiment. William's sister, Myrtle Annie Wood served with the Women's Army Auxiliary Corps in France between July 1918 and December 1919. His brother, Frank Wood, served also in the British Army.

*Amara War Cemetery before its destruction in the 1990s in the First Gulf War.*

# Date of death: 12th June 1916

## Hugo Cholmondeley Arnold: East Kent Regiment

*(A serviceman not on the Alsager War Memorial but with Alsager connection)*

Hugo was the son of Henry Arnold, Vicar of Alsager 1907 -1913. He was born in 1897 in the rectory in the village of Barrow near Chester. His father, Henry, was the vicar of Barrow and his mother was Mary Lyle Arnold, nee Smith. Hugo's grandmother on his father's side was Charlotte Georgiana Cholmondeley of Cholmondeley Castle, Cheshire, hence his middle name. When Henry Arnold became vicar of Alsager he moved into the old vicarage near to Christ Church (demolished in the 1970s) and became responsible for Christ Church and St Mary Magdalene. The family had four female servants and a male gardener. Hugo was sent to school at the Leas, Hoylake, Cheshire, and later, Haileybury School, Hertfordshire, where his father had been educated. Hugo had ambitions to follow his father and grandfather into the ministry but postponed the idea with the onset of war. He enlisted as a private in the East Kent Regiment, service number 18188. On 22nd November 1916 he gained a commission as 2nd Lieutenant in the East Kent Regiment, 4th battalion. By this time his father was Vicar of Wolsingham, Durham, but Hugo's military career was closely followed in Alsager and mentioned in the parish magazine. Hugo proved to be an exceptional soldier and became the "intelligence officer" for his company.

According to the East Kent War Diaries, Hugo was working with the 8th East Kent's on 10th June 1917. The 8th were holding trenches north of English Wood near Damstrasse, near Messines, and underwent heavy barrage as they tried to leave their trenches while being relieved by the 9th Warwickshire Regiment after 9.30 pm on the 10th June 1917. Hugo died of wounds on 12th June 1917 at the military hospital, Camiers, France, and is buried in the Military cemetery, Etaples, grave reference XVII. E. 22.  His commanding officer said of him, *'Shortly after he joined the battalion I picked him out as a most conscientious worker and took him as my Intelligence Officer. He was of great assistance during (what) I suppose will become to be known as the battle of Messines, and his untiring energy surprised me on more than one occasion. On two occasions, I literally had to order him to take some rest. His end was most unfortunate … It was a great shock to me. He was so bright and cheerful and it was never too much trouble for him to do anything. In fact he seemed to take pleasure in doing things for other people. If there was anything doing, he was the first to volunteer. We all miss him very much.'* His major said of Hugo, *'He was one of the best officers we have ever had in the battalion, tremendously keen and very thorough in all he did, and worked hard whenever we were in action.*

*We are all very sorry to have lost him …He had a very high sense of duty and lived up to it at all times. Men like him are difficult to replace.'*

In the July 1917 Alsager Parish Magazine a tribute was made to Hugo Arnold. On hearing her son was wounded Mrs Arnold had set out to France to see him but he died before she reached him. Hugo's father was in hospital in Harrogate at the time of his son's death having being wounded in a shooting accident. On Sunday 24th June prayers were said for the Arnold family in Alsager. Hugo was unmarried.

Hugo was posthumously awarded the British War Medal and Victory Medals. His younger brother's son went on to be Lord Lieutenant of Cheshire. Hugo is commemorated on the war memorial in Wolsingham, Durham.

*Alsager Old Vicarage. Demolished 1960s. The former site is now part of Alsager School. Photo South Cheshire Archives.*

# Date of death: June 22nd 1916

## Lance Sergeant Charles William Yorke: 12th Bn. Northumberland Fusiliers

*(A serviceman not on the Alsager War Memorial but with an Alsager connection)*

Charles Yorke was born in 1879 in Madeley, Shropshire. Charles William was the eldest son of William R. Yorke and his wife Eliza. His father was born in Dawley, Shropshire and in 1891 was a signalman at Hough, Nantwich. The family seemed to have moved frequently: from Shropshire, to Fenton in Stoke-on-Trent, then on to Shavington, Cheshire, and finally Lawton Gate near Alsager. John Henry, younger brother to Charles, also worked on the railways and in 1901 he was employed as a railway goods guard. Another brother, Richard, was also a railway signalman. Charles enlisted in the militia in the Cheshire Regiment on 25th January 1896 in London, and he later transferred to the Northumberland Fusiliers. At his attestation he was described as 5 feet 4 ¾ inches tall with grey eyes and dark brown hair, service number 4882. He began his career with the Northumberlands in Portsmouth. He was appointed Lance Corporal in January 1899 and in 1903 he rose to Corporal. He served in Malta, Crete, South Africa and Mauritius and received the Queen's South African medal with clasp and the King's South African with clasp (1901 & 1902). From 1903 until 1908 he remained in the Reserve. In 1907 he married Betsy Dale at Odd Rode Church.

National Union of Railwaymen records state Charles was a member of the Alsager branch of the union from 3rd July 1910. The 1911 census records Charles as a married 32 year old railway signalman, and living at Railway Cottages, Biddulph. His wife Betsy was visiting relatives at Church Lawton at the time of the census. In October 1914 the Sentinel reported that he was with the Northumberland Fusiliers at Aylesbury and in November that: '*Sergeant Charles Yorke, one of the signalmen from Biddulph Railway Station, a reservist of the Northumberland Fusiliers, has been stationed near Harrow for some time. He came home last Saturday on four days leave, and looks remarkably well. He says that since his promotion (he was a corporal when he re-joined his regiment in August) he has been kept very busy drilling new recruits.*'

The 12th Battalion Northumberland Fusiliers trained at Halton Camp Tring, High Wycombe and Witley Camp, Maidenhead, and with training complete the men were now battle ready. Attaching to 62nd Brigade 21st Division the troops were inspected by Lord Kitchener on 12th August 1915. The following month the division crossed the channel, landing in France on 8th September, and assembled in the Tilques area. The battle of Loos was where Charles was to see his first action on the Western Front. After a long night march, the morning of 26th September brought the battalion to an area known as Bois Hugo, Chalk Pit Wood and Hill 70 redoubt; at the latter the enemy held strong defensive positions. The 12th Northumberlands attacked this redoubt and although the fusiliers fought bravely, the assault which was under unbelievable deteriorating conditions failed, with many casualties. The division were withdrawn to recover, being deployed in a defensive role until the spring of 1916. In the Somme district during early summer the battalion was busy preparing for the forthcoming Battle of the Somme. Charles as a Lance Sergeant would have had extra responsibilities for the preparations; his battalion were in an assembly area north of Becordel-Becourt. Following an enemy artillery bombardment on their position they endured many casualties. Evidently it was in this area that Charles Yorke was to die on Thursday 22nd June 1916. Newspaper reports state that he was killed instantly by a bursting shell. In little more than a week, the Battle of the Somme was to open on 1st July. The Weekly Sentinel of 22nd July 1916 reported that *previous to enlisting he served all through the Boer War and when the present war was declared he was anxious once more to serve his King and country. He enlisted at the end of August 1914 and went to France in September 1915.'* Charles left a widow and four little girls. The Sentinel also reported that Mrs. Yorke had received a letter from him on 28th June (written on the 21st) the day after she had received notification of his death from the chaplain, the Rev. Stanley Keene, in which he wrote to cheer her up, and to *'tell his little girls that Daddy will soon be home now to take them for walks'.* The Battalion Chaplain wrote to Mrs Yorke saying, *'It may be some consolation to you to know that your husband died at once and quite painlessly.'*

The Sentinel newspaper reported Sergeant Yorke's father was Mr. William Yorke, signalman at Alsager station and his brother John was a goods guard at the Junction, also in Alsager. Mrs. Yorke received a letter from Lieutenant J. Brunton in which he wrote: *'At such time as this when you have suffered such an irreparable loss, words of sympathy seem so very inadequate, but I know you will believe me when I say that your husband's death was a very serious blow to myself personally, and also to our company. As his immediate officer your husband and I came very much in contact and I am proud to have had the honour of commanding such an N.C.O.'* Lance Sergeant Yorke now lies in the Dartmoor Cemetery, which today is situated in a beautiful wooded area on the outskirts of the village of Becordel-Becourt. A unique addition to Charles's grave is an old ceramic plaque, presumably placed there by a French person in the 1920s when the cemetery was laid out. The text reads: *'Le Temps Passe Le Souvenir Reste (as time passes the memory remains)'*

*William Yorke's grave. Photo: Commonwealth War Graves*

In Britain Charles is commemorated on the memorial at Stoke-on-Trent railway station, which is dedicated to the men of the North Staffordshire Railway who died in the Great War. He is not included on the Alsager War Memorial but is commemorated on Biddulph war memorials.

William Yorke's medals: Queen's South African medal with clasp and the King's South Africa Medal with clasp; 1914 Star, Victory Medal, British War Medal.

# Date of death: 1st July 1916

The first day of the Battle of the Somme is well documented as the bloodiest day in the history of the British Army – with 58,000 troops falling wounded or killed on that one single day. On that fateful day two men with an Alsager connection died.

## 2nd Lt Norman Andrews Pidduck: 5th North Staffordshire Regiment /Machine Gun Corps

*Norman Andrews Pidduck. Photo Family Archives.*

He was born in Hanley, Staffordshire, in 1895 to Ellen and Frederick Pidduck. His father was the owner of Pidduck's jewellery shops in Hanley and Southport. The family lived at 9 Park Road Hanley in 1901 and moved to 'Brooklyn', Sandbach Road, Alsager, soon afterwards. Norman's sister, Hannah, was born in 1880. In 1911 the family were living in 'Spring Villa' Alsager, Norman being in residence at Mill Hill School, Hendon, Middlesex.

*Norman aged three. Photograph Pidduck Family Archive.*

He was just 20 when he died. He had been educated at Newcastle High School for Boys and then at Mill Hill School. It was at Mill Hill that he received the military training which made him an ideal candidate for a commission. He was a member of the School Officer Training Corps. He enlisted in the 5th North Staffordshire Regiment on 28th August. He was commissioned 2nd Lieutenant on 29th January 1916. He was transferred to serve with the 102nd Machine Gun Corps, responsible for the defence of the Allied trenches at the Somme, close to La Boiselle. Norman would have been all too aware that the 'Big Push' was about to start. From contemporary accounts, it is clear he was excited to do his bit. In the days before July 1st Norman went out, accompanied by his valet, Private James Crockett, and his guide, Private Goodeve, to inspect four guns under his command. On 1st July moments before the advance, Norman borrowed a wristwatch from a fellow officer, after his own stopped working, so he could time the attack in sync with other officers. As the whistle blew to sound the charge, he was first over the parapet, with his men following closely behind. They were raked by enemy machine gun fire, causing devastating casualties.

Lt. Pidduck was one of the first to fall. As he fell, he locked eyes with his company sergeant. Incredibly, Lt. Pidduck smiled while he turned to the sergeant as he fell. In a letter, sent to his father, Lt Pidduck's friend, Lt. Jim Rutherford wrote: *'His sergeant told me that as he fell he turned towards him with a smile as much to say, 'carry on! I am quite all right'. He lay there on his back looking upwards towards the heavens, his mouth partly open and a smile, calm, serene upon his countenance.'*

When he fell, Lt Pidduck was with Corporal D.J. Bavage, who was unhurt in the attack, Private Goodeve and Private James Crockett. His servant Corporal Bavage, who was killed on August 29, 1917, wrote: *'I saw him fall, and when I got to him he was gone. I only wish I could have done more for him for it was a great pleasure. He was the best officer I have ever been with.'*

Sgt F. Clements wrote: *'His death was instantaneous. He had just parted from me and I saw him fall about 20 minutes afterwards. It was a great blow to me and all his men. He died leading his men into action and he died a hero.'* In a letter sent to Mr Pidduck twenty days after the death of his son, Captain Norman Ingpen, who had loaned his Pidduck his wristwatch, described his last meeting with him. He said: *'I last saw him at about 7am on July 1st when going round for the last time to make certain that there would be no hitch anywhere and to wish them all the best of luck. Of course, they were all ready to go and as cheerful as could be at the thought that at last our turn had come. I heard later from one of his men in hospital at the base that he fell near La Boiselle with a bullet through his head, but his men carried on for him the work he had commenced and, I have been told, did splendidly.'*

Norman stands out from many of the casualties of that day because his story can be pieced together through the efforts of his mother, Ellen, and his step-sister, Hannah Harrison, known as Nina. They were determined to find his grave. Although they never succeeded in pinpointing the exact location of Norman's remains, they were able to determine roughly where he fell and where he was likely to lie. It was Ellen's wish to be reunited with her son in death and she expressed a wish that her own ashes should be split it two, with half spread in France. Mark Mills, Norman's great nephew, says of his relative, *'It is quite a sad story, but that is what so many families had to endure. His mother never got over his death. Both she and Norman's step-sister, my grandmother, spent a lot of time trying to find the circumstances of his death and what had become of his body.'* His mother wished for her ashes to be scattered as close as possible to the place where her son may have perished and remained. This action was carried out in 1939, following her death, by her husband and grandson, Neale Harrison. His body was never recovered to be placed into an identified grave.

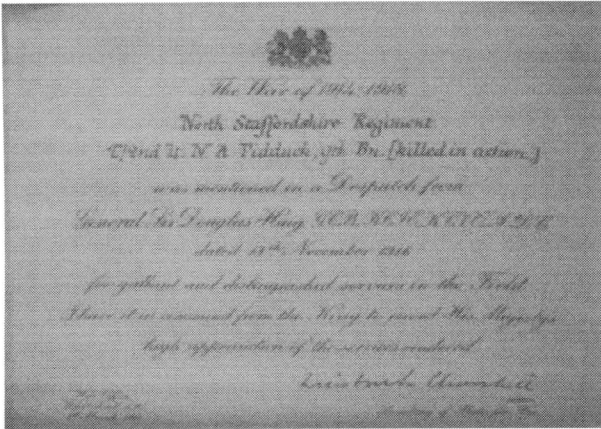

*Mentioned in Despatches citation: Family Archives*

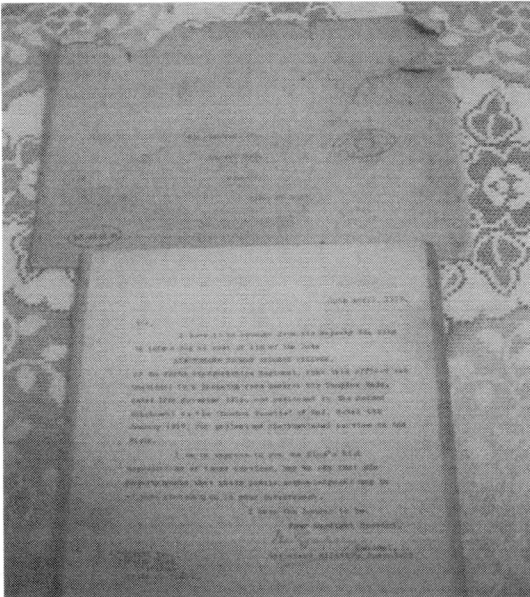

*Mentioned in despatches letter. Family Archives.*

His name is honoured on the Thiepval Memorial in France, Pier and Face 5 C and 12 C,  (along with 72,000 others killed in that sector of The Western Front with no known graves.) He is also commemorated at Mill Hill School

The following letter from Sgt Clements was presumably written in reply to a letter sent by Hannah (Nina) Pidduck who was Norman's half-sister and some sixteen years his senior. She was devoted to him and like their parents, never got over the situation of his death. *'Dear Sir/ Madam, I write these few lines to thank you most sincerely for your kindness to me, for the parcel, which I have received. Someone was very kind to send me a paper with your dear Brother's photo in, I shall keep it as a treasure as long as I live in remembrance of a most brave and Gallant Officer he was, and I see by the paper that he met his death on July 2nd. It is wrong it was July 1st at about 9 a.m. he had just left me and had gone about 50 yards from me when he fell, and God only know how it broke me down to see so gallant a leader, go down, I could not get to him as the Battle was raging for three days Dear Madam he was loved and respected by all officers and men and helped to break away through a strong position which was the beginning of the big push. So dear Sir and Madam, I think this is all I can tell you only he died a Hero and Brave man. Allow me to send you our deepest sympathy on behalf of the section what are left and myself. I remain yours truly, Sgt. Clements. Once more thanking you for your kindness.'*

*2nd Lt Norman Andrews Pidduck's medals. British War Medal, and Victory Medal and Memorial Plaque. Family Archives.*

Had he not been killed in the Great War, Norman would certainly have had an influential and controlling interest in the fortunes of the family jewellery business.

His cousin, Eric Pidduck, from Stoke-on-Trent, was wounded on the same day as Norman was killed and taken prisoner and held a prisoner of war in Bavaria, Germany.

# Date of death: July 1st 1916

### Rifleman Frederick Riley: London Regiment (The Rangers)

Frederick Riley was born in Goldenhill, Staffordshire, in 1897 to Clara Emily (nee Wearing) and Frederick Riley. His father was an Engineer at an Iron Works Foundry and originated from Odd Rode, Cheshire. Frederick's sister Doreen Agnes was born 1900, and his brother in 1901. Frederick's maternal grandparents were James and Agnes Wearing who lived in Tunstall. James Wearing was an Auctioneer & Estate Agent. In 1901 the family lived in Alfred Street, Tunstall. Frederick's family had close links with All Saint's Parish Church, Odd Rode. Fred was a choir boy at the church. In 1911 the family was living in Highfield House Goldenhill, Staffordshire. After Frederick's father died in 1913 Mrs Riley moved to live in Sycamore House, Alsager, with her family in 1916, and she married John L Potter, a Chemist, in 1918.

Frederick Riley enlisted as a Rifleman in the British Army, 12th London Regiment (The Rangers), Service number 4447. His service in France was brief. He had only been six months in training but had been sent to the front aged only just eighteen because he showed promise. He arrived in France on 28th May 1916 and was killed on 1st July in the assault on Gommecourt. The attack at Gommecourt was diversionary to make the enemy believe it was the main attack on 1st July. It was the task of the 48th and 56th Divisions to make the most northerly of these assaults, namely, on the fortress position of Gommecourt Wood. The 48th Division was to drive down behind the wood from the north, the 56th Division was to attack south of the wood in an easterly direction, the idea being that the two assaults should finally link up in the village

The battalion had to cross a wider stretch of No Man's Land than any other in the two divisions attacking Gommecourt Wood. Its orders were to fan out slightly as it crossed No Man's Land (roughly 400 yards wide), and cross the German first and second line trenches. Of the right company (A), a considerable number, including three out of the five officers, became casualties while crossing No Man's Land, and only a few reached the German line untouched. Between the first and second German lines this remnant was enfiladed from the left by a withering machine-gun fire, and took cover in a communication trench. Of the sixteen officers who had gone over, one remained; of the 745 other ranks, 200 remained. Frank is commemorated at Gommecourt Commonwealth Cemetery.

*Commemoration in All Saint's Parish Church Odd Rode Cheshire.* Photograph: Author.

Frederick is also commemorated at All Saint's parish church, Odd Rode, Cheshire in a stained glass window.  The stained glass window was commissioned by Florence Jane Skardon (spinster), in 1940. It was a legacy in her will after her death in 1939. Florence used to live with Agnes Wearing, Frederick's maternal grandmother, in 1901, and in 1911 with Frederick's family at Highfield House, Goldenhill.

Medals posthumously awarded –Victory Medal and British War Medal.

# Date of death: 15th July 1916

## Second Lieutenant Hubert John Goss: Cheshire Regiment.

Photograph: *Sentinel Newspaper*

Hubert John Goss was born in Alsager in 1891. He went to school at the National School by Christ Church School, Alsager, and Newcastle High School, Newcastle-under-Lyme. By 1911 he was a Trainee Solicitor. In 1914 he was articled with Mr Feltham, Town Clerk of Crewe, and on the outbreak of war he was taking his final Solicitor's examinations in London. He enlisted immediately in London in the 10th Royal Fusiliers as a private soldier, service number 1175. He first fought in France on 31st July 1915 and was promoted to Lance Corporal, fighting in Flanders.

Hubert was commissioned 2nd Lieutenant on 26th June 1916 and posted to the Cheshire Regiment 10th Battalion. He was awarded the Military Cross for bravery, the citation reading: *'For conspicuous gallantry in action. He made a bold reconnaissance of a point, and later seized it with 15 men, hanging on till his company arrived. Two days later he did fine work in an attack after his two senior officers were killed. He was himself wounded.'*

He took part in the third Battle of the Somme in July 1916 and was reported missing on July 15th although the ground he had helped to win for the British remained in Allied hands.

According to the Nantwich Guardian, 11th August 1916, Hubert Goss was wounded in the foot but refused to be helped back to the British trenches. A letter to his parents was re-printed in the edition:

'*Letter from an Officer. Recommended for Gallantry: Mr & Mrs Adolphus Goss of Alsager have received a letter from an officer of the Cheshire Regiment respecting their son, Second Lieutenant Hubert Goss, who was reported missing from July 13th. 'On the night of the 14th July I was with his company which made the attack. Owing to the Germans having more machine gun cover in their front than was anticipated the first attack failed when our fellows were about 40 yards from the German trench. Our men did not retire but lay down and took cover in shell holes. It was in one of these that Lieutenant Walter (killed an hour later) found your son, who had been badly wounded in the foot. He refused to be carried back as it would mean another man would have to risk his life in doing it and sent his men back to our trench as they were needed for another attack. Second Lieutenant left him his emergency ration and water, and crawled back to the trench. During the second charge your son was again found in the same hole by a private in A Company, and he again refused to be taken back, but sent the man on with the attacking party. I was in the trench all the next day and when I inquired if your son had been seen I was told by two men they had seen him being carried down the trench on a stretcher, wounded in the foot. But on making inquiries in the dressing station in the trenches I was told he had not passed through their hands, so the men must have made a mistake. The trench was taken by another battalion the next day (16th) so you will probably hear some news of him soon. His loss, even if temporary is felt by both officers and men of the battalion, as although he had not been with us long he was well known and liked by all of us, and as a soldier he was known as a valuable man. I sincerely hope, with you, that he will turn up safe and sound and come back to us.'*

His body was never found. Hubert's name is recorded on the Edward Lutyens' Thiepval Memorial to the missing. The inscription: '*Goss 2nd Lt Hubert John, MC formerly 10th Battalion, Royal Fusiliers, 15th July 1916, aged 26, son of AWH and Sarah Ellen Goss of the Old Villa, Alsager, Cheshire. Enlisted 1914'.* His death was reported in the Staffordshire Weekly Sentinel on August 12th 1916.

*Memorial to Hubert Goss in Christ Church graveyard, Alsager. Photograph: The Author*

In 1927 at the opening of the Goss Memorial Window in St Mary's Alsager, the following was spoken of Hubert Goss. '*Hubert is remembered as thoughtful and reserved, so reserved, that only a few, those intimate with him, knew his real character. He had few friends rather than a host of acquaintances. Many, no doubt, would pass on their way without recognising in him that depth and nobility of character, which he displayed in winning his military decoration, or in sacrificing a chance of his own safety which involved risk to others. I find him acting more than once as a spiritual advisor, and giving that advice with so much sympathy it could not be forgotten.'* Hubert was awarded the Military Cross on 25th August 1916. **The citation:** '*Temp. 2nd Lt. Hubert John Goss. For conspicuous gallantry in action. He made a bold reconnaissance of a point, and later seized it with 15 men, hanging on till his company arrived. Two days later he did fine work in an attack after his two senior officers had been killed. He was himself wounded.'* He was also awarded the 1914/15 Star, Victory Medal, and British War Medal.

# Date of death: 23rd July 1916

## Second Lieutenant Reginald Settle: Royal Flying Corps

*Reg pictured when he was a Sergeant with the Army Service Corps. Photo: Radley School.*

Reginald William Settle was born in Madeley, Staffordshire on 21st January 1891 to Margaret Caroline and Joel Settle. His sister Gwendoline Settle was born in 1887, Violet (1890), Marjorie (1894), and his brother, Mellard, in (1895.) Reginald's father owned a colliery distribution business called Settle, Speakman Colliery Factors. After the war the company was involved in the manufacture of coal trucks.

The family moved to Alsager and lived in 'The Hill', a large detached dwelling overlooking Alsager, which locals called 'Alsager Hall'. Reginald Settle went to preparatory school at Elleray Park, Wallasey, and went to Radley College, Oxford, for his secondary education. After leaving school Reg became a management assistant in his father's business. The works was situated close to Alsager station on the railway line to Kidsgrove. Reg enlisted in the army on 25th November 1914 with the Army Service Corps, Mechanical Transport, and was initially based at Grove Park Army Service Corps M.T. Depot in London. Reg's service record states he was 5 feet 10 inches tall with a 37 inch chest.

Reg had a flair for all things mechanical; engine repairs, and the organisation of motorised transport and his ability was soon recognised by the army. He was the personal driver to General Sir William

Robertson from 1914 to 1915, and was promoted sergeant, service number M2/020578. Robertson was Chief of Army Staff, Europe, based at GHQ in France. Later in 1915 Reg took over responsibility for the upkeep of all vehicles for General Sir Douglas Haig. Despite being in charge of General Haig's motor transport Reg wanted to see more action. In the summer of 1916 he had broken up with his girlfriend and applied for a commission with the Royal Flying Corps. He was given a temporary commission as 2nd Lieutenant on 21st June 1916, service number M2/020578. Returning to France after training Reg served alongside experienced pilots in 15 Squadron before being given the responsibility of flying solo.

His death was reported in the Birmingham Post on 28th July 1916.

> **LIEUT. R. W. SETTLE, ALSAGER (KILLED).**
>
> News has been received by Mr. and Mrs. Joel Settle, The Hill, Alsager, of the death whilst flying over the German lines, of their eldest son, Lieutenant Reginald William Settle. Mr. Joel Settle, who is the managing director of the firm of Messrs. Settle and Speakman, colliery agents and factors, is well known in commercial circles in Birmingham and the Midlands.
>
> Lieutenant Settle, who was 25 years of age, joined the Motor Transport Section as a private in November, 1914. He was engaged in driving the motor-car of Sir William Robertson when he was Quartermaster-General, and afterwards when he was Chief of Staff. On General Robertson's return to England, Mr. Settle, who had been promoted to sergeant, was given charge of the motor-cars of General Sir Douglas Haig at his headquarters. He obtained a commission in the Royal Flying Corps in June.

Flight News reported his death which occurred on 23rd July 1916. He was killed in a small plane with an open cockpit while flying over German lines. He was sitting directly behind the pilot who heard a single shot but thought it had missed them. The plane flew normally but when the plane landed the pilot found Reginald dead with a rifle wound. He wrote to tell Reginald's parents about the circumstances of their son's death. Reg is buried in Beauval Communal Cemetery, Somme, France, grave A. 14. The inscription on his grave reads, *'So Loved So Mourned'*. Reg is also commemorated on the memorial at Radley School, Oxford. His family was awarded back pay of £109. 19. 9d after his death from the Royal Flying Corps and £43 from the Army. Reg left £2,164 to his father, Joel, in his will dated 31st March 1917. In 1919 Joel Settle, Reg's father, asked the War Office to provide the 1914 (Mons) Star for his late son but he was deemed ineligible and was awarded the 1915 Star instead.

# Date of death: 18th August 1916

## Lance Corporal Frank Glover: King's Liverpool Regiment

*Frank Glover (1st row, 1st from right 13th Battalion King's Liverpool Regiment. Photo King's Liverpool Rt.*

Frank Glover was born in Stoke-on-Trent, in 1891 to Hannah and Frederick Bede Glover. His father worked in a tile factory. His sister, Kate Glover was born in1893, Annie (1897), and Rosa (1899). The family lived in Cummings Street, Hartshill. After school Frank became an apprentice electrician with Barrett and Soames Ltd until 1912 when he qualified as an electrician in a colliery. Frank Glover married Daisy Ankers of Linley Farm, Linley Road, on 15th January 1915 at St Mary's Parish Church, Alsager. He enlisted in Manchester as a private in the Kings Liverpool Regiment, 13th Battalion, service number 19569, on 8th August 1914.

Frank is described in the service records as having red hair, *'flaccid'* features and five feet eight tall. He was in 'C Coy' of the 13th Battalion. He embarked to France on 25th September 1915. In January he suffered from dental problems and in March 1916 he suffered from bronchitis and influenza and spent time away from the front line but in June 1916 he enjoyed a brief leave in England between 2nd and 10th June. Mrs Glover was awarded a separation allowance of 9 shillings a week. On 14th July he was promoted to Lance Corporal within the 13th Battalion of the King's Liverpool Regiment. According to his service record he was killed in the field on 18th August 1916, by *'a shell blowing into his dressing station'* according to Alsager Parish Magazine. This implies he had been wounded and invalided to a dressing station which was then subject to attack. He is buried in plot X. A. 3. at the Flatiron Copse Cemetery, Mametz, Somme France. A letter received from his commanding officer

said, *'He carried out his duties with supreme disregard for danger. He has undoubtedly saved many lives by his fine work.'* He was recommended by his officer commanding for the DCM but it was not awarded. Daisy Glover received a widow's pension of 13s 9d from 9th April 1917. She remarried, her name changing to Makin in 1919. Frank Glover was posthumously awarded the 1914/15 Star, The Victory Medal and The British War Medal. He appears on Alsager War Memorial as 'Private. F Glover' not Lance Corporal as indicated on his service records.

*Flatiron Copse Cemetery. Photo: Commonwealth War Graves Commission*

# Date of death: 3rd September 1916

### Private Richard Sant: Manchester Regiment.

Richard John Sant was born in Tunstall, Stoke on Trent in October 1874 to Henry Samuel, and Mary Sant, (nee Stanway) His father was a potter's agent. His older brother, Samuel, was born in1866, Frederick, (1867) Ernest (1873) Gertrude (1871). In 1881 the family were living in Albert Cottage, Alsager. Richard was educated at the National School by Christ Church, Alsager. In 1891 the family had moved back to live in Stoke in Waterloo Road. Richard was living with his widowed mother in Cobridge and Richard was working as a clerk in a pottery factory. By 1911 Richard had moved back in Alsager and living in 'West View,' Audley Road, with his widowed mother but he was not in employment. His brother Samuel was living in the same address and worked as a 'Factor' in the pottery business.

At the age of 42 and unmarried Richard enlisted in the 20th Service Battalion of the Manchester Regiment, service number 26626, the 5th Manchester Pals as they are known. He enlisted in 1916 in Congleton and was involved in fighting in the Somme region of France. On 1st July his regiment moved to Fricourt in C1 Sector of the Somme battlefield and saw action in the 'Quarry', 300 yards south east of the Bois Francais to Mametz-Becordel road attacking at 2:30pm. Richard survived the attack but a hundred and ten of his battalion were killed, twenty nine were missing, and one hundred and seventy one were wounded.   On 3rd July the regiment were pulled out of front line, but regrouped to take part on 14th July on the attack on Bazentin Wood. In August they were rested in billets at Dernancourt. The regiment, part of 4th Division, took part in the attack on Delville Wood and Ginchy. The Germans had been slowly pushed out of positions in Delville Wood during August, and on 30th August the British front line had been pushed north and east of the woods. On 31st August the Germans made yet another counterattack, recapturing a narrow band in the north east corner of the wood. A British counterattack failed to retake this narrow band of the wood on 3rd September. Richard Sant went missing killed in this counterattack. After this counterattack only 130 of the 5th Manchester Pals were left alive.

The Manchester Evening News, 14 November 1916, published this report of Private Sant:

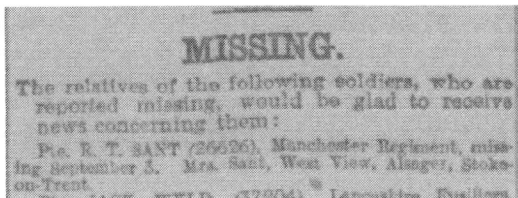

Richard Sant is commemorated on Thiepval Memorial, Pier and Face 13 A and 14 C. He was posthumously awarded the Victory Medal, and British War Medal.

*Thiepval Memorial Photo: Commonwealth War Graves Commission.*

# Date of death: 16th September 1916

**Private Henry Christopher Dale: North Staffordshire Regiment.**

*Photograph: Sentinel newspaper.*

Henry Christopher Dale was born in Alsager in 1897 to Amelia and George Dale. George Dale was a carter of coal. His sister Nellie was born in 1891; Frederick (1894), Reginald (1899), and Sarah Constance (1898). The family lived in Sandbach Road, Alsager, and moved to Shady Grove before 1911.

Henry worked as a 'Farmer's Servant' in 1911 but by the outbreak of war was working as a *'blacksmith's striker'*. On 28th December 1914 he enlisted as 'Christopher Dale' with the North Staffordshire Regiment in Tunstall, service number 16132. He is recorded as being 5 feet 6 inches tall, chest 36 inches, dark hair, blue eyes, and fresh complexion.

Dale embarked to France on 5th May 1915 from Devonport. On 28th May 1915 he was transferred to the 3rd Battalion Duke of Wellington's (West Riding) Regiment, service number 16400. He was wounded on the first day of the battle of the Somme on the 1st July 1916 with a forearm wound and was evacuated to the 11th General Hospital, Camiers, France. He was released back to 2nd Battalion, West Riding Regiment, on 27th July 1916. On 16th September he was killed in action on the Somme but his body was never found. He is commemorated on the Thiepval Memorial, Somme, France, Pier and Face 6 A and 6 B. Christopher is also remembered on a Dale family grave in Christ Church

73

graveyard. He was granted the 1914/15 Star, the British War Medal, and the Victory Medal. His father, George, received Christopher's personal effects in February 1917.

*Dale Family Grave, Christ Church, Alsager. Photograph: Author*

# Alsager in 1917

In February 1917 there was a strong appeal to parishioners to join War Savings schemes and two Sunday Schools (Christ Church and St Mary's), the Church of England Men's Society, Girls' Club, and Girls' Friendly Society all started savings associations. An appeal for the work of the Girls' Friendly Society was made in women's munition factories, and the church made a donation to St Dunstan's Home for Blind Soldiers. The Church magazine also reprinted the Food Controller's regulations on food restrictions, and in 1917 the King's Proclamation on Food Economies was read out on four successive Sundays. The title of the article was '*Ration yourself and your family*'.

Early in 1917 Germany announced unrestricted submarine warfare which meant British merchant ships transporting food from overseas would be at risk of being sunk, worsening the food shortages. With men conscripted to join the army there was pressure on food production. The authorities had to take action. In 1917 the Women's Land Army was formed to provide extra voluntary labour, with 'Land Girls' replacing servicemen who had left the farms to fight. The government also created propaganda campaigns encouraging people all over the country to start growing their own food. A scheme of voluntary rationing was promoted on 1st February 1917, with the aim of reducing the consumption of food in short supply, and to show how to avoid waste when cooking. In June the Vicar asked the people of Alsager to be '*public spirited*' and join the food economy campaign.

The allowance under this scheme was based on three staples of the daily diet - bread, meat, and sugar. The weekly allowance was for:

• *Bread including cakes, puddings etc. - 4lbs (1.8 kg)*

• *Meat including bacon, ham, sausages, game, rabbits, poultry, and tinned meat - 2½ lbs (1.1 kg)*

• *Sugar ¾ lb (340 grams)*

Shortages continued and although wealthier people could still afford food, malnutrition was seen in poor communities. To try to make things fairer and ensure that everyone received their fair share, the government introduced rationing in 1918.

Ration cards were issued and everyone had to register with a local butcher and grocer. The first item to be rationed was sugar in January 1918, but by the end of April meat, butter, cheese and margarine were added to the list.

In October 1917 the Nantwich Guardian reported the people of Alsager were complaining about the quality of 'War Bread', despite regulations to ensure its quality from January 1917.

## Canadian Aviator

On 4th May 1917 the Nantwich Guardian reported a Canadian Aviator passing over Alsager had trouble with his engine and had to land in a field in Thurlwood. He landed safely managed to resolve the engine problem and soon proceeded on his way.

## The Alsager Military Tribunal in 1917.

In April 1917 Mr J.J. Nelson, Clerk to Alsager Council reported that Mr Samuel, Sub-Commissioner of the District, had asked him to send out Military enrolment forms to every man in the Alsager area between the ages of 18 and 61. The Council employed volunteers to distribute the forms but the results of the attempt to recruit more men were unknown. The work of the Alsager Military Tribunal became crucial in getting more men into the services but the needs of the local economy, particularly food production, were just as important.

In May 1917 the Alsager Tribunal heard that two cases from the local Tribunal to the County Appeal Tribunal at Chester had been dismissed. The County Tribunal backed the original decision taken by the Alsager Tribunal. In the May hearings the case of an Alsager joiner aged 37 was dismissed. His employers had wanted to find a replacement for him before he enlisted. An Alsager bricklayer aged 24, single, who had suffered two bouts of pneumonia and was only one of two bricklayers left in the town was given 3 months exemption provided he found work of national importance. A press photographer married with two children who had had several attacks of pneumonia was given six months exemption. An insurance inspector aged 39 and married who had been working 3 days a week at a quarry was given 2 months exemption conditional on him remaining at the same place and joining the Volunteers. A corn merchant, 27, with five children was given six months exemption provided he joined the Volunteers.

In June 1917, an Alsager farmer appealed against a Tribunal decision he must serve with the Volunteers for part of the week. He claimed he could not do all the work on the farm and drill for the Volunteers. He had a son in the army and the help he obtained from off duty soldiers was insufficient. His appeal was allowed.

In July 1917 several cases were heard most giving three months exemption conditional on the appellants working one or more days a week on a farm or on munitions at Crewe. A grocer appealed for temporary exemption for his son aged 18 on the grounds he was his only assistant. He was given three months final exemption. At the September meeting of the Tribunal several appellants were given three months exemption, including a boot and shoe dealer, a bricklayer, a gardener, and a house painter. The Military Representative, Lieutenant Mason, appealed against the exemption of an insurance agent, aged 41, on the grounds he had not complied with the condition imposed by the Tribunal that he should find work of national importance. The Military Representative's appeal was successful. At the end of business a vote of condolence was given for the loss in battle of Second Lieutenant W.R.G Holland. His uncle was a member of the Tribunal. The soldier was said to be *'unassuming in civil life, but with a heart of steel in battle'* and he had gained the honour of a Military Cross by his conspicuous gallantry.

## The Red Cross Hospital at Rode Hall in 1917

A new hospital for wounded soldiers was planned for the Alsager area. Rode Hall, the home of the Baker Wilbraham family, had often been used before the war as centre for the Red Cross and the St John Ambulance events.

*A photograph in the Weekly Sentinel from 1912. A Red Cross event in the grounds of the Hall.*

The Baker Wilbraham family was keen to help the war effort and on 4th May 1917 the Rode Heath Red Cross Hospital was opened officially by Katharine, Duchess of Westminster. The event was reported in the Chester Chronicle on the same day. Sir Edward Cotton-Jodrell made a speech saying the Red Cross had been concerned of rumours its staff were being moved to France but he said they would not be opening Rode Hospital if that was the case. Mrs Ffoulkes, the new hospital's Commandant, said the hospital offered forty five beds, a singing and games room and an office. It had a complement of 35 nurses and Dr Henry Freeland Kington from Alsager provided specialist medical advice and became Chief Medical Officer from November 1917. His wife, Mary Elizabeth Kington, became a full time nurse. Katharine Mary Ffoulkes, who was Sir Philip Baker Wilbraham's sister, wrote to the Chronicle on 17th August 1917 to inform them the first patients had arrived from Stockport on 3rd May 1917 with further convoys on 5th and 8th May. The hospital was practically full. The cost of equipping the hospital was £145 and the cost of running it in the first two months was £465 with the government paying £237 of this cost. Mrs Ffoulkes praised the many people who had donated towards the running of the hospital and said they still needed help. She hoped the hospital would remain open longer than the initial six months guaranteed. A long list of benefactors was added to the Alsager Parish Magazine in July 1917. Most were Alsager families, including families who had lost loved ones in the war.

*Photo. Rode Hall*

Alsager Urban District Council agreed to allow the hospital to hold its meetings in the downstairs Council room on Friday afternoons to receive gifts from the public. On 11th May1917 the first service was held in the Hall Chapel. On 17th May Private Telford, a patient in the hospital, Northumberland Volunteers heard he had been awarded the Military Medal for bravery. On 30th May Nurse Robinson heard her brother had been killed in action. Nurse Booth's husband was also killed. On 15th November 1917 a concert was given by the patients in aid of the French Red Cross. There was a crowded audience and a sum of £7. 2s. 0d was collected in donations.

**War News**

In August a list of war decorations awarded to Alsager men was printed in the Parish Magazine.

Rawlin Holland awarded the Military Cross and Hubert John Goss, the Military Cross for gallantry.

Capt. Robert Ellis was awarded the Military Cross for special service at a dressing station. Norman Pidduck and Frank Glover (both killed) were Mentioned in Despatches. In October 1917 it was reported in the Parish Magazine that Victor Maddock had been awarded the Military Cross.

**Crime and Public Morale in Alsager**

A concert was held in St Mary's Schoolroom in July 1917 under the auspices of the of 'the Wounded Soldiers' Entertainment Committee'. Tea was provided by Mr Paxton Barrett, and songs were sung by local classical artists. There was also a performance by J. Redfern, Humourist. There was a large audience including the Entertainment's Committee which included A.Goss, J Pidduck, and the Maddock family.

It was the responsibility of the police to ensure the lighting regulations were enforced. Many must have thought it irrelevant whether Alsager's lights were extinguished but the proximity of important railway lines, the munitions works at Crewe and sheds at Alsager meant the restrictions would deter Zeppelin attacks. The lighting regulations appear to have been contradictory On 24th August 1917, Thomas Burgess, a farmer from Oakhanger, was fined £1 for being drunk in charge of a horse and for assaulting a Police Constable Whelton. Burgess had been stopped not having lights on his vehicle. Whelton was struck in the chest and kicked. Sergeant Lythgoe arrived and arrested Burgess and his companion and they were locked up in Alsager cells overnight. Burgess was fined 10 shillings for no lights, 2 shillings and sixpence costs. His companion was fined £1. On 19th October 1917 Arthur James Band of Alsager was fined 10 shillings for having unshaded incandescent lights in his house on 22nd September. Band said he had just arrived home and was suffering an asthma attack. PC Edward Bell said he had warned Band about lighting infringements a few days earlier. It appears that regulations for vehicles were different from static lights in buildings. Bell may have been overzealous in his duties. He may also have been concerned about his son, Harry Bell, who was just about to be posted to France with the Monmouthshire Regiment.

Life was difficult for farmers trying to work with reduced manpower and farmers were reluctant to send their children to school. On 19th October 1917 George Nicholson, farmer, of Betchton, was fined for not sending his daughter, Christina, to school. Nicholson had repeatedly failed to send his daughter to the Alsager National School.

In February 1917 the parish magazine was concerned with the vulnerability and temptations faced by women munition workers many of which were living far from home. Rev. Waller put out a plea for parishioners to give funds to the Girls' Friendly Society War Emergency Fund providing money to fund hostels, rest rooms and lodging for women munition workers. £20 5s. was collected.

**Tragedy**

In May the vicar's ten year old daughter, Emily Waller died, extending the gloom in Alsager. The churches played an important part in keeping up morale in the town and this personal tragedy for the Reverend Waller was a blow to both him and the community.

**The Alsager Volunteers in 1917**

There was an appeal for older men to join the Home Defence Corps. (Volunteer Training Corps) and Major Royds wrote an urgent letter in July to the people of Alsager pointing out *'lads of 17 can join section C and thus would have the advantage of good instruction, which will stand them in good stead when they have to join up though it does not mean they will be sent out earlier.'* In September it was proposed to set up cadet companies for boys aged 14 and over. Target practice and competitions continued at the Alsager shooting ranges. Having done a musketry course men could keep a small supply of ammunition for range practice. In June 1917 the Volunteers drilled in Crewe Park under Major Royds. They now had their own rifles, bayonets and equipment. A Sergeant Major was recruited to drill them. On 20th July the Alsager and Sandbach Volunteers took part in a parade in Northwich and afterwards took part in a mock battle to defend Vale Royal Abbey. The Alsager contingent assisted in the capture of a company defending the Hall at the rear of the building. After the successful event and refreshments a collection of motors brought them back to Alsager from Whitegate Church. A more spectacular training event took place in the Alsager area on 3rd August 1917. Lieutenant Maddock leading the Alsager and Barthomley contingent were ordered to defend the railway station at Hassall against an 'attack' by 40 members of the Sandbach Volunteers. The action took place after midnight. The aim was for the Sandbach Volunteers to get within a quarter of a mile of Hassall Hall without being put out of action. The Alsager men wearing white armbands started out from Hassall Hall at 9.30 pm to search for the attackers. Unknown to them a scouting party from Sandbach monitored their whereabouts and instructed the main Sandbach force to take another route. The Sandbach men outflanked the defenders and were able to capture their objective of Lodly Smithy despite Lieutenant Maddock trying to resist with a small detachment of men. It was nearly 3am when the exercise was completed. It had been very dark and a soldier from Sandbach admitted he had seen what he thought were an Alsager man's white markings and stealthily worked his way up to him, only to find it was a calf with white markings. The adventures of the Volunteers were a world away from the horrors of actual battle.

The Church Magazine continued to add its sympathy on the loss of individual servicemen. By November 1917 a total of twenty five men from the town had been killed in the war and were remembered at a special All Soul's Day communion service.

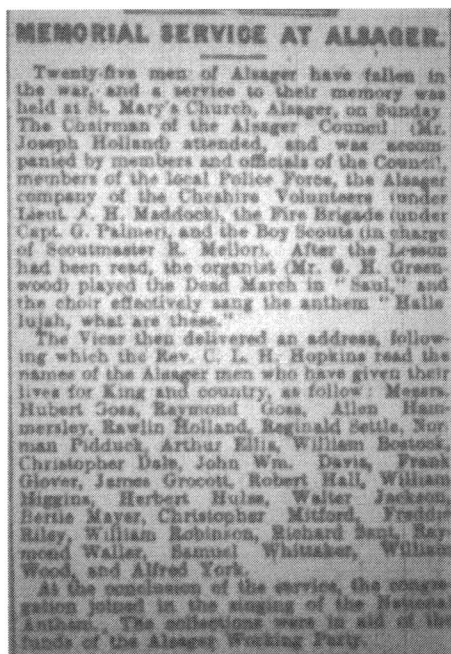

*Sentinel Newspaper*

A paper shortage began to limit church publications in late 1917. Food restrictions stopped refreshments being served at the annual Parish Tea. Monthly takings for the Alsager Working Party fell to £13 a month as the deprivation caused by the war increased. Collections for the Prince of Wales' Relief Fund seemed to have stopped altogether. The death toll grew.

*St Mary's Church Harvest Festival. An effort was made to keep traditions.*

*Photograph: St Mary Magdalene, Alsager*

# Deaths of Alsager servicemen in 1917

## Date of death: 26th January 1917

### Lance Corporal William Bostock: North Staffordshire Regiment.

William was born in 1895 in Hanchurch near Trentham, Staffordshire, to Hannah and Job Bostock. His father was a farm worker. His brother Thomas Bostock was born in 1894, Ellen (1897) Alice (1899) James (1904) Albert (1907) and Mary (1911).

In 1901 the family lived in Lane House, Whitmore, Staffordshire. By 1911 William had left home and was lodging at nearby Moat Farm owned by his employer, Mr Sumner. William worked as a wagoner on the farm. By 1914 William had moved to Alsager and lived at 1 Crewe Road. He was employed as a farm labourer.

He enlisted at Tunstall in the 11th Battalion of the North Staffordshire Regiment on 25th October 1915. His service record gives the following details: Height; 5 feet 5 inches, chest measurement, 36 inches. He had fresh complexion, hazel eyes and dark hair.

William was promoted Lance Corporal on 12th June 1916. He trained with the 11th Battalion until 26th June 1916 and then transferred to the 7th Battalion North Staffordshire Regiment. Travelling first to Bombay in India, he then embarked to Mesopotamia (modern Iraq) arriving in Basra on 16th September 1916. The British Army had recently suffered the humiliation of surrendering its garrison at Kut and its aim became the recapture of Kut and the area of the Tigris River. On 7th and 8th January 1917 General Maude's forces launched a series of minor diversionary attacks nearby as a lead-in to what turned out to be an unusually effective bombardment by artillery on 9th January at Khadairi Bend, a heavily fortified town in a loop of the Tigris north of Kut. The resulting battle continued for almost three weeks, including two counterattacks by the Turks, before the town fell on 29th January.

On 11th January the Battalion War Diary reads …

### 25th January 1917

*The Battalion took part on an assault on the first Turkish line on West Bank of the river. The assault was delivered at 9.45 a.m. (after an intense artillery bombardment and behind their barrage) in four waves by A, B & C Companies in columns of platoons at 50 yards distance, but no interval between companies. Order of companies from E to W was C, B and A. D Coy was held in reserve finding the platoons to dig communication trenches if the assault was successful. Lewis Gunners and Bombers were sent behind the first wave in order to assist in consolidating. The assault was partially successful, the right Coy having but little difficulty, while the left was held up by machine gun fire and compelled to close in onto the right. At 11 a.m. the enemy counter attacked using bombers freely, and although "A" Company was practically isolated and partly driven back, and although the Battalion of the right flank of the North Staffs. Regt. gave way, "B" & "C" Companies held their guard for some considerable time, until the Royal Warwicks came up in support and the line was regained. From that time until 4 p.m. with only one officer, 2nd*

82

*Lieut. McDowell left, A,B & C Companies held what ground they could until overwhelmed by enemy bombers; they finally evacuated the line and fell back to the position from which the assault had been delivered.'*

William was killed in action the following day. He is commemorated at the Amara Commonwealth Graves Cemetery, Amara, Iraq. The cemetery was destroyed by the Iraqis in the 1st Gulf War, but all the headstones had been removed in 1933 due to salts denuding them. William's identity disc was returned to his mother in August 1917.

William was posthumously awarded the Victory Medal, and British War Medal. The Commonwealth War Graves records state:

*'Bostock, Lance Corporal, William 19230, 7th Btn. North Staffs Regiment, 26th January 1917. Son of Job Bostock of Mill Cottage, Madeley, near Crewe Plot: IXVI. B. 6.'*

# Date of death: 25th February 1917

### Private Stanley Allman: North Staffordshire Regiment.

Stanley Leese Allman was born in Alsager in 1893 to Ellen and John Allman. His father was a signalman on the railway and later a jobbing gardener. Stanley's sister, Florence Evelyn was born 1881, Wilfred (1882), Edith (1883) and John Sydney (1892). The family lived in Crewe Road, Alsager. In 1911 Stanley is recorded as working as a gardener for one of the wealthy Alsager families. When he enlisted in the army in 1914 he was working with his father as a gardener at Beech Villas, Alsager.

Stanley joined the North Staffordshire Regiment, 4th Battalion, in Burslem on 2nd September 1914 and remained on home service in Britain until 1916. According to his service record he had grey eyes and was five 5 feet 8 inches tall. He had black hair. On 24th June 1916 he was posted to the 7th Battalion, North Staffordshire Regiment, and on the following day left Devonport to sail to Basra, Mesopotamia, where he arrived on 31st May 1916.

In 16th December 1916 he went into Amara hospital with anaemia and was released to his regiment three days later. On 27th February 1917 Stanley was reported missing presumed dead. His family received photographs, a post card, and a pocket book of Stanley's from the army. Mrs Allman wrote to the army to ask, how and where his possessions were discovered when such small items would normally be carried on his person. There is no reply in the records.

Mrs Allman's letters to the Army, part transcription:

*Crewe Road, Alsager. Feb 8th '18*

*Referring to my letters of Nov 15th sent along with official form acknowledging receipt of pocket book, photographs and postcards which were the personal belongings of my son, 14349, Pte. Stanley Allman, 7th North Staffordshire Regiment, posted as missing 25th July 1917. I should be glad of a reply to same in which I asked how the things sent on came into your possession....the things were certainly his and would be things carried about in his pocket, it stands to common sense that someone has some information and say what became of him. It seems to me very strange to me his things were sent on a year later.....Will you agree a reply is needed and as it stands at present it is most unsatisfactory to me and his father and the rest of the family. If these things had not turned up it is quite possible you could give no further information but now I think I should know how the articles came into your possession. I enclose a stamped addressed envelope as my last letters have been ignored, so I trust I shall receive a reply to this one,*

*Yours faithfully,*

*E. Allman*

*Basra War Memorial (re-sited) Photo: Commonwealth War Graves.*

Stanley was commemorated on the Basra Memorial, Iraq. He was granted the British War Medal and Victory Medal.

Until 1997 the Basra Memorial was located on the main quay of the naval dockyard at Maqil, on the west bank of the Shatt-al-Arab, about 8 kilometres north of Basra. Because of the sensitivity of the site, the Memorial was moved by Presidential Decree. The move, carried out by the authorities in Iraq, involved a considerable amount of manpower, transport costs and sheer engineering on their part, and the Memorial has been re-erected in its entirety. The Basra Memorial is now located 32 kilometres along the road to Nasiriyah, in the middle of what was a major battleground during the First Gulf War.

# Date of death: 13th March 1917

## Second Lieutenant Anthony Hammersley: North Staffordshire Regiment

*Photo the Sentinel*

Alan George 'Tony' Hammersley was born on 27th September 1895 in Alsager. Alan was the son of Gilbert and Helena Hammersley. Gilbert was a partner in the china manufacturing company Hammersley & Co, based in Longton, Stoke on Trent. It traded his ware under 'Alsager China'. Helena originated from Evesham, Worcester. Gilbert Hammersley died in 1909 aged 50.

Alan's brother, Eric Victor Hammersley, was born 1894. Leslie (1899) Doris Maud (1901) and Vera Hilda (1910) eight months after her father's death. Two other siblings died in infancy.

In the 1901 census 'Tony' was living with his family in The Avenue, Alsager. Gilbert Hammersley was described as *'a china manufacturer & employer'* in the census. The family employed a governess, Amy Chambers aged 20, and general servant Mary Hamlet, aged 20.

Tony attended the National School, Alsager, and went on to study at Newcastle-under-Lyme School. In the 1911 census Tony is described as living in Church Road, Alsager, with his widowed mother, Helena, siblings Eric (apprentice to a manufacturer of china), Leslie and Doris (both at school) and Vera, aged 10 months. Their governess, Amy Chambers, and general domestic servant Olive Mayer, aged 25, also lived in the house.

On 29th December 1914 Alan enlisted as a Private with the 5th Battalion North Staffordshire Regiment, service number 2754. He was promoted Lance Corporal (date unknown) and posted to France on the 3rd March 1915. Alan was commissioned as Second Lieutenant on 11th Aug 1915. He went on to serve in France with the 5th Battalion. In October 1915 Tony was wounded in action. This was reported in The Sentinel newspaper on 19th October 1915. He convalesced in Herne Bay, Kent. By July 1916 he had regained health enough to re-join the army and was training at Catterick, returning to France by 26th September 1916. Alan was killed in action whilst *gallantly leading his men against the enemy trenches'* on 14th March 1917 in France.

The report in the Birmingham Post of 21st March 1917 states:

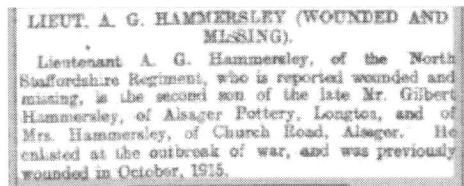

LIEUT. A. G. HAMMERSLEY (WOUNDED AND MISSING).

Lieutenant A. G. Hammersley, of the North Staffordshire Regiment, who is reported wounded and missing, is the second son of the late Mr. Gilbert Hammersley, of Alsager Pottery, Longton, and of Mrs. Hammersley, of Church Road, Alsager. He enlisted at the outbreak of war, and was previously wounded in October, 1915.

The War Diary of 14th March contains a report by Lt. Col. A.E.F Fawcus, Commanding Officer, 1/5 North Staffs Battalion. The object of the attack was to enemy attack positions in Bucquoy. Alan managed to reach the enemy wire but could not breach it and was killed by incoming fire. The battalion was forced to retreat and defend against a counter attack. Alan Hammersley was buried in Shrine Cemetery, Bucquoy, Pas de Calais, France, in grave number I.A.5.

His death was announced in the Liverpool Echo. No details of his death were given but it was noted he was wounded in October 1915.

On 7th April 1917 in the Cheltenham Chronicle, Gloucestershire, a piece appeared recounting how Alan died and describing him as *'the grandson of the late Dr A.S. Haynes of Tower House, Evesham'.*

Hammersley was awarded the 1914/15 Star (as a Lance Corporal serving with the 5th Btn. North Staffordshire Regt). He was also awarded the British War Medal & Victory Medal.

*Photo: IWM.*

LIEUT. A. G. HAMMERSLEY.

*Alan Hammersley commemorated on a family grave at Christ Church, Alsager. Photo: Author*

*Tony Hammersley's grave in Shrine Cemetery, Bucquoy, Pas de Calais, France. Photo Commonwealth War Graves*

# Date of death: 3rd May 1917

## Private Herbert Trevor Wood: East Kent Regiment

*(A serviceman not on the Alsager War Memorial but was an Alsager connection)*

Herbert Trevor Wood was born at 62 Crewe Road, Alsager, Cheshire, in 1890 to Mary and Sam Wood, an Agent in a colliery. A brother, Douglas Trevor, died in infancy. Herbert was raised in Sandbach Road, Alsager. In the 1901 census he was staying in Southport. It is not known if he went to school there. In 1911 Herbert was single and living with his parents in 'Newlyn,' Sandbach Road, Alsager and is recorded as working as a bank clerk. His father died on 14th May 1911 and was buried in Christ Church graveyard. After the outbreak of war Herbert enlisted in the Buffs, the East Kent Regiment, 7th Battalion, Service number 20839. The 7th (Service) Battalion was formed at Canterbury in September 1914. It came under the command of the 5th Brigade, 18th (Eastern) Division. Herbert was killed in action whilst serving as a Private with the 7th Battalion. On 1st May1917 the Regiment moved up to north east of Neuville Vitasse to relieve the 7th Queen's on the front line. On the 3rd May 'A' and 'B' companies prepared for an attack and 'C' Company were in support. 'D' Company was held in reserve. The attack commenced in complete darkness at 3.45am and the attack was well clear of British lines when the enemy fired back. The enemy retaliated with heavy machine gun and rifle fire and artillery barrage. The attack reached the streets of Cherisy and then the Sensee River. Following counterattacks new attacks were necessary on Cable Trench and the southern part of Cherisy village. In the action the 7th Battalion lost 12 officers and 368 other ranks including Private H.T. Wood.

When he enlisted Herbert had been staying with his widowed mother, Mary Trevor Wood, at 40 Richmond Mount, Headingley, Leeds, Yorkshire. Mary was still living in Leeds in 1917, after Herbert's death. Herbert is commemorated on Bay 2 of the Arras Memorial, Faubourg D'Amiens Cemetery, Arras, Pas de Calais, France. A memorial stone was also laid on the family grave at Christ Church Alsager. The inscription reads: *'Herbert Trevor Wood, The Buffs, East Kent's, killed in Action May 3rd 1917 aged 26 All Honour to the Brave ....The Nation's Best'* He was posthumously awarded The British War Medal, and the Victory Medal.

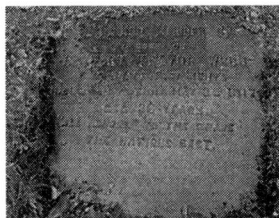

*Memorial stone to Herbert Trevor Wood, in Christ Church, Alsager. Photo: Author*

# Date of death: 22nd May 1917.

## Frank Asbury: Military Mounted Police

*(A serviceman not on the Alsager War Memorial but with an Alsager connection)*

Frank Asbury was born in Haslington on 13th May 1891 at Mill Farm, close to Haslington Hall, to Ann and John Hilditch Asbury. He was baptised at Sandbach Primitive Methodist circuit church on 31st May 1891. His father was a corn miller. After he left school Frank became a locomotive engine cleaner with the North Staffordshire Railway Company. He joined the Military Police and was promoted to become Lance Corporal in the Mounted Police Section. In 1917 he became sick whilst working in Aldershot at the military barracks. His probate record states his home address was Grove Farm, Radway Green near Alsager. His will states he died at Aldershot Isolation Hospital on 22nd May 1917. He left £226. 13s. 0d. to John Hilditch Asbury.

*Chester Chronicle 2nd June 1917*

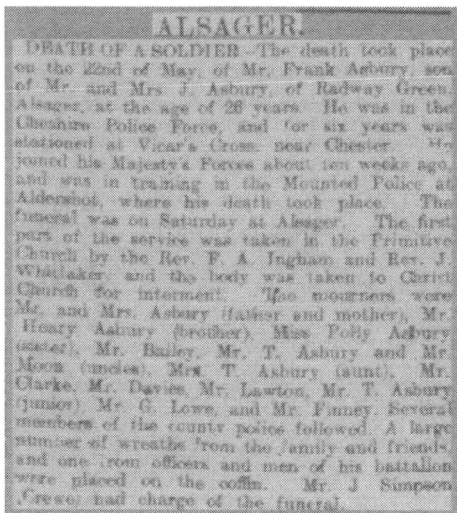

Frank is buried in Christ Church Alsager in a designated Commonwealth War Grave (Plot: East; Row: 1; Grave 7.) Frank was not included on Alsager Memorial but he is commemorated on the Haslington War Memorial in St Mathews Church.

# Date of death: 25th July 1917

## Private William Higgins: Army Service Corps

William Higgins was born in Odd Rode, Cheshire, in 1893, to Alice and Frank Higgins. Frank worked as a collier. William's sister Evelyn was born in 1895, Olive (1897) Ada (1900) and Winifred (1902.) In 1901 the family were living in 'The Fields,' but later moved to Rose Cottage, Close Lane, Alsager. In 1911 William took a job as a dairyman at Manor Farm, Alsager, and worked for Mr Heler.

In the 1915 Electoral Register he is shown as living in Chancery Lane. Before the war he took a job as a *motor car driver* and it was this skill which prompted him to enlist with the Army Service Corps (Military Transport) in Coventry on 22nd April 1915. His army number was M2/079437. His service record states he was 5 feet 5 inches tall, had fair complexion and a chest measurement of 32 inches. He was unmarried. William was based in Devon for a short period before embarkation to France on S.S. Onward on 12th July 1915. He was attached to X1 Corps before transferring to 50 Army Service Corps (ACS) on 7th August 1916. He spent a short period working in the ASC Repair Shop before being attached to 72 Field Ambulance working near the front line in the Ypres Salient. On 25th July 1917 while on duty he was hit by a shell and received wounds to his neck and head. He died on the same day. He is buried at the Dickebusch New Military Cemetery Extension, West-Vlaanderen, Belgium in plot III. F. 1. In his army will he left £3. 11s. 8d. to his father and sisters. He had been at home on leave shortly before his death and he had spoken very hopefully about returning home and peace before the end of the year. His father was a lifelong member of Christ Church choir for many years. William was posthumously awarded the 1914/15 Star, the British War Medal, and the Victory Medal

*Dickebusch New Military Cemetery. Photo: Author*

*Family Grave commemoration, Christ Church, Alsager. Photo: Author*

# Date of death: 9th August 1917

### 2nd Lieutenant Charles Raymond Waller: Royal Flying Corps.

Charles Raymond Waller was born on 19th June 1898, in Allahabad, Bengal, India .His father was Edward Harry Mansfield Waller, a clergyman, who went on to become the Bishop of Madras in India. His uncle, Alfred Waller, was the Vicar of Alsager during the Great War. According to the Parish Magazine Bishop Edward Waller preached in Alsager on two occasions when visiting his brother from India.

Charles' mother was Irene Juliana Louisa Waller (nee Doudney.) His brother, David, died in infancy in 1912.

For his education Charles returned to England from India. He sailed from Calcutta on *S.S Algeria* arriving in London on 25th May 1909 to attend Hilltop School in Hastings, Sussex. He was the only passenger in the 3rd or 'seafaring' class.

In the 1911 census Charles is described as living in Hastings Sussex aged 12 and born in Allahabad, India. After school Charles went to Jesus College, Cambridge. His name is among those Jesuans killed in the war listed in The Chanticleer (Michaelmas 1919.)

Charles was living in Alsager at the parsonage with his uncle before leaving to commence training with the Royal Flying Corps on 15th February 1917. He was commissioned with effect from 24th May 1917 as 2nd Lieutenant in the Royal Flying Corps following training as a cadet in Oxford from 13th April 1917. Charles joined 52 Squadron and continued his training at Hounslow Aerodrome, Middlesex. He died on 9th August 1917, in a flying accident whilst taking an altitude test. He had practically finished his training when the accident happened. A description of the accident was recorded in Flight magazine, 16th August 1917 page 840.

*'Fatal Accidents. In an inquest held on August 11th on 2nd Lieut. C. R. Waller, who was killed at Hounslow on August 9th it was stated that the pilot went up for an altitude test. He had never before flown more than 3,000 ft. up, but on this occasion he went up to 16,000 ft. The machine then nose-dived, righted itself, dived again, rolled over and collapsed, the pieces being scattered over a large area. It was suggested that the deceased became faint or had a heart attack. A verdict of "Accidental Death" was returned.'*

*Photo: a standard B.E.2c aeroplane*

*Photo Wikipedia*

The plane was a reconnaissance, light bomber, a night fighter, trainer, and coastal patrol aircraft. This plane had a particularly poor stability but a good accident record. This plane was used at Hounslow Aerodrome, and was probably the type of plane flown by C.R Waller

Below is a passage from The Straits Times, 29th September 1917 page 15.

*'Fainted at 16,000 feet. Unusual flight of an Airman.*

*When he had ascended to a height of 16,000 feet, Sec-Lieut. C. R. Waller, of Meopham, Kent, fainted in the air. An explosion occurred, and Lieut. Waller was killed. This was stated at the inquest at Hounslow, when the symptoms of air faintness were described. The machine, it was stated, nose-dived, righted itself, then dived again and rolled over. When the explosion took place, the machine was blown to pieces. Captain C. P. Inglefield said that Lieut. Waller had never before flown more than 3,000 feet up, and it was unusual and dangerous to fly 16,000 feet at a first attempt. He thought that the officer must have become faint or had a heart attack. The Coroner: 'How can you tell that?" –*

*"His flying cap was strapped under his chin before he went up, but it was found unstrapped two miles away. One of the first things a flying man does if he feels faint is to unloose the strap. The first symptom of faintness", said Captain Inglefield, "is stars moving before the eyes, when an airman should come down at once. Fainting would cause a man to fall forward and lose absolute control of the machine. It would need a strong man to fly at such a height."*

*A Juror asked: "Would he know the air pressure?" –*

*"No."*

*The Coroner asked: "Would it not be useful to have an air pressure gauge on the machine?"*

*"It would be very useful," replied Inglefield. The jury returned a verdict of accidental death.'*

Charles left his father, the Rt. Rev Edwards Harry Mansfield Waller, £56.00 in his will.

He is buried in Heston (St Leonard) Cemetery, Middlesex, England. Grave reference E. 20.

*Heston (St Leonard) Cemetery. Photo Flickr.*

Charles's name is inscribed on the war memorial in Alsager, primarily because his uncle Alfred Hamilton Waller was his closest relative living in Britain. His uncle was the Vicar of Alsager between 1913 and 1924. Charles is also commemorated on the Jesus College, Cambridge, War Memorial.

# Date of death: 18th September 1917

## Second Lieutenant William Holland M.C.: West Yorkshire Regiment.

*Photograph: Sentinel newspaper*

William Rawlinson Garside Holland was born in Alsager in 1893 to Sarah and William Holland. His father was a farmer. They lived at Brook Farm, Wheelock, but after William Holland senior's death the family moved to 'Ingleside' Lawton Road, Alsager. 'Rawlin', as he preferred to be called, attended Newcastle-under-Lyme School, Staffordshire, and on leaving school he became a bank clerk in the National Provincial Bank in Hanley. He was a Sunday school teacher at Christ Church for some years and was the founder of the Sunday School library. He was also the organist at the Linley Mission and occasionally played at St Mary's. He was one of the inaugurators of the Alsager Junior Constitutional Association. He moved to Leeds because of work, lodging at 25 Roman Grove, Roundhay, working as a bank clerk with the National Provincial Bank. On 5th December 1915 he enlisted with the West Riding Regiment in Leeds, army number 4333. His service record states he was 6 feet 1 inch tall and had a chest measurement of 38 inches. He trained with the 89th Training Battalion but suffered an appendicitis in March 1916 which interrupted his training. In July 1916 he was promoted Lance Sergeant. He was posted to the West Yorkshire Regiment on 18th September 1916. On 10th November 1916 he was reported in the London Gazette as being promoted to 2nd Lieutenant from 25th October 1916. He embarked to France on 13th December 1916 and was posted to the 50th Trench Mortar Battery from the 10th Battalion, West Yorkshire Regiment in 1917.

On 16th August 1917 he was awarded the Military Cross: *'for conspicuous gallantry and devotion to duty in handling his mortar battery with great skill and coolness during a critical time when the enemy were threatening to rush our position. His mortars were under heavy shell fire in the front line, and inflicted great loss on the attacking enemy.'*

He was due home to receive the Military Cross from the King but was wounded and on the 18th September 1917 he died of wounds and was buried at Sunken Road Cemetery, Fampoux (near Arras), Pas de Calais, France.

A report of his death was reported in the Birmingham Post on 25th September 1917.

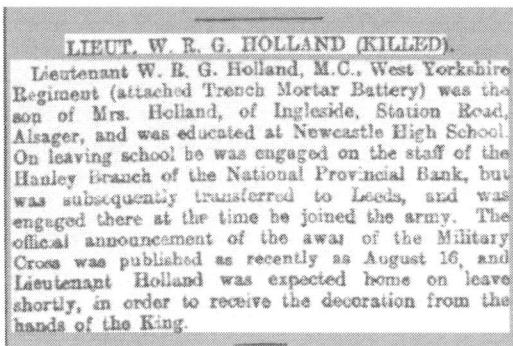

**LIEUT. W. R. G. HOLLAND (KILLED).**

Lieutenant W. R. G. Holland, M.C., West Yorkshire Regiment (attached Trench Mortar Battery) was the son of Mrs. Holland, of Ingleside, Station Road, Alsager, and was educated at Newcastle High School. On leaving school he was engaged on the staff of the Hanley Branch of the National Provincial Bank, but was subsequently transferred to Leeds, and was engaged there at the time he joined the army. The official announcement of the award of the Military Cross was published as recently as August 16, and Lieutenant Holland was expected home on leave shortly, in order to receive the decoration from the hands of the King.

*Birmingham Post*

The news of Lt Holland's death came as a great shock to his mother and sister as they had received a letter from him the previous Sunday in which he said he had been resting and was not expecting to go into the firing line. He spoke of coming home for his Investiture of the Military Cross he was to receive from the King's hands.

*William Rawlinson Garside Holland's*

*Military Cross. Photo from sale catalogue. It was sold at auction in 2005.*

William is also commemorated on the Moor Allerton St John's Church memorial, Leeds, and on a wall plaque at Wheelock Methodist Church.

William's headstone bears the words

*'Out of the stress of the doing into the peace of the done.'*

William was posthumously awarded the Military Cross, Victory Medal and the British War Medal.

# Date of death: 27<sup>th</sup> September 1917

## Pte. Frederick Henry Shipley: North Staffordshire Regiment.

*(A serviceman not on the Alsager War Memorial but with an Alsager connection)*

Fred Shipley was born in Cobridge, Staffordshire, in 1898 to Alice and Enoch Shipley. His brother, Harry Hollis Shipley, was born in1907. The family lived in Hanley in the early part of the century and after school Fred worked as a parcels porter with the North Staffordshire Railway Company. After Fred enlisted in the 2/5<sup>th</sup> North Staffordshire Regiment on 9<sup>th</sup> May 1916 his family moved to live in Alsager at Moorhouse Farm where Enoch was employed as a worker. Fred was 5 feet 6 inches tall and had a 36 inch chest and served as a private, army number 202979. He embarked to France on 25<sup>th</sup> February 1917 and served in 'C' Company. He was wounded in action on 27<sup>th</sup> September 1917 on active service and was treated in a field hospital where he died on the same day. His belongings, found on his body, were his identity disc, letters, photos, his railway company employment card, and a church attendance card. Fred was a staunch Methodist. He is buried in Bridge House Cemetery, West-Vlaanderen, Belgium, reference A 14. The Commonwealth War Graves record states, *'Son of Enoch and Alice Shipley, of Morehouse (sic) Farm, Alsager, Stoke-on-Trent. Native of Hanley'* Fred received the British War Medal and Victory Medal. He was 19 when he died and was unmarried.

Items found on Pte F Shipley

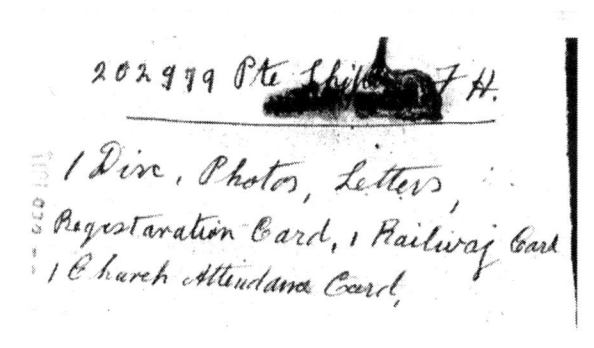

*Card sent to Pte. Shipley's next of kin*

# Date of death: 9th October 1917

### Private Herbert Morris: Manchester Regiment.

*Herbert Morris – a blurred photograph from the Sentinel newspaper 1917*

Herbert Morris was born in April 1898 to Emma Morris and Thomas Hulse. His father was a coal hewer. The family lived with Emma's father in Crewe Road, Alsager. His brother, Thomas Morris, was born in 1895, Elsie (1901) and May (1903). Herbert was a platelayer for the North Staffordshire Railway Company based in Alsager sidings. His trade union record erroneously states he left railway employment in 1919.

Herbert enlisted in Alsager with the 2/9th Battalion, the Manchester Regiment after 1916, army number 352567. The 2/9th Battalion, Manchester Regiment, was formed at Ashton-under-Lyne in August 1914 as a second line unit. It was nicknamed, 'The Ashton Pals.' In November 1914 the Battalion was placed under command of 198th Brigade in 66th (2nd East Lancashire) Division. It moved to Crowborough in May 1915, and went on to Colchester in March 1916. In February 1917 it landed in France as part of XI Corps. The Division remained in France and Flanders and took part in the following engagements: The Operations on the Flanders Coast (Operation Hush) (26th June – 25th September 1917) and the Battle of Poelcapelle 1917, a phase of the Third Battle of Ypres (6th - 10th October 1917) Herbert Morris was killed during the second day of the battle near Potijze. He was identified by his identity disc and buried in Potijze Chateau Grounds Cemetery, West-Vlaanderen, Belgium, plot II. C. 14. For almost the entire period of the First World War the village of Potijze was held by the Commonwealth forces but stood directly behind the Allied trenches and was well within range of German guns. It was here that soldiers entered the communication and support trenches that led to the front-line. Although subject to constant shell fire Potijze Chateau, a country house dating from the nineteenth century, remained intact throughout the war and was occupied and used by Commonwealth troops. The ground floor was later used as an Advanced Dressing Station while the first floor, which commanded views of the German lines, served as an observation post. For much of the war the Chateau was surrounded by a cluster of dug-outs and trenches and a large shed on the grounds, known to soldiers as 'Lancer Farm', housed ammunition and trench stores. Working parties would pause here to collect tools, coils of barbed wire, duckboards, bombs and other supplies before moving up the line. The Nantwich Guardian reported on 26th October 1917 that Morris had been killed while carrying supplies up to the Royal Engineers. Half way on the second journey they made that evening there was severe shelling and Morris was hit.

*Cemetery, Vlaanderen, Belgium. Photo Commonwealth War graves Commission*

Many people in Alsager knew Herbert as Herbert Hulse, his father's name, though official records put his name as Morris. Alsager Parish Magazine reported his death as Herbert Hulse in November 1917. Herbert was granted the Victory Medal and British War Medal. His mother was entitled to £5 war gratuity and £4 back pay.

The inscription on Herbert Morris's headstone written by his mother; *"Time Heals Many Things but Memory like Ivy Clings"*

He is also commemorated on the Ashton Pals Roll of Honour.

Pte. 352567 HERBERT MORRIS. Born Alsager, Cheshire.
Enlisted Alsager. Killed in Action in France & Flanders 9.10.1917.

*Ashton Pals Roll of Honour*

# Date of death: 16<sup>th</sup> October 1917

### Corporal Walter Amos Jackson : North Staffordshire Regiment.

Walter Amos Jackson was born in Alsager Cheshire, in 1896 to Ann and Amos Jackson. His father was an agent for a monumental mason company. Walter's brother William Hodkinson Jackson was born in 1890. The family lived in Lawton Road, Alsager. In 1911 Walter worked as an errand boy for local Alsager shops. He then worked for the Post Office. Walter enlisted in the 1/5<sup>th</sup> North Staffordshire Regiment in March 1916, army number 5168, in Shelton near Hanley, and saw action in France in 1917. Walter's brother, William, fought with the Cheshire Regiment. Walter was promoted to Corporal to lead a section in his company, and his army number was changed to 201574. He was killed in action on 16<sup>th</sup> October 1917. According to the Battalion War Diary only one man in the regiment was killed on 16<sup>th</sup> October 1917.

Walter was killed by enemy mortar fire when the regiment was in trenches near to Hulluch. He was buried at the Philosophe British Cemetery Mazingarbe, Pas de Calais, France in plot II. V. 5, His headstone reads,

*'He fought the good fight, he kept the faith. Son of Amos and Ann Elizabeth Jackson, of Windsor Cottage, Alsager, Stoke-on-Trent.'*

Walter was posthumously awarded the Victory Medal and British War Medal

*Philosophe British Cemetery Mazingarbe, Pas de Calais, France. Photo: Commonwealth War Graves Commission*

Walter Amos Jackson was a member of Wesley Place Methodist Church and is commemorated on their Great War Memorial plaque.

# Date of death: 16th October 1917

### Lance Corporal James Edward Grocott: Grenadier Guards

James Edward Grocott was the son of Jane and Thomas Grocott and was born in Alsager in August 1893. His father was a gardener. He had five brothers and one sister; George born 1886, Thomas (1888) Arthur (1895) Jesse (1898) and Horace (1895) His sister, Harriet, was born in 1895. The family lived at 95 Crewe Road, Alsager, in 1901, and by 1911 they were living in 'The Fields', Alsager. In 1911 James was working as a general labourer, and his brothers were railwaymen. The Nantwich Guardian reports he was in the police force in Rockferry before he enlisted. James enlisted in the Grenadier Guards, 1st Battalion, in July 1914 as a professional soldier, service number 17130. In October 1914 the Battalion embarked to Zeebrugge but James did not join them until 12th November. He was involved in the final stages of the first battle of Ypres in late November 1914 after which only 4 officers and 200 men of the Battalion survived. The 1st Battalion transferred to the 3rd Guards Brigade of the Guards Division and it was engaged in various action on the Western Front including the Battle of Flers-Courcelette and The Battle of Morval in 1916. During 1917 the Germans retreated to the Hindenburg Line, and James Grocott was involved in the Battle of Pilkem, and the Battle of the Menin Road. He was promoted to Lance Corporal and transferred to the 3rd Battalion Grenadier Guards. He was wounded during the 3rd Battalion's attack on 7th October 1917.

In the history of the Battalion by Ponsonby he writes, '*At 5.20 a.m. the attack commenced, and the leading Battalions started off preceded by a barrage. The Broembeek was crossed without difficulty, and the first objective was secured according to the scheduled time. The companies in support then passed through and captured the second objective. The 3rd Battalion Grenadiers and 1st Battalion Coldstream Guards received instructions not to cross the Broembeek until the first objective had been secured..... Barring the way of the 3rd Battalion Grenadiers was a concrete block-house, the garrison of which no doubt thought it held an impregnable position.*'

J.E. Grocott was wounded in the action and evacuated from the field. He died on 16th October 1917 and is buried at Etaples Military Cemetery, Pas de Calais, and not in the 'Guards Cemetery' at Lesboueffs. This indicates he must have been evacuated to a military hospital near Etaples before his death. He is commemorated at the Etaples Military Cemetery, Pas de Calais. His grave is located in plot XXX. D. 15. On 20th February 1918 James' mother was awarded £17. 7s. 11d. of James' back pay, and on 25th November 1919, £18. 10s. 0d. a 'War Gratuity'. James was posthumously awarded the 1914 Star with clasp, Victory Medal, and British War Medal.

*Etaples Commonwealth War Graves Cemetery-resting place of Lance Corporal James Edward Grocott. Photo: Commonwealth War Graves Commission*

# Date of death: 22nd October 1917

### Sergeant Frank Greenwood: Cheshire Regiment

Sergt. F. GREENWOOD

Frank Greenwood was born in Lawton Heath End, Betchton, near Alsager, Cheshire, in August 1890 to Fanny and William Greenwood. His father was a foreman plate layer on the railways.

His brothers and sisters: Aaron Greenwood was born 1874, John ( 1876) Harry ( 1880) Polly ( 1881), William ( 1883), Enoch ( 1885) Percy ( 1886), Lilly ( 1893) Frances ( 1896) and Annie ( 1900.) In 1901 the family was living in Wesley Street, off Lawton Road in Alsager. The family were associated with the Wesley Place Chapel and Frank attended the Wesleyan Sunday School for some years. Some of Frank's older brothers moved away to work on farms or the railways. Frank obtained work as a farm labourer on a local farm but in 1907 he followed his brother Percy into the army, enlisting in Crewe with the 2nd Battalion The Cheshire Regiment for seven years, service number 8697. Percy joined the Royal Field Artillery. After basic training Frank was based with the 2nd Battalion in England until the regiment went to India on 1st February 1910. Frank was based in Secunderabad, located in the Indian state of Telangana. Frank's service records show he was ill periodically with Indian sub-continent ailments and fevers. In August 1914 he was based in Jubbulpore, India, but with the commencement of hostilities the battalion returned to England, landing at Devonport on 24th December 1914. The battalion came under orders of 84th Brigade, 28th Division, at Winchester. It Landed at Le Havre on 17th January 1915. In 1915 Frank's mother, not knowing her son's whereabouts and Frank not answering her letters, wrote to the Cheshire Regiment to find out where he was serving. He was in the retreat from Mons and suffered severely from frostbite during the winter of 1914/15. In October 1915 the battalion moved to Egypt where he served until 8th June 1916. Frank was promoted to Lance Corporal on 20th December 1915. But on 16th May 1916 the Staffordshire Sentinel Newspaper reported he was recovering from illness in hospital. He was partially buried after a shell burst and remained trapped for eight hours before being rescued. It also reported Frank was one of five Greenwood brothers and one grandson serving in the colours. In January 1916 he was invited to apply for a commission but he returned to France without taking it up. On 20th July 1916 Frank transferred to the 10th Battalion of the Cheshire Regiment and served with them in France until November of that year. He returned to France on 8th March 1917 and was promoted to Sergeant on 13th April 1917, transferring to the 16th Battalion of the Cheshire's. The 16th Battalion were known as the *'Bantams'* because of their short height. In France they were known as *'piccaninni soldats'*. The regiment was soon involved in the Arras sector. On 22nd October 1917 the battalion was involved in a frontal attack near Houlthurst Forest near Arras towards Marchal Farm in bitterly cold weather. Frank was killed in the action along with nine officers and 329 other ranks in the battle which was later called *Passchendaele*. His body was never found. He is commemorated on the Tyne Cot memorial, Belgium, on panel 63 and 64. In 1920 his medals, the 1914/15 Star, the British Medal, and the Victory Medal were sent to his mother, Fanny Greenwood.

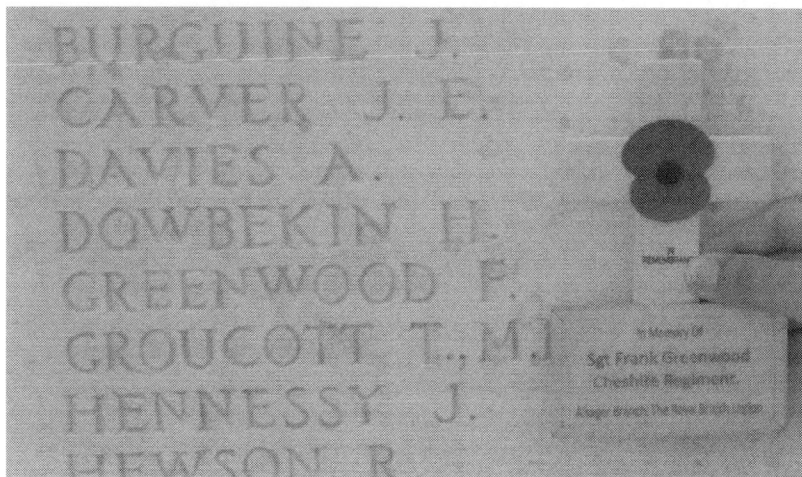

*Tyne Cot Memorial, Belgium. Photo Mr Voller.*

Frank Greenwood was a member of Wesley Place Methodist Church and is commemorated on their Great War Memorial plaque.

# Date of death: 30<sup>th</sup> October 1917

**Private George Henry 'Harry' Whipp: 2/6<sup>th</sup> Kings Liverpool Regiment.**

George Henry 'Harry' Whipp was born in Poynton, Cheshire, in 1898 to Frank Thomas and Mary Ann Whipp. His brother, Frank Ewart was born in 1894, and his sister Edith Ann Whipp, was born in 1897. In 1900 his family moved to Alsager, where his father worked as a dairyman. In 1901 the family lived in Crewe Road and by 1911 they moved to 'Oaklands,' Station Road. George went to school in Alsager at the National School, Church Road, and later worked at Settle Speakman, Alsager. In 1914 the family moved to Dinorwic Rd., Birkdale, Southport. George joined the 2/6th King's Liverpool (Rifle) Battalion, Service number 63883.

The Regiment had been formed in Liverpool on 10<sup>th</sup> September 1914 as a second line battalion. On 8<sup>th</sup> February 1915 the regiment came under orders of 171<sup>st</sup> Brigade, 57<sup>th</sup> (2<sup>nd</sup> West Lancashire) Division. George Henry served under the name of 'Harry' Whipp. Harry probably enlisted in 1916 as he was not awarded the 1915 Star. On 14<sup>th</sup> February 1917 the battalion landed in France. Harry was killed at the third battle of Ypres ('Passchendaele') on 30<sup>th</sup> October 1917.

On 28<sup>th</sup> October the battalion moved from Mousin Farm to Eagle trench in the vicinity of Schaap-Balie north west of Westroozebeke relieving the 2<sup>nd</sup> /5<sup>th</sup> Battalion and taking up position in old German pillboxes. As the regiment moved up it was attacked by gas projectiles but moved into front positions at Reben's and Gravel Farm suffering twenty casualties. However they discovered they were out of position. On 28<sup>th</sup> October Lieutenant C.W Clarke and Sergeant Stubbs and seven other ranks moved from Besace Farm and advanced 1000 yards to reconnoitre enemy positions. During the night of 29<sup>th</sup>/30<sup>th</sup> October 'B' Company made attempts to take Memling and Ruben's Farm enemy positions but were held up at both locations by machine gun fire. British artillery opened up heavy fire and the enemy responded with their large guns. The regiment again attempted to take Memling Farm without success taking 3 officer casualties and 70 other ranks. 25 men were missing. Harry Whipp was amongst the casualties during this action.

Harry's death was reported in the Weekly Sentinel on 24<sup>th</sup> November 1917.

*'Pte. Whipp, King's Liverpool Regiment, has been killed in action. Son of Mr & Mrs Whipp of Southport, previously Alsager, worked Messrs Settle Speakman Co. of Alsager.'*

Harry is buried at the British Cemetery, Poelcappelle, Belgium in grave XXXV. D. 9. His parents had the following inscription placed on his grave, *' Free from harm in His Shepherd's arms'*. In 1919 his parents were awarded their son's Victory and British War medals.

*Poelcappelle British Cemetery. Photo: Commonwealth War Graves Commission*

# Date of death: 20<sup>th</sup> November 1917

## 2<sup>nd</sup> Lieutenant M.F W Leek: West Yorkshire Regiment.

Leek was christened Major Frederick William Leek, but was generally known as 'Freddy'. He was born in May 1890 in 11, Ironmarket, Newcastle-under-Lyme to William Edward and Lucy Leek. He was christened at St Giles Parish Church on 1<sup>st</sup> June 1890. His sister Constance was born in 1886. His father was a shoe manufacturer and merchant in Newcastle. In 1901 the family were living in London Road, Stoke-upon-Trent. Frederick attended Newcastle under Lyme School, where he is commemorated on the school war memorial. After school Frederick worked in the Manchester and District Bank in Stoke. His family moved to Alsager and lived at Coniston Lodge in the Avenue. His father died in 1913. He was a member of the B'hoys Society of Alsager. Freddy is on the Electoral Register at Coniston Lodge, Alsager, in 1915. Frederick joined the 28<sup>th</sup> City of London Regiment, the Artists' Rifles, as a private soldier, service number 3472. The serial number indicates Freddy enlisted in March 1915. On 29<sup>th</sup> July 1915 Frederick was commissioned 2<sup>nd</sup> Lieutenant in the West Yorkshire Regiment which was reported in the London Gazette on August 4<sup>th</sup>, 1915, and in the autumn of 1915 he transferred to the Tank Corps. The Artist's Rifles particularly attracted recruits from public schools and universities; on this basis, following the outbreak of the First World War, a number of enlisted members of The Artists Rifles were selected to be officers This exercise was so successful that, early in 1915, selected Artists officers and NCOs were transferred to form a separate Officers Training Corps, in which poet Wilfred Owen trained before posting to the Manchester Regiment.

On 20<sup>th</sup> November 1917 Frederick was involved in the first tank advance of the battle of Cambrai. He was a commander in 'D' Battalion tasked to assist 51<sup>st</sup> Highland Division to capture the village of Flesquières; the unit talking heavy casualties as they pressed home their attack against well positioned German artillery. To the south of Flesquières, long columns of black smoke rising from the destroyed and burning tanks clearly indicated that something was wrong. Due to a fierce resistance by the German field artillery, the tanks were stopped. The 51st Highland Division, too far

106

away to help, was not able to prevent the disaster. Frederick was killed in the action. A Major of the Corps wrote '...*Lieut. Leek showed dash and skill quite remarkable in an officer who was taking a tank into action for the first time.*'

On 23rd November, the remaining 14 Mark IV tanks attacked Bourlon Wood and the heights to the west; all tanks rallied despite severe enemy fire. Frederick's body was never found. Frederick is commemorated on panel 13, Cambrai memorial, Louverval, Departement du Nord, France. In his will he left £4,120. 16s.10d. to his mother and his sister, Mrs Constance Rimell.

Freddy was posthumously awarded the 1914/15 Star, British War Medal, and Victory Medal.

*Tank Corps 1917.*
Photo: Wikipedia.

In 1992 his medals were auctioned by Christie's in London along with those belonging to another Tank Officer. The medals realised £330. The catalogue erroneously stated that Frederick joined the Royal Flying Corps before joining the Tank Corps. There is no record of this.

*'Through mud and blood to the green fields beyond'*
Tank Corps motto.

# Alsager in 1918

Dr Kington's medical report to Alsager Urban District Council in January 1918 looked back at the year 1916. He reported 657 houses in Alsager were occupied in 1916 and 13 were empty. The population was 2,716 and there had been 36 deaths that year. There had been one case of scarlet fever, four of measles, and nine cases of tuberculosis. In June and July thesere had been numerous cases of indigestion and diarrhoea caused by poor 'war bread'. (Regulations had subsequently been introduced to ensure the quality of bread.) On the face of it the war had not significantly changed the health of the people of Alsager but the emotional strain of war was bound to be considerable.

The local government electoral register containing the 'Absent Voters' list in 1918 records one hundred and eighty five men serving in a wide range of Army regiments and in the Royal Flying Corps/ Royal Air Force and Royal Navy. The register was probably drawn up in early 1918. The men were included on the electoral register despite being absent from their home residence on active service. In 1914 twenty nine out of the first seventy eight recruits had enlisted in the North Staffordshire Regiment. In 1918 only ten Alsager men on the Absent Voters list were still serving the North Staffords compared to sixteen men in the Artillery and ten in the Royal Flying Corps/RAF. After 1916 men were allocated to training regiments and on to regiments where they were needed and fewer Alsager men were serving alongside their brothers or friends. After 1st September 1916, regimental distinctions disappeared and the reserve units of the regiments were instead designated as battalions of the Training Reserve. They were organised into new brigades. Men who were posted to the Training (TR) battalions were not allocated to any particular regiment when the time came for them to be posted. So from this time on it is not safe to assume that a recruit would serve with his local regiment. Later, from May 1917, this arrangement was itself altered when the units of the TR became Graduated and Young Soldier Battalions and were once again aligned with specific regiments. The register included men like Reg Savory and Fred Challinor, both killed in final year of the war. The one hundred and eighty five men were still serving in 1918 constituted 6.7% of the town population. If you include the men killed or invalided out of the forces, and women serving in the nursing Voluntary Aid Detachment (V.A.D), the percentage of the total population involving in the direct war effort was nearer 11%. Men still serving within the 'Absent Voters' list in 1918 included several prisoners of war, Harry Johnson, George Jacobs, Mellard Settle and Frank Lucas. On the general Electoral Register for 1918 women with voting rights are included for the first time but none are recorded as Absent Voters who may have been serving in the forces. Only two women with an Alsager connection joined the Women's Auxiliary Army Corps (WAAC), Myrtle Wood and Kathleen O'Brien, who were both serving in France in 1918. Raised first in 1917 the WAAC enrolled 57, 00 volunteers. The WAAC were run on military lines though members served as workers: drivers, administrators, technicians. The equivalent of Private Soldiers were called Workers, and their Officers were called Controllers. The WAAC was later called the Queen Mary Auxiliary Army Corps (QMAAC)

**The German Spring Offensive. Several Alsager men become prisoners of war.**

March 1918 brought difficult news to Alsager. Several men became prisoners of war during the German spring offensive. On 5th April the Nantwich Guardian reported Lt Col. Harry Johnson, Captain Mellard Settle, and Lt Joseph Spite, all of the North Staffordshire Regiment, and Lt. John Dickinson, Liverpool Regiment, had been captured and were in Germany. News later trickled out about less senior soldiers taken prisoner including Privates E. Lucas, Jack Howarth, and Charlie Young, of the Shropshire Light Infantry. When servicemen became prisoners of war their relatives were informed by means of post cards sent via the International Red Cross.

**The Church Magazine**

In 1918 the Alsager Church Parish Magazine was brought out in thin brown paper because of the shortage of quality paper. In January it was suggested to parishioners they should cut out of the Parish Magazine the list of food restrictions and pin it to their dining room walls.

*Men on heavy industrial or agricultural work, bread, 8lbs per week*

*Men on ordinary or menial work, bread, 7 lbs a week*

*Men engaged in sedentary work, bread, 4 and a half pounds a week*

*Women on heavy industrial or agricultural work, bread, 5 lbs a week*

*Women on ordinary industrial or domestic service, bread 4lbs a week*

*Women engaged in sedentary work, bread, three and a half pounds a week.*

*For all classes. Other cereals: 12 ounces a week. Meat 2lbs a week. Butter, lard, margarine 10 ounces a week, Sugar half a pound a week.*

*Any person may take half a pound of meat instead of half a pound of bread or take half a pound of bread instead of half a pound of meat.*

On January 6th open air services were held in Alsager and the King's latest proclamations read out along with the names of local men serving in the colours. The open air services were held at the following places: Linley Bridge 9am; the Station, 9.20; Shady Grove, 9.45; Corner of Church Road/Lodge Lane 2pm; Bickerton's Corner (junction of Crewe Road and Station Road) 2.15; Band's Corner (Bank Corner), 2.40pm.

Freddy Leek's death was mentioned in the January edition of the Parish Magazine as well as it celebrating the allies' victory at the battle of Cambrai.

The Nantwich Guardian reported that several Alsager men were taken to work in France on road building. In response to the appeal for comforts for these men the Council sent 2 guineas subscription towards the appeal in January 1918.

## Food and Fuel Shortages

Food distribution was becoming a major problem and in January 1918 a conference of all the local council debated the problem. It was proposed the area should have a distribution system similar to the existing one for sugar for tea, margarine, butter, and other products. There was a big shortage of meat in the district. Stocks in the markets were less than 50% of what butchers were entitled to sell.

In January a deputation from Crewe and Alsager went to London to discuss arrangements to improve the access to food. J.J. Nelson from Alsager proposed the deputation.

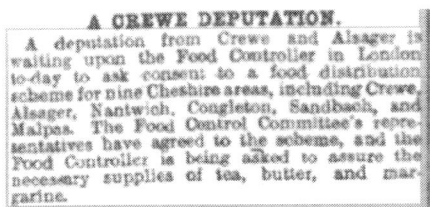

**A CREWE DEPUTATION.**

A deputation from Crewe and Alsager is waiting upon the Food Controller in London to-day to ask consent to a food distribution scheme for nine Cheshire areas, including Crewe, Alsager, Nantwich, Congleton, Sandbach, and Malpas. The Food Control Committee's representatives have agreed to the scheme, and the Food Controller is being asked to assure the necessary supplies of tea, butter, and margarine.

By May 1918 because of the Board of Agriculture's delay in delivering seed potatoes Alsager allotment holders declined to accept them. The council was stuck with 7cwt of unwanted potatoes. It is possible the potatoes were useless by this time and were not worth planting. The Council was also concerned about the shortage of coal. A proposal was discussed to ration coal to households based on the number of occupied rooms. By September the Local Government Board issued a leaflet, 'Hard Facts on the Coal Situation,' saying all areas must reduce their consumption of coal electricity and gas. J.J.Nelson, for the Council, responded that *we can hardly do any more in Alsager*. Only two street gas lamps were lit in Alsager during the last winter. Councillor Owen, said, to laughter, that a lamp was needed to find the two street lamps there was so little light from them. *We would not miss them*. The Council *did* propose to employ a scavenging contractor to re-use waste products like iron, cans, waste paper and household refuse to raise money.

Food shortages led to incidents of theft from farms in a few cases. On 8th February 1918 the Nantwich Guardian announced the arrest of culprits from Tunstall who had stolen and killed sheep from John Barker of Ash Bank Farm, Alsager. After sheep stealing they had killed them on a bridge crossing the North Stafford railway line. When the criminals returned on another occasion they were apprehended by police and committed for trial. This and other incidents of crime were rare however in Alsager but when it did occur the police were successful in solving them. In June 1918 John Mason from Rode Heath stole Treasury Notes (bank notes) from Percy Morris while they were both working and living at Alsager Hall Farm. Mason also stole 42 gun cartridges from Morris and went on to sell some of them to W. Ankers, blacksmith, of Alsager. When Mason disappeared from the farm he started to boast about having a treasury note and he was arrested. He was imprisoned for two months with hard labour.

## The Alsager Military Tribunal and the Volunteers in 1918

At its meeting in early April 1918 two appeals for exemption from military service were refused; a plumber's labourer, and a wagoner, 18, and single. A motor plough driver, 41, married was allowed for three months provided he remained on tractor or farm business. A munitions worker, 35, with 5 children was given 3 months provided he joined the Volunteers. A driver of a bread van, single, 18, whose brother was in the army, his parents dead, and who was the guardian of four young brothers and sisters was given 3 months exemption provided he joined the Volunteers. This seems a severe decision when the care of children was at risk but the Tribunals did not want to set a precedent for other single men to be exempted from military service. In July 1918, 12 cases were considered. A milk seller whose case had been adjourned for medical examination was given three months exemption. A hay cutter's claim was adjourned pending a decision by the War Agricultural Committee. Most cases were given three months exemption. These men would have avoided having to fight as the war ended in November but may well have still been conscripted into the services.

The Alsager Volunteers continued to drill in Alsager and participate in training with local detachments. In January they took part in a mock battle to attack Crewe Hall with men from Sandbach, the hall being defended by the Crewe and Barthomley detachments. The Volunteers were a visible presence and good for local morale though practically they contributed little to winning the war. They turned up to civic events, drilled, made a good show, and they would have been used if Britain were attacked by invasion but serving soldiers in France would have probably ridiculed them.

Military events abroad were raised and discussed in Alsager. The victory over the Turkish army and the re-taking of Jerusalem was described in the Parish Magazine as *'the dawn of a new era in world history'*. The Church of England Men's Society debated trade with Germany after the war and the collapse of the government in Russia. The new Curate announced he was to work on a farm three days a week to help with food production.

## Rode Hall Hospital

In the summer soldiers from Rode Hospital were entertained by the church. On 5th June the M.P. Ernest Craig, held a garden party at Milton House to entertain troops from Rode Hall Hospital. There was a tennis tournament, music from Mr Hughes orchestra, and there was a parade of decorated cycles and at 5.30 pm the soldiers had tea. Entertainment was provided by the 'Jingle Jonnies' who came from Stoke-on-Trent to entertain the wounded troops. Sergeant Hughes gave a vote of thanks to Mr Craig for his hospitality and this was carried with loud cheers. All through the summer of 1918 there was a big effort to collect for the Rode Hall Hospital. The Congregational Sunday School collected £16, Wesleyan Sunday School, £113, and St Mary's £138. The Primitive Methodist Sunday School raised over £19. This was in addition to numerous gifts of food, old linen, and pillows; and Mr Settle donated a truck load of coal.

## The influenza epidemic 1918

In May 1918 the parish magazine announced several servicemen were recovering from the epidemic, including Air Mechanic 1, Douglas Rowley Whalley, of Cherry Tree Cottage, Lawton Road, and Malcolm Harrison. Later in the year it would have a more devastating effect on the army in particular.

## Alsager's own aeroplane

An 'aeroplane week' was held in the area in July 1918 and the town asked to raise £10,000 towards this fund. One aeroplane was to be called Alsager. It was funded by the purchase of war bonds. With a total population of 2,700 Alsager had raised £20,000 for 'Tank Week' (equivalent to £1,025,000 in 2016) only four months previously. In the Nantwich Guardian, 5th July, it was reported £7,500 had already been collected in war bonds for the aeroplane. At a packed public meeting in Scholar Green Adolphus Goss asked people to use their savings to invest in war bonds. On the 19th July the Nantwich Guardian reported £10,400 had been raided, a staggering amount equal to £530,065 in 2015 (*source: Bank of England Inflation calculator.*) The funds would not just have covered the cost of aeroplane manufacture but also running costs. The various war savings schemes also contributed to the amount collected. There were ten Savings Associations in Alsager; Alsager Gardeners, St Mary's, Christ Church Senior, Christ Church Junior, Wesleyan, Congregational, Church of England Men's Society, Railway Station, Alsager Institute, and Girls' Friendly Society. By 26th July the total, including money from Lawton, totalled £11,404. This is equivalent to £584,321 in 2015. (*Source: Bank of England inflation calculator.*)The personal sacrifice by Alsager people led to a significant drain on their personal savings. Why were such huge amounts given? In the spring of 1918 the German offensive had nearly broken through the defences of the Allied Powers. The enemy had taken hundreds of British prisoners, including several Alsager men, and the British people were worried they were going to lose the war. Investing in an aeroplane seems like a token gesture but was a tangible way in which Alsager could help the war effort.

In the autumn of 1918 heating and lighting restrictions reduced the number of church services and evening services were cancelled. In Alsager the end of the war had been expected and brought about a huge release of emotion and relief.

On Armistice Day in Alsager, 11th November 1918, the Christ Church bells rang out, school children cheered and the streets were filled with flag-waving crowds. The churches were full for thanksgiving services. The Vicar Rev Alfred Waller, wrote, *'I don't think any of us will ever forget Monday*

*11<sup>th</sup> Nov as long as we live. We had all been on tip toe of expectation for several days, and one night ringers were actually in the Belfry and about to ring the joy peal which was to tell the tell the glad tidings the war was ended...'*

*Five days previously the last man to commence his Great War Service was William Mandeville. He served on S.S Tunisian a merchant vessel escorting vessels across the Atlantic. He was born in Alsager in 1902 and was only 16 when he enlisted. Despite only serving six days before the Armistice he still gained his Mercantile Marine Medal.*

*William Mandeville. Photo: Southampton Archives*

On 22<sup>nd</sup> November a thanksgiving service was held in St Mary's church and collections were made for a War Memorial Fund.

In some ways Alsager carried on as if the war had not ended. On 22<sup>nd</sup> November the Council elected twelve members of a 'Food Control Committee'. By statute two members had to be women, and Miss Sarjenson and Mrs Nelson were elected on to the twelve member grouping. The *'Guns Week'* campaign, started in Alsager on Tuesday 26<sup>th</sup> November with a procession through the town consisting of councillors, children, scouts, Volunteers, and a Chester brass band. A six inch howitzer, *'properly camouflaged'*, was placed on a trailer and drawn by a tractor at the rear of the procession. Speeches were made, including one by Miss Sarjenson, and the village was promised if it raised £8,400 it would be presented with an engraved 15 inch shell, *'a permanent memento to their aid to their country's finances'*. On 6<sup>th</sup> December 1918 the *Nantwich Guardian* reported that the *'Guns Week'* had brought in £30,471 (value: £1.56 m. in 2016. *Source, Bank of England inflation calculator*) invested by Alsager Banks and Post Office which included £10,000 invested by Prudential Insurance. It was as if the fighting might restart and the country must be ready for it. What ever happened to Alsager's engraved shell?

The Alsager peace celebrations were postponed until 1919. The community must have decided it should await the return of servicemen and women and hope hostilities would nor recommence before celebrations could take place.

# Deaths of Alsager servicemen in 1918

## Date of death: 23rd February 1918

**Fourth Engineer Officer Samuel Percy Jones: '*S.S. British Viscount*',
Mercantile Marine.**

Samuel is the only sailor from the Great War commemorated on the Alsager War Memorial.

Samuel Percy Jones was born in Seacombe, Cheshire, in 1884 to Frances and John Jones. John Jones was an accountant. Samuel's brother Francis Jones was born 1879, and his brother, Arthur Owen Jones was born 1883. Both of Samuel's brothers were involved in mercantile engineering. In 1891 the family were living in Seacombe, Birkenhead, Cheshire, and moved to Eccles, Lancashire before 1901. Samuel Percy joined the merchant navy as a cabin boy and when he was 17 he was recorded on the 1901 census abroad ship in dock in Antrim, Ireland. In 1911 Samuel's family moved to live in Shady Grove, Alsager, Cheshire. In 1914 Samuel was appointed an Artificer Engineer (equivalent to Warrant Engineer) as recorded in the Navy List 1914 and 1916. In the war Samuel worked on ships requisitioned for war duty. He was Fourth Engineer on the 'British Viscount,' a Tanker of 3,287 tons, a ship built in Britain in 1889 by Mordaunt & Co., Southampton. The ship was licenced to Petroleum SS. Co. Ltd. (British Tanker Co. Ltd.), London. On 23rd February 1918 the ship was sunk 12 miles N by W ½ W from the Skerries, near Anglesey en route from Liverpool to Queenstown, Ireland. It was torpedoed by U Boat U91, commanded by Alfred von Glasenapp. Samuel Percy was one of six casualties. The ship was carrying a cargo of fuel oil.

*Map of wreck site S.S.
British Viscount.*

Samuel's body was not recovered. Samuel, who was unmarried, is commemorated on the memorial on Tower Hill, London, to sailors who died at sea.

*Tower Hill Memorial, London.*

*Photo Commonwealth War Graves Commission.*

Samuel was posthumously awarded the 1914 Star, the Victory Medal and the British War Medal.

# Date of death: 18th March 1918

## Arthur Thomas Davies: Air Mechanic 2nd Class

A.T. Davies was born in Alsager in 1897 to Lily and Arthur Thomas Davies. His father worked as a bricklayer. The family lived in Station Road, and later moved to Beech Terrace, Crewe Road, Alsager.

His brothers and sisters were: Edith M. Davies (born 1895), Lilian Davies (1898), Mary Davies (1900), Frederick Davies (1902), Robert Davies (1904), Elaine Davies (1906), and Annie Davies (1910.)

Arthur Davies was Secretary of Christ Church Sunday School, a regular member of the choir, and a bell ringer at the church. He is recorded in the Central Council of Bell Ringers records as a casualty of The Great War.

Arthur was an engineer's pattern maker in a foundry. He attested for military service in December 1915 but was put on the Army reserve because of his occupation. His service record states he was five feet ten inches tall and had a chest measurement of thirty seven inches. He joined the Royal Flying Corps as a mechanic on 9th October 1917 at Farnborough, Hampshire. His service number was 97951. He died on 18th March 1918 near Newmarket, Cambridgeshire. He died of sudden heart failure. He was buried with full military honours in Christ Church graveyard, (plot - Old Ground 8.83) on 22nd March 1918. He is buried in a designated Commonwealth War Grave. Arthur's father lived until the age of 91 and lived at 93 Crewe Road Alsager until his death in February 1961. Arthur's mother died one month after her husband, on 7th March 1961 aged 88.

*A.T. Davies' grave in Christ Church, Alsager. Photo: Author*

Because of his family connections A.T Davies is also commemorated on the Welsh National War Memorial, Cathays Park Cardiff.

# Date of death: 21st March 1918

### Private Frederick Charles Challinor: King's Shropshire Light Infantry.

Frederick Charles Challinor was born in Crewe, Cheshire in 1896 to Martha (nee Henshall) and Ralph Challinor. His father was a railway guard, later becoming a foreman for a railway company. Frederick's brothers and sisters were as follows: Alfred was born 1897, followed by Marion (1899) John William Challinor (1901), Ralph Clifford (1903), and Irene (1908). Between 1901 and 1911 the family lived in Wesley Street, Alsager, and in 1914 they were living in Lawton Road, afterwards moving to Sandy Lane, (Ashmore's Lane) Alsager. In 1911 Frederick worked as a Grocer's errand boy in Alsager.

He was a member of Rev Harold Thomas's Sunday school class at St Mary's Church in 1912 but became a member of Wesley Place Methodist Church and is commemorated on their Great War Memorial plaque.

On 27th June 1915 Fred was admitted to the National Union of Railwaymen trade union, working on Alsager Station as signalman and porter for the North Staffordshire Railway Company. He then went on to work at Mow Cop station. He enlisted in the army in May 1917. His death in the trade union record is given as June 1918, which is an error. It says he died on active service. His name is crossed out in the Trade Union records.

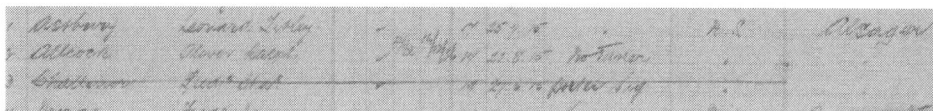

Frederick enlisted in the 1st Battalion King's Shropshire Light Infantry, service number 20407. He first saw active service overseas in October 1917. In January 1918, the battalion was serving with 5th Army and met the brunt of the great German Spring Offensive on 21st March, being just about annihilated at Lagnicourt - not one combatant officer was left and only 53 other ranks came out alive. The battalion was part of the 16th Infantry Brigade. The battalion was completely re-formed under Lt. Col. Meynell and within ten days of being all but destroyed, was back in the line at Ypres and fought continuously in the salient until late August. Frederick was killed in action on 21st March 1918, the first day of the Battle of St Quentin. The British infantry and the most forward-placed artillery faced the 'perfect storm' on the morning of 21st March: they were attacked in overwhelming strength in thick fog, wearing gas masks for much of the day, finding that fast-moving enemy infantry had broken through gaps in the defences and were rounding them up from behind. Thousands were killed and more captured. Many British soldiers held out although surrounded, but the Germans drove deep into the British positions in several areas, precipitating retreat and chaos that developed over the next few days. Frederick Charles Challinor's body was never found. He is commemorated on Bay 7 of the Arras Memorial Pas de Calais. According to records Frederick's father was awarded £10. 17. 6d. back pay owing to Frederick and a £3 war gratuity. At the time of Frederick's death he was recorded on the Absent Voters' list for Alsager stating his home address was Sandy Lane, Alsager. His brother Alfred also served on active service abroad.

*Fred Challinor (in uniform) photographed with his family during the war. Left to right: Marion Challinor, Amy Lump (Fred's fiancée), Ralph Challinor, Fred Challinor (in uniform) Martha Challinor, John Challinor, Ann Wildblood. Children sitting (front) Irene Challinor, Clifford Challinor. Photo: South Cheshire Archives, Crewe. Frederick was posthumously awarded the Victory Medal and the British War Medal*

# Date of death: 23rd March 1918

**Private Percy Nutt: Royal Fusiliers (London Regiment).**

*Percy Nutt. Photo: Sentinel*

Percy Nutt was born in Alsager Cheshire, in February 1899 to Elizabeth and Joseph Nutt. His father was a locomotive engine driver for the North Staffordshire Railway Company. His brother William was born in 1893. The family lived in Audley Road, Alsager throughout Percy's childhood. After school, Percy worked for the North Staffordshire Railway Company. In 1917 he enlisted in the 106th Training Battalion, 30th (Reserve) Battalion, service number GS/70879. Percy was allocated to the Royal Fusiliers, 7th Battalion, (London Regiment *The Shiny Seventh*), and embarked to France on 12th March 1918. He was killed in action only a few days later on 23rd March 1918 following a major German attack on the Western Front in the battle of St Quentin.

On 23rd March the British Fifth Army's line had gone back an average of four to six miles (this included retirements of up to eight miles in some sectors). Percy was missing presumed dead. He is commemorated on the Arras Memorial Faubourg D'Amiens Cemetery, Arras, Pas de Calais, bay 3. The Commonwealth War Graves record states, *'Son of Joseph Nutt, of 4, Frederick Avenue, Penkhull, Stoke-on-Trent'*. By 1918 Joseph Nutt, Percy's father, had moved to Penkhull, Staffordshire. Percy's brother, William, was a wireless operator with the Royal Engineers.

Percy was posthumously awarded the Victory Medal and the British War Medal

# Date of death: 8<sup>th</sup> May 1918

## Private James Yates. King's Liverpool Regiment

*(A serviceman not on the Alsager War Memorial but with an Alsager connection)*

James Young was born in Alsager in 1881. He was 35 when he enlisted in 1917, first in the Cheshire Regiment, and afterwards with the 17<sup>th</sup> Battalion, King's Liverpool Regiment, one of the first 'Pals Battalions'. By profession he was a house painter working in the town. At the time of enlisting, probably by conscription, he was living with his widowed mother in Lawton Road. He had been born in Shady Grove and had never lived anywhere else but Alsager. He had an older brother, John, two sisters, and a younger brother, Edward. His father, also called James, was a publican and later a potato merchant. He originally enlisted in Chester but his service with the Cheshire Regiment has been lost.

*James Yates Tyne Cot Memorial. Photo: Mr Voller*

James' second regiment, the 17<sup>th</sup> (Service) Battalion (1<sup>st</sup> City), landed in Boulogne in November 1915. The Liverpool Pals (17<sup>th</sup> - 20<sup>th</sup> Battalions) wore the 'eagle & child' crest of Lord Derby. In May 1918 the regiment was fighting in the Ypres Salient and James was killed, his body never found. He is commemorated on the Tyne Cot Memorial: panel- Addenda, 165. His family were given his British War Medal and the Victory Medal. James was not included on the Alsager war memorial despite his close links to the town. His mother died in Alsager in 1928.

# Date of death: 14th May 1918

## Private Benjamin Mitchell : Loyal North Lancashire Regiment.

Benjamin Mitchell was born in Crewe Road, Alsager, Cheshire, in 1899 to Emily and George Mitchell who were living at the time with George's mother, Hannah Mitchell in Crewe Road, Alsager. George Mitchell was a labourer. Benjamin's siblings were: step brother Henry Mottram born 1892, step sister Florence Mottram born 1893, and brother, Arthur Mitchell who was born in 1901. By 1901 the family were living in Red Street, Chesterton, but by 1911 Benjamin was living with his grandmother in Crewe Road, Alsager. Benjamin worked as a farm labourer and after the outbreak of war the family moved to Church Street, Butt Lane, Staffordshire.

Benjamin was posted to the 4/5th Loyal North Lancashire Regiment in Chester on 7th October 1916, service number 9777. He did his basic training in England. Records state he was five feet five tall and had a chest measurement of thirty two inches. The regiment received a warning order on 5th January 1917 that it would soon depart for France. The units crossed the Channel between the 7th and 22nd February and completed concentration at Merris on 23rd February 1917. Benjamin embarked from Folkestone on 12th February 1917 to Boulogne. Benjamin was given a new service number 244671 and posted to the North Loyal Lancs1/5th Battalion. Three days later the regiment took over the right sector of II Anzac Corps, north of Le Tilleloy.

SIR OR MADAM,

I am directed to forward the undermentioned articles of private property of the late No. 244671 Rank Private Name Benjamin Mitchell Regt. 1/5th Loyal North Lancs. and would ask that you will kindly acknowledge receipt of the same on the form opposite:—

1 Identity Disc, 1 Letter, Photographs, 1 Wallet, 2 Cards, 1 Spoon

*Items returned to Benjamin Mitchell's family in 1918. National Archives.*

The Division remained in France and Flanders and took part in the following engagements: The Second Battle of Passchendaele (26th October – 7th November) phases of the Third Battle of the Ypres. Benjamin then fought in 1918 in The Battles of the Lys (9th -29th April) He was attached to 170 Trench Battery Company. He was killed in action near Gommecourt, France on 14th May 1918. He is buried in the Couin New British Cemetery, Pas de Calais, grave E. 12. The cemetery is 15 kilometres east of Doullens. Benjamin was identified by his identity disc. In his possession were photographs and a letter from home which were returned to his father. Benjamin was unmarried. Benjamin was posthumously awarded the Victory Medal and the British War Medal.

**Date of death 15th May 1918**

**Herbert James Hines: 22nd Durham Light Infantry**

*(A serviceman not on the Alsager War Memorial but with an Alsager connection)*

Herbert Hines was born in Alsager 1898. In 1901 the family lived in Ashmore Road (Ashmore's Lane.) He had two sisters, Ann and Clara. His father was a 'Domestic Gardener'. In 1911 the family moved to Lichfield.

He enlisted on 27th May 1917 in Lichfield Staffordshire with the North Staffordshire Regiment., service number 45945. He was a Railway Porter, 5 feet 4 inches tall with a 32 inch chest, and joined the ranks on 14th June. He transferred to the Durham Light Infantry, service number 66531, on 21st June 1917. He trained in a Training Battalion connected with that regiment and served in Britain until 21st December 1917 before embarkation to France. He was posted to the 22nd Durham Light Infantry. He went missing in the field on 15th June 1918 and on 27th June he was presumed dead. In 1921 his father wrote to the War Office asking if his son's body had been found because he felt *'unsettled here in Lichfield'*, and his wife was *'broken hearted'*, and he would like to receive the memorial plaque to remember him by. The army replied that Herbert's body had not been discovered and there was no evidence of a will being made by Herbert. Where there was no proof of death families grieved more than if a body had been recovered. He is commemorated on the Soissons Memorial, Picardy, France. He is also commemorated on the Alrewas and Lichfield War Memorials.

Herbert was posthumously issued with the British War Medal and Victory Medal.

# Date of death: 21st August 1918

**Private Thomas Cartwright:  9th Queen's Royal Lancers.**

*Thomas Cartwright in 1913. Photo: South Cheshire Archives.*

Thomas Cartwright was born in Alsager, Cheshire, in 1899 to Florence and William Cartwright. William was a blacksmith. Thomas had five brothers: Albert Edward, born 1895, George (1896), Arthur (1901), Ernest (1902), and Norman (1904.) In 1901 the family lived in Audley Road, Alsager, and were still living in the same house in 1911. After the outbreak of war the family moved to Talke Road. He worked as a painter for Mr Kennerly in Alsager. Thomas was a bell ringer at Christ Church and he is commemorated in the Central Council of Church Bell Ringers Great War Casualties. When Thomas Cartwright reached the age of eighteen in 1917 he enlisted in the 9th (Queen's Royal) Lancers. He was a competent horseman and the drill and skills needed to be a Lancer were considerable. Although most of the Lancers' operations were fighting in the trenches after 1914, by 1918 the regiment were again operating in the saddle as the war became more mobile. According to the War Diaries, on 21st August 1918 the 9th Lancers were crossing the Courcelles to Le Comte and on to the Ablainzelle Road in heavy mist in support of Infantry and tanks. The Regiment had saddled up at 4.30am and moved through Jewell Valley south west of Ayette. They entered a smokescreen and could not see more than 10 yards ahead. Machine gun fire from the wood held by the enemy caused the first casualties. The Lancers lost 29 horses, three men killed, and three wounded believed killed.

*Badge of the 9th Lancers*

The Regiment had to stay in column formation because of the poor terrain. It could not be deployed because of shell holes. The regiment retired and reached Sarston at 7pm. Because of losses a new draft of horses were needed on 23rd August.

Thomas Cartwright's body was never discovered. He is commemorated on the Vis-en-Artois memorial, Pas de Calais on panel 3. Vis-en-Artois and Haucourt are villages on the straight main road from Arras to Cambrai about 10 kilometres south-east of Arras. The Memorial is the back drop to the Vis-en-Artois British Cemetery, which is west of Haucourt on the north side of the main road. At the time of his death Thomas Cartwright was on the Absent Voters List for Alsager with his home address as Talke Road. Medals: Victory Medal and British War Medal. On 15th November 1918 the Nantwich Guardian reported a portrait of Tom Cartwright was unveiled at Christ Church Sunday School.

# Date of death: 21st August 1918

### Corporal Harry Jenkinson. Royal Fusiliers.

*(A serviceman not on the Alsager War Memorial but with an Alsager connection)*

Harry Jenkinson was killed on 21st August 1918. His death is recorded in St Mary's parish magazine. Although Harry is commemorated on the Barthomley and Church Lawton War Memorials he has close associations with Alsager. He attended St Mary's Sunday School and was in Rev H.A Thomas's confirmation class. The magazine states he enlisted early in the war. On 18th September 1914 the Nantwich Guardian included H. Jenkinson in the '*Roll of Honour, of Alsager men who had enlisted*'. He lived at Peel Cottage, Church Lawton with his wife Emma. He was born in Talke in 1892 but the family moved to Peel Cottage, Church Lawton after 1901. Harry worked as a clerk in a colliery. He enlisted in Stoke-on-Trent and served with the Royal Fusiliers, 13th Battalion (The London Regiment), service number 2382.

He was promoted Corporal before August 1915. He served in France and Belgium from 13th August 1915 until 9th October 1915. There was then a gap in his service, presumably because he was wounded, because he did not resume service in France until 15th June 1916, transferring to the 12th Battalion of the same regiment but he only served until 6th September. He was almost certainly suffering from wounds because he transferred to the Labour Corps and served with them in France from 16th February 1917. He eventually re-joined the 13th Royal Fusiliers on 24th June 1918. He was killed at Gommecourt and is buried in the Commonwealth War Grave Gommecourt near Hebuterne, grave reference v.g.21. Harry Jenkinson is also commemorated on the Church Lawton War Memorial.

His medal card wrongly says he was killed in action on 16th November 1916, but confirms he was awarded the 1914/15 Star, British War Medal and Victory Medal.

He married Emma Elizabeth Copleland Darlington in Barthomley 1916 and left her £141.00 in his will proved in 1919. His wife originated from Barthomley. There is a memorial stone to him in Talke cemetery.

Harry's brother, Second Lieutenant Arthur John Jenkinson, served with the North Staffordshire

Regiment.

*Photo: Memorial stone Harry Jenkinson. Author*

# Date of death: 25<sup>th</sup> October 1918

## Corporal Albert Edward Riley M.M.: Argyll and Sutherland Highlanders

*(A serviceman not on the Alsager War Memorial but with an Alsager connection)*

Albert Edward Riley was born in Chesterton, Staffordshire, in 1889 to Eliza and Albert Riley. His father was a farmer. His sister, Florence Riley was born 1891 and his brother, Clarence Riley, in 1893. They lived at Partridge's Nest Farm, Spring Wood, Chesterton, Staffordshire. In 1901 the family had a servant to help out caring for the children. In 1915 Albert married Eleanor Smart in Chesterton and they lived in Mona Terrace, Alsager. Albert worked on the family farm before he enlisted in the army after conscription and was posted to the 2<sup>nd</sup> Battalion Argyll and Sutherland Highlanders. He was promoted to Acting Corporal in 'C' Company, service number 14783. He served in France and was killed in action on 25<sup>th</sup> October 1918. He is buried at Quietiste Military Cemetery, Le Cateau, Nord, France in grave 'C 10.' The Commonwealth War grave states Albert was *'Husband of Mrs. H. Riley, of Mona Terrace, Alsager, Cheshire. Native of Chesterton'*. Albert was posthumously awarded the British War Medal and Victory Medal. On 11<sup>th</sup> March 1919 Albert was awarded posthumously the Military Medal for bravery in the field. After her husband's death Eleanor moved to Gawsworth, Cheshire, where she died in 1962. She never remarried. Her husband is commemorated on Eleanor's grave in St James, churchyard, Gawsworth.

*Posthumous award of Military Medal (Alsager misspelt 'Alsayer.') in the London Gazette.*

*Albert Riley recorded on his wife's grave in Gawsworth, Cheshire. Photo: Author.*

A.E Riley was awarded the Military Medal and posthumously awarded the 1914/15 Star, The British War Medal, and the Victory Medal. It is not known if Riley is commemorated on any war memorial.

# Date of death: 8th November 1918

**Sapper Cyril Scarlett Jackson: Royal Engineers.**

Photo: Sentinel Newspaper

Cyril Scarlett Jackson was born in Stoke-on-Trent, United Kingdom in 1897 to Ada Beatrice Jackson nee Scarlett and Bertie Jackson. Ada Beatrice Jackson nee Scarlett, was born in Alsager, Cheshire. Bertie Jackson, Cyril's father, was an agent for a brewery. Cyril's brother, Douglas Jackson, was born in 1900. The family lived in King's Terrace, Hartshill, Stoke-on-Trent in 1901, and by 1911 were living in Shady Grove, Alsager. In the 1911 census Cyril is recorded as visiting his paternal uncle in Market Drayton, Shropshire. He was living with his uncle and studying at Rosemont School, Newport, Shropshire. Cyril became a Sunday school teacher and a devoted member of his church. In 1915 according to the electoral register, the Jackson family were still living in Shady Grove. Cyril worked in the claims department at Stoke Station and later for the Post Office before enlisting with the Royal Engineers in Hanley on 15th May 1916 as a Driver, service number 2590. He was later attached to the Royal Field Artillery, and given the service number 805636. By 1918 Cyril was attached to 146th Division (West Riding Brigade), Signal Company, as a Sapper. He died of influenza in RAMC Number 50 Casualty Clearing Station, Bohain, Picardy, France on 8th November 1918, three days before the Armistice.

Premont village had been captured by the 30th American Division on 8th October 1918. Premont British Cemetery was made and used by four Casualty Clearing Stations (the 20th, 50th, 55th and 61st), which came to Bohain in October 1918. Cyril is buried at Premont British Cemetery, Premont, Departement de l'Aisne, Picardie, France, Plot: II. C. 16.

*Cyril Jackson's Commonwealth War grave citation:*

'*146th Div. Signal Company, Royal Engineers. Died of influenza. Son of Bertie and Ada Beatrice Jackson, of Richmond Terrace, Goldenhill, Stoke-on-Trent. Age: 21*'. On Cyril Jackson's grave it reads, '*Cyril Jackson, a life full of promise*'.

The Jackson family had moved from Alsager to Goldenhill between 1916 and 1918. On 27th November 1918 the Sentinel newspaper reported Cyril's death saying, '*he was loved by all with whom he came into contact*'.

*Premont British Cemetery. Photo: Commonwealth Graves Commission.*

# The Men who died after the Armistice on 11th November 1918

The great influenza pandemic killed several servicemen after the war ended on 11th November 1918. Others succumbed to wounds incurred during the fighting. Men like William Beech and Reg Coomer, who both died in 1920, may have been too late to be included on the Alsager War Memorial. The Influenza pandemic was out of control throughout the world. There was great misunderstanding about the illness and several manufacturers of drinks and potions ran dubious advertising campaigns in newspapers implying they could help cure influenza victims.

## Date of death: 19th November 1918

### Gunner Francis Knight Lucas: Royal Field Artillery.

*St Mary's choir in 1912. Photo St Mary Magdalene Church, Alsager*

Francis (Frank) Knight Lucas was born on 11th May 1897 in Alsager to William Thomas Lucas and his wife Annie Elizabeth. In 1901 the family lived in Hawthorn Cottage, Sandbach Road, and by 1911 they had moved to a house called the Limes in Sandbach Road. William Lucas was a pottery agent with a ceramic manufacturing firm. In 1911 they employed two servants at their home. Francis was the only boy in a family of six. Dorothy Rachel born 1885, Marjorie (1899), Vera (1901), Ruth (1902), and Marion Gertrude (1908.) In 1912 Frank was a member of the St Mary's Church Choir.

He enlisted in 1916 and was posted to the Royal Field Artillery. The local artillery regiment in Stoke-on-Trent was called the 1st Staffordshire Artillery Volunteers but in 1913 it was renamed the 2nd North Midland Brigade Royal Field Artillery (Territorial Force.) It had its headquarters at the Drill Hall, Victoria Square, Shelton, Stoke-on-Trent. After the commencement of hostilities it became part of 296 Brigade Royal Field Artillery. On 21st March 1918 Frank was taken prisoner at Ecouet, France and taken to Dulmen Prisoner of War Camp in Germany.

According to National Probate and Army Records, Francis died on 19th November 1918 in Gravenbroikling in the province of Dusseldorf. The cause of death is not specified though he probably died of influenza. He is buried in the Cologne Southern Cemetery, Germany. The motto on Francis's grave is '*Altiora etiam Petamus*' (*'Let us seek even higher'*). This indicates that Frank probably attended Hanley High School, Stoke-upon-Trent, as this was the school motto. After his death his father was awarded £80. 9s. 0d. back pay belonging to his son. His father was Chairman of Alsager District Council in 1926.

Francis was posthumously awarded the Victory Medal and British War Medal.

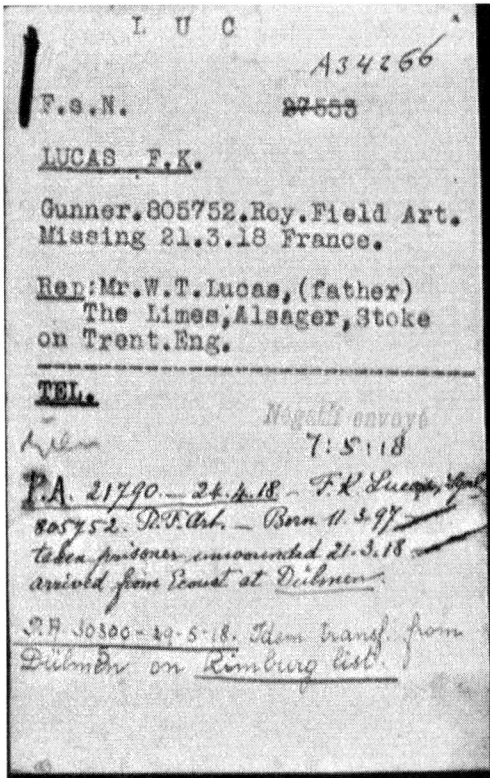

*Photograph of document from the International Red Cross*

# Date of death: 23rd December 1918

**Captain Mellard Settle: 5th North Staffordshire Regiment.**

Mellard Settle was born in Madeley, Staffordshire, United Kingdom in 1895 to Margaret Caroline and Joel Settle. His father was a civil engineer and owner of Settle Collieries. Mellard's sister, Gwendoline was born in 1887. Violet (1890) Reginald (1890) Marjorie (1894) and Isobel (1897.) The family lived at 'The Hill' Alsager.

Mellard went to school at Elleray Park, Wallasey, and Radley College, Oxford as did his brother Reginald. After school Mellard took a position as manager at his father's firm, Settle Speakman Colliery Factors.

In August 1914 Mellard enlisted in the 2/5 North Staffordshire Regiment, and after basic training spent 1915 on home duty. On 2nd November 1914 he was commissioned Temporary 2nd Lieutenant and was made Temporary Lieutenant on 17th January 1916. On 27th July 1917 the London Gazette announced he had been promoted Captain, the appointment backdated to 1st June 1916. Mellard embarked to France with his regiment on 7th November 1917. He commanded 'C' Company, 5th Battalion North Staffordshire Regiment. In January 1918 the Regiment were training at Liencourt preparing for front line duty.

*Mellard Settle, 2nd left, Reginald Settle, 2nd right, with their sisters, in 1915*

On 19th March the 2nd/6th Battalion North Staffordshire Regiment relieved Settle's 5th Battalion in the front line trenches at Bellancourt. On the 20th the Germans broke through the line and the 5th Battalion was cut off. On 21st March 1918 Mellard was involved in defending an attack by the enemy. On 2nd April 1918 the Sentinel reported Captain Settle was wounded and missing. A fellow officer wrote to Mr and Mrs Settle to inform them Mellard was wounded but would not leave his post and he was not seen again by him. Later it was reported he had been captured at Bellancourt, Somme, Picardy, France, and initially taken to Rastatt and then to Mainz in Germany. The Germans informed the International Red Cross that Mellard was a prisoner at Mainz on 2nd July 1918. The Battalion War Diary says Mellard's Battalion lost 22 Officers and 539 other men during the attack at Bellancourt.

*German Registers of prisoners, Mainz. International Red Cross Records*

Mellard Settle died in Germany. The Times newspaper provided an obituary explaining Mellard died from 'Influenza while in the German prisoner of war camp. After the Armistice Mellard had been unable to return home because of influenza complicated by pneumonia and pleurisy.' According to the Weekly Sentinel January 1919, when the French Army occupied Mainz they rushed nurses to the prisoner of war camp to help the influenza sufferers but in Mellard's case to no avail. He died on 28th December 1918. The newly appointed French commanding officer of Mainz, General Mangrin, paid tribute to Mellard Settle and gave a guard of honour as the cortège carried Mellard's body from the camp, personally saluting as the body passed by. The body was first interred in Mainz, a guard of honour formed at the graveside and the Chaplain of British Forces officiating at the ceremony. Later Mellard's body was repatriated home and he was reburied in the Settle family grave in Christ Church, Alsager on 19th May 1920. It is a designated Commonwealth War Grave, (Plot: New Ground; Row: 8; Grave: 632.)Mellard was posthumously awarded the Victory Medal and British War Medal.

*Mellard Settle's Grave in Christ Church, Alsager. Photo: Author*

# Date of death: 28th December 1918

**Private 1st Class Robert Dickinson: Royal Air Force.**

Robert Dickinson was born in Kidsgrove, Staffordshire, in January 1899 to Eliza Meron and Robert Dickinson. His father owned a draper's shop in Kidsgrove, The family moved to Alsager and lived in Lawton Road in 1918 before moving to Station Road in a house called 'Hill Rise'. Dickinson opened a draper's shop in Crewe Road. Robert had several siblings; John born in 1895, Frederick (1903) and Evelyn May Dickinson (1906.) After school Robert gained a position in Barclays Bank as a clerk. He joined the Royal Flying Corps squadron on 12th March 1917 aged seventeen and a half. He enlisted as an Air Mechanic, 2nd Class but his function was as a Royal Flying Corps Motor Cyclist. He was transferred to 149 Squadron on 1st April 1918 as Private 1st Class. No. 149 Squadron, RFC, was formed at Yapton, Sussex, on 3rd March 1918, as a night-bomber unit and three months later went to France equipped with Farman Experimental (FE2b) planes. Engaged in bombing enemy communications, airfields, as well as on reconnaissance duties on the Second Army Front, it dropped more than 80 tons of bombs and made 161 reconnaissance flights. Two interesting details worthy of mention concern the squadron's equipment. All the planes were fitted with a "flame reducer" designed by an officer of the squadron – Captain C.E.S. Russell. This successfully damped all exhaust flame, an important requirement for night-flying aircraft. All aircraft were fitted with special racks, designed by one of the squadron's mechanics which could carry either Michelin flares or bombs without modification.

*Farman Experimental planes (FE2bs) Photo: Wikipedia*

The FE2bs were therefore instantly adaptable for either bombing or reconnaissance. Of the squadron's original 18 Farman Experimentals which flew to France in June 1918, seven were still in service on Armistice Day.

After the Armistice No. 149 was the only Farman Experimental squadron chosen to accompany the Army of Occupation into Germany. Robert Dickinson fell ill with influenza suddenly on 26th December 1918 and was sent to the No. 48 Casualty Clearing Station, Namur, where he died on 28th December. He is buried in 'Belgrade' Cemetery Namur, France, grave 1V. C. 2. The Commonwealth War Graves Commission misspells Robert's surname as 'Dickenson'. He was posthumously awarded The British War Medal, and the Victory Medal.

# Date of death: 20th February 1919

**Private Charles Henry Reginald Savory: The Kings Liverpool Regiment.**

Charles Henry Reginald Savory was born in Market Drayton in 1883 to Henry and Sarah Ann Savory. His father was an engine driver for a railway company. In 1891 the family lived in Bowstead Street, Stoke-on-Trent. Charles' brothers were Edward, born in 1886, and William (1890- died in infancy.) By 1901 the family had moved to Ashmore's Road, Alsager before settling in Shady Grove. In 1904 Charles married Florence Mary Holland in Coppenhall Crewe. Charles was working at the time as a railway clerk. Charles and Florence had four children, Constance born 1904, Audrey Beryl, (1906), Lily Kathleen, (1910), and John Selwyn (1915). Charles and his family lived with his parents in Shady Grove, Alsager. In December 1915 Charles enlisted under the name 'Reginald Savory' at Kidsgrove Staffordshire and was assigned to The Kings Liverpool Regiment but he was placed on the army reserve because he was in a reserved occupation working as a chemical distiller at the Birchenwood Iron and Steel Company, Kidsgrove. He was involved in the manufacture and use of TNT explosives. He remained on the army reserve until March 1917 when he was called back into the army and assigned to the Labour Corps 1st Battalion, and then 29th Company. His service record states that Private Savory was 5 feet 9 inches tall, had a chest measurement of 38 inches, and had blue eyes with brown hair. He embarked to France on 29th June 1917. Reginald, as he preferred to be called, served in France for the remainder of the war and after the armistice was transferred to 254 Divisional Employment Company. The company was involved in salvage work. In the crises of March and April 1918 on the Western Front, Labour Corps units were used as emergency infantry. The Corps always suffered from its treatment as something of a second class organisation, and the men who died are commemorated under their original regiment, with Labour Corps being secondary. The Spanish Influenza disease spread through France in late 1918 and early 1919. Reginald fell ill and was sent to the 14th General Hospital, Wimeraux. In 1919 Wimeraux became the General Headquarters of the British Army in Europe. Reginald died on 20th February 1919. On 27th February the army sent a telegraph to Florence Savory in Shady Grove, Alsager notifying her of her husband's death. His effects were returned to her and she was awarded a pension of 36 shillings a week. Reginald is buried and commemorated at Terlincthun British Cemetery Wimille, France, reference X111. E.4. The inscription on his grave reads: '*And Jesus Said Come unto me and rest forever. Remembered by his wife and children*'. Reg Savory was a member of Wesley Place Methodist Church and is commemorated on their Great War Memorial plaque.

The Commonwealth War Grave record also reads: *Rank: Private. Service No. 80181. Date of Death: 20/02/1919. Age: 36 Regiment/Service: The King's (Liverpool Regiment) Infantry Labour Bn. Transf. to (194144) 254th Div. Employment Coy. Labour Corps Son of Henry and Sarah Ann Savory, of Market Drayton; husband of Florence Mary Savory, of Shady Grove, Alsager, Stoke-on-Trent.*

Charles was posthumously awarded The British War Medal and the Victory Medal.

*Terlincthun British Cemetery. Photo: Commonwealth War Graves Commission.*

# Date of death: 10th October 1919.

## Private Bertram Marklew: Connaught Rangers

*(A serviceman not on the Alsager War Memorial but with an Alsager connection)*

Bertram James Marklew was born in Hednesford, Staffordshire in 1886 to Mary and James Marklew. His father was a bootmaker. The family moved to Burslem in North Staffordshire, where Mary Marklew originated, in 1890. In 1901 the family lived in Dartmouth Street, Burslem. Bert is recorded as being an errand boy on the 1901 census. Bert married Lily Stanier in 1908 and in the same year a daughter, Dorothy Marklew, was born. In 1910 a son, Stanley, was born who died in infancy. In the 1911 census the family are living in Burslem and Bert worked as a Grocer's Porter. Bert enlisted on 8th April 1915 in Burslem Staffordshire and was posted to the 3rd Connaught Rangers, service number 5607. The records record Bert was 5 feet 4 inches tall, he had dark brown hair and brown eyes, and he had a chest measurement of 35 ½ inches. He was a porter at the date of enlistment and his address was Chancery Lane, Alsager, his Burslem address being crossed out. This is likely because his wife died in April 1915 and he moved to live with his sisters, Frances and Miriam, in Chancery Lane, Alsager. Bert's daughter, Dorothy, was being cared for by her aunts. Bert's brother, Lawrence Marklew, also served with the Connaught Rangers, service number 5669, 1st Battalion.

During his time with the Connaught Rangers Bert became a *'motor driver'*. He was posted to the 5th Connaught Rangers on 27th Jun 1916 and embarked with the Mediterranean Expeditionary Force to the Balkans. While in Salonika he began to develop tuberculosis in July 1917, and his weight dropped to 7 stones 11 pounds. He was moved from Salonika to Alexandra on 5th September 1917 with his regiment, then moved to Gaza and admitted to hospital on 5th October 1917. He was evacuated back home on 7th November 1917. The medical board meeting on 18th November in Birmingham stated Bert had total incapacity and recommended he be discharged from the Army as unfit to serve. His TB had been aggravated by military service. His commanding officer referred to him as being, *'Very good, an honest, sober, and well behaved Man'*. He was discharged from the army on 7th December 1917. A medical report in Bert's service record states Bert's sister, (Miriam), died of TB in 1917. Bert was given a pension of 27 shillings and 6 pence and a 5 shillings allowance for his daughter. He was given a Silver Badge award to demonstrate he had served with the army but was no longer well enough to serve. In 1918 Bert continued to receive his pension and the Medical Board recommended him for treatment in a TB sanatorium He continued to live in Chancery Lane until his death on 10th October 1919. His daughter, Dorothy Marklew married Frederick Pass in 1936 and died in 1987. Bert's brother, Lawrence, survived the war and was demobbed in 1919. Bertram James Marklew is buried in Christ Church graveyard, Alsager plot 3.9 in the 'New Ground' in a Commonwealth War Grave memorial. He was buried on October 15th 1919. He was not included on the Alsager War Memorial.

*Grave of B.J. Marklew, Christ Church, Alsager. Photo Author.*

He was posthumously awarded the 1914/15 Star, The British War Medal, and the Victory Medal.

# Date of death 27<sup>th</sup> May 1920

## Private William Beech: Royal Army Medical Corps.

*(A serviceman not on the Alsager War Memorial but with an Alsager connection)*

William Beech was born in Lawton, Cheshire, in 1898 to Lucy and William Beech. His father was a Railway Signalman. His sister Lucy was born in 1893. In 1901 the family were living in Linley near Alsager. In 1911 the family lived in Linley, Talk o'th' Hill, Stoke-on-Trent. According to the National Railway Museum records William was employed by the North Staffordshire Railway Company. William enlisted as a private in the British Army, Royal Army Medical Corps. Service number 119649 on 13<sup>th</sup> May 1916 and served overseas. William was discharged from the army under Kings Regulations 392 xvi (sickness) on 23<sup>rd</sup> February 1918, and was awarded a Silver War Badge (no 380288) on July 18<sup>th</sup> 1918 and returned to live with his mother living then at Thorneycroft, Audley Road, Alsager. He died on 27<sup>th</sup> May 1920 and is buried in Christ Church graveyard, (Plot: New Ground; Row: 32; Grave: 439.) William is buried with his mother Lucy Mary Beech (d.1935).William is buried in a designated Commonwealth War Grave. He was posthumously awarded The British War Medal, and the Victory Medal.

*Grave of William Beech, Christ Church, Alsager. Photo: Author.*

# Date of death: 4th September 1920

## Private Reginald Coomer: Manchester Regiment

*(A serviceman not on the Alsager War Memorial but with an Alsager connection)*

*Reginald Coomer, photographed in 1914 (family archive)*

Reginald William Coomer was born in Tetton, Warmingham, Cheshire, in 1899 to Sarah Elizabeth and Thomas Coomer. His father was a 'Hay and Straw Dealer'. The family lived in Lawton Road, Alsager. His older brothers worked as a house painter and a butcher in the town. Reginald went to school at the National School, Alsager and was later employed by Mr Kennerly, butcher, of Rode Heath. He enlisted in 1916 and after being in a training battalion joined the 18th Manchester Regiment, service number 61209.He was only in France a week when he was taken as a prisoner of war by the enemy. On 13th December 1918 he was repatriated to England. After being demobbed Reginald became ill and was transferred in 1920 to the St Asaph Isolation Hospital, Flintshire where he died on 4th September 1920. His name was not added to Alsager War Memorial but his grave in Christ Church, Alsager, constitutes a Commonwealth War Grave (Plot New Ground; Row:15; Grave:612.) He was posthumously awarded The British War Medal, and the Victory Medal.

# Date of death unknown

## Gunner J. Higgins

Gunner J. Higgins is listed on the Alsager War Memorial but it has not been possible to identify him. One of the candidates for J. Higgins was James Henry Higgins born in Thurlwood, Rode Heath, Cheshire in 1890. His birth was registered in Congleton in that year. He was baptised at Odd Rode Church, Cheshire in 1890, his parents being given as John and Elizabeth Higgins. According to marriage records John Higgins married Elizabeth Woodward in 1878 in Congleton *(National Archives Marriage index reference 1878, 8A, page 442, July to September.)*

In the 1891 census James Henry is shown living in Thurlwood with his father John, a canal labourer, and his wife Elizabeth, sisters Fanny, Lily and Mary and his brother, John. In 1901, after his mother's death, James Henry was living with his father at 85 Crewe Road, Alsager. His father, John, was described as a 'widower', and a 'canal labourer' by profession. His sister Lily was living with them.

By 1911 James Henry was living with the Cooke family at Hall Farm, Fallibroome and Prestbury, Cheshire. The Cooke family originated from Alsager. James Henry worked as a wagoner on the farm.

In 1911 James' father was living in Station Road, Alsager, with his sister Fanny Smith and her family. John's father's occupation was described as a 'Boat repairer'.

In the Alsager Parish Magazine in January 1915 J. Higgins is listed as one of the men who enlisted before December 1914. His regiment is given as 1st Battalion Cheshire Regiment. In early 1915 he was one of the recipients of the Red Cross Alsager Working Party who sent him clothes.

James Higgins, service number 16697, is recorded on a medal card for the Cheshire Regiment. He enlisted on 14th September 1914 and embarked to France on 25th September 1915. He is recorded as being discharged from the army because of 'wounds' on 7th September 1916. He was awarded a Silver War badge to demonstrate he could no longer serve in the ranks. He served in the 1st Battalion and other Battalions of the Cheshire Regiment. He fought in France from 25th September 1915.

| Regtl No. | Rank | Name (in full) | Unit discharged from | No. of Badge and Certificate (To be completed at War Office) | Date of Enlistment | Date of Discharge | Cause of Discharge (Wounds or Sickness and para. of K.R.) | | Whether served Overseas (Yes or No) |
|---|---|---|---|---|---|---|---|---|---|
| 13582 | Pte. | Rutherford, Tom, S. | Depot. | 87066 | 24.8.14. | 3.8.18. | Para 392 XVI | Wounds | Yes. |
| 15933 | A/Cpl. | Kent, Joseph. | 3rd Bn. | 87067 | 5.9.16. | 23.6.18. | " | Sickness | No. |
| 286 | Pte. | Crosbie, James. | 15th Bn | 87068 | 5.9.14. | 1.6.15. | " | Sickness | No. |
| 26805 | " | Troughton, Henry | 3rd Battn. | 87069 | 7.5.15. | 29.3.18. | " | Sickness | No. |
| 11035 | " | O'Hare, George | Depot. | 87070 | 29.8.14 | 30.5.18. | " | Heart Disease | Yes. |
| 16697 | " | Higgins, James. | Command Depot. | 87071 | 14.9.14. | 10.10.16. | " | Wounds. | " |
| 15063 | " | Reade, Wallace, B. | Depot. | 87072 | 1.9.14. | 7.9.16. | " | Sickness | " |

The man recorded on Alsager War Memorial is *Gunner* J Higgins. We cannot prove James Higgins, service number 16697, is the man commemorated on Alsager War Memorial. The Cheshire Regiment had its own artillery brigade, the 267th. They were part of the Cheshire Regiment until December 1916 when the brigade was re-designated and became part of the Royal Field Artillery. It is possible that James Higgins was part of the 267 Artillery Brigade, (Cheshire Regiment.)

No man recorded with the Commonwealth War Graves Commission fits James Higgin's description. The four Gunner J Higgins in Commonwealth War Graves Commission cemeteries came from Lancashire or Gloucestershire.

Gunner J. Higgins must remain Alsager's mystery soldier, unknown but not forgotten. He is not included in the list of men killed 1914-17 who were listed in a church service in St Mary's Church in 1917 and nor is he mentioned in any Commonwealth War Grave as he probably died in England after 1917. James Higgins is not mentioned on the 'Absent Voters List.' James's sister Lily Higgins died in Alsager in 1919 and was buried at Christ Church on 27th March aged 35. James' uncle, also called James Henry Higgins (born 1872) served in the Great War and survived the war. In 1921 he was licensee of the Rising Sun Inn Mow Cop.

James Henry Higgins was unrelated to Private William Higgins commemorated on Alsager War Memorial.

# The Survivors

The 1920 'Absent Voters List' for Alsager gives the names of the citizens still serving in the forces over a year after the armistice  In early 1918 the 'Absent Voters List' had detailed 185 men still serving, but by 1919 and with wide scale de-mobilisation only nineteen men living in Alsager were still in the ranks. The list includes Robert and Henry Ellis who fought all through the war, and George Jacobs who had been a prisoner of war for five years. The list does not include the Alsager men who had moved away from the town but were still in the army, such as Dick and Vernon Goss.

From an analysis of the Police Gazette 1914-20 there are no records of any man or woman from Alsager deserting or being absent without leave from the services. Adolphus Goss, Chairman of the Alsager Military Appeals Tribunal, boasted he never had cause to hear an appeal from a conscientious objector during the war.

*List of 'Absent Voters' serving in the Forces in 1919*

**Short biographies of servicemen and women with Alsager connections who survived the Great War. (The biographies are in alphabetical order)**

These biographies people who all survived the war. Some went on to have distinguished careers, others settled back into humdrum jobs. Some bore terrible wounds and died prematurely; a few lived on until old age. Most never talked about their war and what remains is their service records.

### Private William Affleck:  Royal Army Medical Corps

William Affleck was born in 1895 in Alsager to William and Anna Affleck. His father originated from Scotland. William was the oldest of three children. Aged 15 William was living with his family in Sandbach Road, Alsager and was working as an auctioneer's clerk. He enlisted in 1917 and went to France in the summer of that year, service number 22426. On August 14th 1917 he was awarded the Military Medal for bravery in the field. After the war he married Harriet Munton and they lived in Liverpool Road West in Church Lawton. William went back to his job as Auctioneer's Clerk. He died in 1956.

### Lieutenant Reginald McKay Alcock: Royal Field Artillery.

Reginald was born in 1888 in Audley Road, Alsager. His father, Frank, was a bricklayer. His mother's name was Caroline. He had a brother, Frank, and sisters Evangeline and Hilda. Before the war he worked as a clerk in a colliery and then cashier at the Longton office of Messrs Settle Speakman.

Reginald Alcock joined the Royal Field Artillery in December 1914 and joined officer training in March 1916. He was commissioned 2nd Lieutenant in September 1916. On 22nd August 1917 the Weekly Sentinel reported Reginald had been severely wounded in France. After the war he married Helene Louise and moved to Tunbridge Wells. He died in 1928. His brother Frank who sang in the choir at St Mary's Church remained in Alsager and lived until he was 92.

*Reg Alcock. Photograph from the Sentinel*

## Phillip Arthur Band: Air Mechanic Class 3

Arthur Phillip Band was born on 29<sup>th</sup> December 1898 in Alsager to Mary Jane and Arthur James Band. His father was a caretaker at a bank. Arthur Band preferred to be known as Phillip and after childhood called himself *Phillip Arthur* Band. He lived in Crewe Road, Alsager along with his sister Muriel Gwendoline, born in 1897, and a brother, Reginald, born in 1907. After school Phillip became a motor mechanic and worked in that job until he attested in the Royal Flying Corps on February 1917 and enlisted on 31<sup>st</sup> October 1917. According to his service record he was 5'6" tall and his service number was 106760. He worked as a fitter on aeroplanes and was posted to France in April 1918. He remained with the Royal Air Force, as it became, in France until April 1919. He was discharged from the RAF in May 1919 and remained in the reserve. After the war Phillip married Mary Sharratt in 1920 and managed the Bands hardware shop in Sandbach Road started by his grandfather, William, in the late 19<sup>th</sup> century. While the business is now not owned by the Band family the business is still called 'Bands.' (2016) He was awarded the British War Medal and Victory Medal. Arthur Phillip Band died in 1983.

*Bands Hardware Shop. Photo: South Cheshire Archives*

## Corporal Francis Allen Barker

*A brave soldier wounded three times in the Great War*

Francis Allen Barker was born in Colwich, Staffordshire, United Kingdom in 1887 to Martha and George Barker. Francis' sister, Naomi Barker, was born 1880 and brother, Herbert William Barker, in 1881. Aged three in 1890 he attended the National School in Colwich as identified on the school admissions register. His father was a railway worker and the family moved to Alsager in 1900. George worked as a 'Shedman Engine Tenter' who oversaw the operation of factory machinery in the Alsager locomotive sheds. The family lived in Talke Road near to the railway station. In 1911 Francis was working a 'wagoner lifter, wagon preparing,' employed by the Birmingham Wagon and Carriage Company at Alsager sidings. He was still working for the company at the outbreak of war.

On 5th September 1914 Francis enlisted in the North Staffordshire Regiment, service number 13663, joining in Lichfield on 1st October 1914 for basic training. He was posted to the 8th Battalion. He was 5 feet 8 inches tall with a 35 inch chest and had a *'sallow'* complexion and dark hair and eyes. He moved to Salisbury Plain, went into billets in Bristol in December 1914 and in February 1915 to Weston-Super-Mare before going to Tidworth in April. On the 1st June he was promoted to Lance Corporal and on the 18th July 1915 he embarked with the regiment to France. His first action was at Pietre, in a diversionary action supporting the Battle of Loos. In 1916 he was in action during the Battle of the Somme, capturing La Boisselle and being involved in the attacks on High Wood, The Battles of Pozieres Ridge, the Ancre Heights and the Ancre. On 6th July 1916 during the battle of the Somme, Francis suffered shell shock was sent to hospital in Etaples, but on the 11th July he had recovered enough to leave hospital and was posted to the 8th Battalion South Staffordshire Regiment on 15th July.

On 18th August 1916 he was wrongly reported as killed in action but the record was partially erased from the service sheet. On 22nd April 1917 Francis was wounded by a bullet through the left shoulder and was evacuated from the field and returned to England on Hospital Ship *Brighton*. He convalesced in England but in 1918 was fit enough to re-join his regiment in France. On April 1st 1918 he was posted to the 2nd Battalion South Staffordshire Regiment. On 27th September 1918 Francis was wounded by a machine gun bullet through his left thigh and evacuated to the 5th Northern General Hospital, Leicester, then at the Stapleford Park Hospital, Melton Mowbray, Leicestershire. Francis claimed a disability pension in 1919 but was turned down. He was discharged from the army in March 1919. In the same year he married Jessie Martin and settled in Alsager. Francis never recovered fully from his war wounds and died in 1927.

He was awarded the 1914/15 Star, the British War Medal and the Victory Medal.

### Sapper Herbert Barker

Herbert, Francis Barker's older brother, Herbert, joined the Royal Engineers, Railways Operating Division, service number 97513 in the Great War. Before the war he was a fireman in a locomotive engine. Herbert married Edith Hackney in 1905. Once in France, as a sapper Herbert would have been assigned to a 'Construction Train,' of which there were eight in operation in mid-1915. Each 'Construction Train' would have a complement of up to two complete Railway Companies, with a Captain as officer commanding the train. This enabled the sappers to carry both themselves and all their necessary tools and equipment to and from wherever the next work was required. The Companies would pitch tents for accommodation, as required. Large-scale work would include the construction of the major stores and ammunition dump at Audruicq, ten miles from Calais. Here, and at numerous other locations such as the nearby major ammunition dump at Zeneghem Yard, there was great use of Chinese Labour Companies and Royal Engineers Labour Companies to prepare the ground, ready for the plate laying sappers. Herbert was awarded the Victory Medal and British War Medal. After the war he returned to live in Talke Road, Alsager. He worked for the railways in Stoke on Trent as a *'Steam Raiser'* with the role of cleaning boilers and raising the steam in the locomotive ready for the driver and fireman. He was a member of the National Union of Railwaymen. He died in 1925.

## Frederick John Barrett: Royal Field Artillery

Fred Barrett served in France and earned 3 wound stripes. A single man aged 37 when he enlisted in December 1915, he was the son of Alsager's Post Mistress, Sarah Barrett, of Sandbach Road, Alsager. Alsager Post Office was run as a family business, Sarah as Post Mistress, her two daughters, Isobel and Elsie as clerks. Fred was employed as a copper plate engraver. He was born in 1878 in Alsager when his father, John was Postmaster. Fred enlisted in Kidsgrove in December 1915 and joined the Royal Field Artillery, service number 118757. He trained as a gunner and transferred to the 21st Reserve Battery, RFA on 11th October 1916 when he arrived in France with the British Expeditionary Force. According to his Service Record Fred was 5 feet 8 inches tall and had a 38 inch chest, and he weighed 146 lbs. During his service in France he was wounded three times spending some time at the 53rd Casualty clearing station. Perhaps because of his wounds or his age he transferred to the Labour Corps on 30th August 1917. He remained in France, not returning to England until February 1919 when he was discharged from the army. Fred married in 1923, Elizabeth Brammer, when he was 48 years old. He worked as an insurance agent and later moved to live in Stoke-on-Trent.

## Private James Henry Baylis: Royal Marines. M.M.

According to Royal Navy records James Baylis was born on 5th October 1895 in Warwick but in the *1939 Register* gives his date of birth as 7th October 1896. His birth registration district was in Erdington Birmingham. His family moved to Alsager and lived in Wesley Street. He worshipped at St Mary's Church. He is recorded on trade union records as being a porter on Alsager Station in 1913 aged 16. He joined the Royal Marines Medical Unit service number 3583 enlisting on 23rd March 1915 and was initially based at Royal Marines, Deal, Kent. He then served in Gallipoli. His Royal Marines record gives him as five feet eight inches tall, brown eyes and hair. His unit was part of the Royal Naval Division. The Division sailed via Egypt to Gallipoli in Turkey and fought at Anzac Cove. Casualties before the battle commenced included officer and poet, Rupert Brooke, who died from illness at sea on 23rd April 1915. The Royal Naval Division was one of two British divisions (the other being the Regular Army 29th Division) at the Gallipoli landings. Eleven troopships, the battleship *Canopus*, and the destroyers *Dartmouth and Doris*, and trawlers patrolled off Bulair before dawn. The warships began a day-long bombardment just after daybreak. A destroyer made a close pass off the beach and later on in the late afternoon men began to embark on landing craft which headed for the shore just before dark. During the night Lieutenant-Commander B. C. Freyberg swam ashore and lit flares along the beach, crept inland and observed the Ottoman defences, which he found to be dummies and returned safely. Just after dawn the decoy force sailed south to join the main landings, coming ashore on 30 April 1915. Baylis came ashore and worked in the 2nd Field Ambulance.

Baylis wrote letters to the Vicar which were published in the Parish Magazine.

Following his service in Gallipoli James served in France landing in Marseilles on 23rd May 1916. He was awarded the Military Medal for bravery in the field on 16th August 1916 (London Gazette number 3034/16.) He was wounded on 13th November 1916 in France. He was discharged from the services on 23rd February 1919. In 1921 he was living in 'Sunnyside,' Alsager. In 1939 he was living at 53 Audley Road, Alsager, with his wife Catherine and was described as a 'Foreman Porter (Retired)'. He died in 1959.

James was awarded the Military Medal, the 1914/15 Star, the Victory Medal, and the British War Medal.

### Private Harry Bell: Monmouthshire Regiment

Harry Bell was the son of one of Alsager's police constables, Edward Bell, who originated from Oakmere, Cheshire, and had served in Bredbury near Stockport where Harry was born in 1898. Harry had five siblings and they initially lived in Lawton Road when they moved to Alsager before moving to Sandy Lane before the Great War. Harry went to school in Alsager before finding work on a local farm as an Assistant Dairyman. He was working in that occupation when he enlisted on 14th July 1916 in Crewe. He was born on 12th July 1898. He passed the medical but records say he only had a 31" chest, very thin. He was 5'6" tall. Whether by choice or not he was assigned to the Monmouthshire Regiment 4th Battalion but he was not called up until February 1917. It is possible his military career was postponed because he was working on a farm where labour was scarce. He was transferred to the 1st Battalion, Monmouthshire Regiment and sailed with them to France on November 13th 1917. It was a Pioneer Battalion part of the 46th (North Midland) Division. I January 1918 he lost seven days' pay for losing his cap badge. The regiment was involved in fighting and Harry was slightly wounded by a gas shell on 31st May 1918 and received treatment in a field hospital and returned to duty the next day. On October 7th 1918 he was given leave in England and was supposed to return to France on 31st October but fell ill and was in hospital there from 15th November, just after the armistice. He re-joined the regiment at its base unit but in January 1919 he was transferred to the Royal Welch Fusiliers was posted to Egypt with them. Harry was one of the last Alsager men to be demobilized, in February 1920. After the war he applied for a job in the Civil Service and asked the army for a reference. He became a postman and married Hannah Ollerhead from Alsager in 1924. In 1939 he was living in Wistaston near Crewe and was working as a postman. He died in 1977. He was awarded the British War Medal and Victory Medal.

### Nurse Eveline Bickerton: Voluntary Aid Detachment

Eveline was born in Hassall near Alsager in 1895 and lived with her aunt Mary in Chancery Lane, Alsager in 1911. She was living from *'private means'*. In October 1916 she enlisted as a nurse at Rode Hall Hospital. Her record states her home address was Harpfield Villa, Alsager and she went to work at Congleton Red Cross Hospital for three months followed by seven months at the Military Hospital Whalley. She then went to work at the Orthopaedic Hospital in Birmingham as a nurse where she was still serving in May 1919.

### Edwin Archer 'Archie' Boffey: Royal Field Artillery.

Edwin Archer Boffey was born in Smallwood, Cheshire, in 1892 to Isobel and Edwin Boffey. His father was an agricultural labourer. In 1901 the family were living in Lawton Road Alsager. By 1911 Edwin was living in a boarding house in Church Street, Hanley, and working as a *'Grocer'* in a shop. At this time he called himself, 'Archie', after his middle name but he enlisted with the name Arthur Boffey'. He enlisted in the Royal Garrison Artillery, service number 24598, and entered service on 20th October 1914. He entered France on 9th December 1914 with 107 Company, half of which later became the 5th Siege Battery. The remainder of the company stayed at home to form a heavy siege company based in Plymouth and responsible for South Western Coast Defences. The 5th Siege Battery fired a 30-cwt (hundredweight) version of the 6-inch Howitzer. This type had been introduced into service in 1895. It fired a 100-pound (weight) shell to a maximum range of 6,000 yards. Archie was a Gunner working on the howitzer.

At some stage in the war Archie transferred to work in the North Midland Field Hospital, a mobile team of over 200 men in the 46th Division. He first served as a private soldier and was later promoted Sergeant. We can deduce he was unable to carry on working as a Gunner and was transferred to lighter duties. The Field Ambulance he served with assisted troops who saw action in the Battle of the St Quentin canal, the Battle of the Beaurevoir Line, and the Battle of Cambrai. E.A Boffey was demobilized on 21st February 1919 and returned to live in Alsager. He married Harriet Black in 1915. His second marriage was to Gladys Earnshaw in 1923. In the Second World War he served as a Special Constable. He worked as a clerk in a colliery and resided at 46 Audley Road when he died in 1959.

## Corporal Arthur Bossons: Machine Gun Corps

Arthur Bossons was born in Alsager on 7th August and baptised in Alsager in Christ Church on 4th September 1887. His parents were Arthur and Martha Bossons and the family lived in Rose Cottage, Sandy Lane, Alsager. His father was a bricklayer. His brother Herbert, who died in infancy, was born in 1891. Arthur was a copper engraver working in the printing industry. His sister, Gwendoline, was born in 1898. In July 1915 the Alsager Parish Magazine recorded he was fighting with the Motor Machine Gun Corps. He enlisted with the Royal West Surrey Regiment service number 6449 transferring to the Machine Gun Corps, service number 10935. One of his letters to the Vicar was included in the church magazine in October 1916.

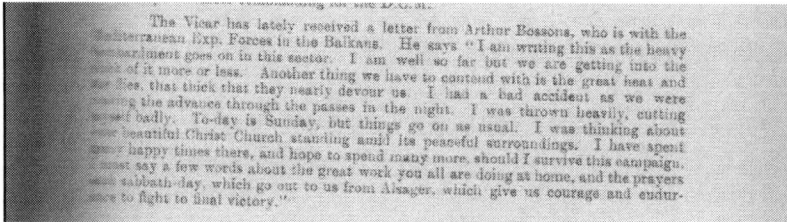

The Vicar has lately received a letter from Arthur Bossons, who is with the Mediterranean Exp. Forces in the Balkans. He says "I am writing this as the heavy bombardment goes on in this sector. I am well so far but we are getting into the worst of it more or less. Another thing we have to contend with is the great heat and the flies, that thick that they nearly devour us. I had a bad accident as we were making the advance through the passes in the night. I was thrown heavily, cutting myself badly. To-day is Sunday, but things go on as usual. I was thinking about our beautiful Christ Church standing amid its peaceful surroundings. I have spent many happy times there, and hope to spend many more, should I survive this campaign. Let me say a few words about the great work you all are doing at home, and the prayers that go out to us from Alsager, which give us courage and endurance to fight to final victory."

Bossons was discharged from the army on 3rd February 1919 and was later awarded the Victory Medal and British War Medal. In 1939 Arthur Bossons lived at 2 Well Lane. He was a horticultural salesman.

## Sergeant Charles William Bourne: Royal Fusiliers

*Charlie Bourne (wearing his cricket umpire's coat in 1960) Photo: South Cheshire Archives*

Charles Bourne was the son of George and Mary Bourne of Wesley Street, Alsager. He was born in 1899 and before the Great War worked at Boyce Adams grocers in Crewe Road, Alsager. He served in the 2nd Battalion Royal Fusiliers, service number 8397, arriving in France on 23rd September 1915, and later served in the 2nd and 9th Battalions, service number 19945, Royal Sussex Regiment, in

France. In August 1918 the Sentinel newspaper reported Charles had been gassed. Charles survived the war and remained in the army until 1923. He was a member of Alsager British Legion. He married Elsie King in 1925. Charles was associated with Alsager Cricket Club all his life and became Club President He died in 1985. He was awarded the 1914/15 Star, the British War Medal, and the Victory Medal.

### Corporal George Frederick Bullock: Royal Warwickshire Regiment

He was a soldier who suffered mental health problems due to war service. George Frederick Bullock was born in Gloucester, United Kingdom in 1881 to Louisa and Charles Bullock. They moved to Stoke-on-Trent before 1891 and lived in Elm Street, Shelton. His father was a linotype printer in the pottery industry. George's first job was as a caster in the pottery industry. In 1901 George married Lillian Rosa Cox and they moved to Alsager. In 1911 he was living Sparkbrook, Birmingham where he worked as a clerk. George joined the Royal Warwickshire Regiment on 11th November 1914 in the 8th Battalion. He was promoted Corporal and by 1918 was serving in the 7th Battalion, Royal Warwickshire Regiment, service number 305863. He was discharged from the army on 22nd October 1918. After the war he settled in Alsager at 53 Crewe Road but suffered from mental health problems due to his war service in 1917. He was a member of Alsager British Legion for many years. In 1939 he died in a mental hospital Macclesfield run by Cheshire County Council, but the inquest concluded George did not die from his mental condition but because of the gunshot wounds he received in 1917 which kept opening and would not heal properly. He had one son, Charles W Bullock. George was awarded the British War Medal and Victory Medal.

### Mary Helen Christien: Worker.

Mary Helen, 'Nellie' Smith was born in 1897 in Burslem. She lived at Grove House, Alsager. She enlisted at Rode Hospital in April 1917 and worked as a nurse for five months. From January 1918 she was paid £20 a year and received a clothing allowance. She then worked at the 12th General Hospital, Trouville, France from April 1918 until 4th November 1918 as a Ward Maid. She married John Ainsworth Christien, 7th Royal Fusiliers in July 1918. In November 1918 she transferred to the 24th American Hospital, 24 Kensington Palace Gardens in London where she was Kit Orderly. She was still serving there at 12th June 1919. After the war she was awarded the British War Medal and Victory Medal.

### Maurice Clowes: Royal Field Artillery

*Enlisted in September 1914 and was invalided out of the army in 1916*

Maurice, born in 1896 in Rode Heath, was the son of a miner, John Clowes and his wife. He was baptised at Odd Rode Church on 27th July 1896. By 1901 the family were living in Linley. By 1911 Maurice was working as a miner himself, working on a compressed air machine underground. By 1914 he was working as a *'Delivery Wagoner'*. Maurice enlisted as a gunner in the Royal Field Artillery on 14th August 1914 in Stoke-on-Trent, service number 79777. In November he was re-designated

Bombardier in 174 Battery, and in January 1915 transferred to the 54th Brigade. Maurice was nearly 5 feet 9 inches tall, with grey eyes, brown hair, and fresh complexion. On 7th July 1915 Maurice embarked with the Mediterranean Expeditionary Force to Egypt. The brigade sailed from Devonport on 7th July 1915 for operations in the Mediterranean, and arrived at Alexandria in Egypt two weeks later. It moved to Mudros, the forward base for operations at Gallipoli, arriving on 11th September 1915 but did not proceed into that theatre of war. It left Mudros on 5th October 1915 and arrived at Salonika, Greece, on 10th October. On 21st November Maurice was promoted Corporal. He was admitted to Giza hospital in late November and on 7th December 1915 transferred to Cairo with dysentery and frost bite. On 4th January he was evacuated to Britain and by 10th January he entered 2nd General Hospital Manchester. He was transferred to the 50th Reserve Battery in England. Maurice did not adequately recover from his illness and on 10th June he appeared before a medical board hearing in Bedford and was discharged from the army on grounds of sickness. He proceeded back home to Linley on 16th June 1916, given £1 and a plain suit of clothes and told to await further details concerning his army discharge. He was officially discharged on 24th June 1916 and issued with a silver war badge on 1st February 1917, badge 56368. He was also awarded the 1915 Star, the Brutish War Medal, and the Victory Medal. In 1939 Maurice was single and living in Stockport and was a Master Builder. He died in Surrey in 1985.

## Private Moses Corfield: Royal Army Medical Corps.

*Headmaster of Alsager National School*

Born on 18th March 1878 in Sheepbridge, Normanton, Derbyshire, Moses studied at York Teacher Training College and began his teaching career in Alsager in 1901. He married Helena Edwards in 1905 and lived at his father in law's home in Woodside, Alsager. He became the Headmaster at the National School, Alsager after the retirement of Mr John Peacock. In November 1915 the Nantwich Guardian reported Corfield had been presented with a gift of a pipe and tobacco by the boys of his school before he left for military training. They had collected small sums for him. Members of Alsager Institute, of which he was Secretary, presented him with a silver wrist watch.

He was posted to the Royal Army Medical Corps in March 1916 and served in Albert. On 10th November 1917 he was awarded a 'Good Conduct stripe.' On 12th April it was reported in the Nantwich Guardian that Moses Corfield had been taken seriously ill at the front and had been invalided to England for convalescence. In May 1918 he was posted to Ireland and worked in Randaltown and Belfast before being posted to Litherland, Lancashire, with an exemption from service 'P' Class Army Reserve, to work as a Schoolteacher on 27th June 1918. He was awarded an army pension in 1919. He returned to Alsager and continued to work as headmaster and live at Woodside House. He was a strong disciplinarian and would stand by the central door with a cane behind his back. His son George, was also a schoolteacher. Corfield was Secretary and later President of Alsager British Legion and attended many events on their behalf. He was awarded the British War Medal and Victory Medal for his war service. Moses Coffield died in June 1945.

## Private Andrew Milligan Cowden: RAMC

Born in Kirkmaiden, Wigtownshire, Scotland on 26th July 1871, Andrew came from a large family. In 1891 he moved to England and lived with his uncle in Ardwick, Manchester and according to the census worked as a 'Draper's Salesman.' Andrew married Ethel Parton from Alsager in 1899, and in 1900 he lodged with his brother John Cowden in the Poplars taking two rooms and paying £50 a year rent. In 1901 he moved house to Talke Road Alsager and was still working as a 'Draper's Salesman.' His sons were all born in Alsager: John W Cowden was born in 1900, Reginald (1902) Harold (1904) and Leslie (1908).

Andrew joined the B'hoys club in Alsager in 1911 and sang at the 1912 annual dinner.

He was still living in Talke Road in 1911 and the family had a servant to look help after the children.

After the commencement of hostilities Andrew joined the Army Veterinary Corps (RAVC 1918) service number 11600. He was posted to France on 26th October 1915 and would have been responsible for the welfare of mules and horses carrying supplies.

Andrew was awarded the 1914/15 Star, Victory Medal and the British War Medal.

In 1939, aged 68, he was living in Wesley Avenue and was described as an *'Unemployed Draper'*. His wife died in 1940. He died on 21st November 1960 in Alsager. His brother Corporal **Joseph Cowden** also served in the Army Veterinary Corps in the Mediterranean Expeditionary Force, enlisting in June 1915 aged 41, embarking with them to Salonika on 17th October 1915 and returning on 29th July 1916.

# Farrier Sergeant George Henry Cummings: 7th Hussars

*George Cummings presented with British Legion certificate for long service 1955. Photo: South Cheshire Archives.*

George. Cummings was born in Haslington, Cheshire on 21st July 1887. He was raised as a foster child, or *'Nurse Child'*, as described in the 1891 census, at Far Heath Farm, Hassall near Alsager. By the age of 13 he was living in Crewe Road with Mary Barker and her family. He trained as a blacksmith and aged 19 on 11th November 1907 he enlisted with the 7th (Queen's Own) Hussars, army number 1538, at Albuhera Barracks, Aldershot, and was employed as a shoeing smith for the cavalry. He had dark brown hair, weighed 145 pounds, was 5 feet 5 inches tall and had grey eyes. He was made a Shoeing Smith on 11th August 1908 and a Shoeing Smith Corporal on 2nd November 1911. With the commencement of the Great War, George served abroad and on 15th November 1917 he was promoted Farrier Sergeant with the 7th Hussars. They were stationed at Bangalore until the start of the First World War, moving to Secunderabad with detachments keeping order in Delhi. In 1917 the regiment sailed to the River Tigris near Basra to fight against the Turks as part of 11th Indian Cavalry Brigade. His service record states he suffered from mild malaria and was returned to England in February 1918. Following recovery he worked with the 2nd Royal Canadian Regiment attached to the 7th Hussars. At the end of the war he continued to serve and was not discharged until 4th November 1919. He was awarded the British War Medal and Victory Medal and was awarded an army pension. On 9th September 1919 he married Maud Painter in St Mary's Church, Alsager and the couple lived in Crewe Road, Alsager. George worked as a blacksmith for a railway company. In 1939, following the start of the 2nd World War, George was a Sergeant Major in the St John Ambulance Corps and applied to become an ARP Warden. He lived at 44 Audley Road, Alsager. He was from 1924 a founder member of Alsager British Legion serving as Standard Bearer from 1927 to 1955. He died in December 1979.

His granddaughter, Dorothy Clarice Smith, says of George;

'My Grandfather George would have his Sunday dinner at his my dad's house after he lost his wife, Maud. After dinner my two brothers and I would have to watch our Ps and Qs. He was a straight John Bull sort of man. He was kind and had a very dry sense of humour we would double up with laughter at the things he said. If grandad felt like it we would sit crossed-legged at his feet and he would tell us some amazing tales of when he was in India and the Khyber Pass. He was also very lucky as he was shot in the head just behind the ear while he was serving in the Hussars but I believe it was Malaria that finished his service career. Grandad and Grandma had two children, my Dad, George Henry Cummings, and Ernest Painter Cummings. Grandad made us very proud of the years he carried the British Legion Flag.'

## Able Bodied Seaman Ernest Dale: Royal Navy.

*An Alsager sailor who fought in the battle of Jutland in 1916*

Ernest Dale was born in Alsager on 4th May 1898 to William Ernest and Julia Ann Dale. He was the oldest child of a large family. His father worked as a collier. In 1911 the family lived in The Fields Alsager, and aged 13 Ernest left school and did labouring work. On 1st January 1914 he joined the navy as a boy sailor on *HMS Impregnable*, a training ship. In December 1914 he was listed in Alsager Parish Magazine as being one of the original 78 Alsager men to be in the services. In early May 1916 he was transferred to *HMS Thunderer* and during the Battle of Jutland the ship took part in the action. *Thunderer* first came to action at 18:30 when indistinct ranges of 18,000 to 22,000 yards (16,000 to 20,000 m) were obtained on some German ships. Due to poor visibility from smoke she did not open fire, and it must be remembered that *Thunderer* was at the rear of the 2nd Division and her visibility would have been affected by the smoke of the three leading ships. At 19:15 *Thunderer* sighted two enemy battleships visible between *Royal Oak* and *Iron Duke*. She fired two salvoes of common percussion capped shells at the leading ship, but no hits were made and the second salvo was actually fired over the top of *Iron Duke*. *Thunderer* did not see the enemy again. However, during the German fleet's run to the south after breaking off the engagement, Moltke sighted four large ships at 22:40. These were the four Orion-class ships, so *Iron Duke* had a lucky escape in that the British lookouts did not see her. In total *Thunderer* fired just 37 rounds of 13.5-inch ammunition, all common percussion capped. Her 4-inch batteries were unused.

Dale went on to serve on several ships including *Vivid*. After the Armistice Dale served on the *Warsprite* and in 1925 transferred to *HMS Cockchafer*, a gun boat patrolling the Yangtsee River in China. On 20th March 1926 Dale was reported missing, presumed drowned. He was 27. A court of enquiry did not conclude any foul play and the drowning was accidental. Handwritten on Dale's service record it states Ernest was probably 'drunk' and had fallen overboard.

For his service in the Great War he was awarded the 1914 Star, British War Medal, and Victory Medal

*The sailors on HMS Impregnable 1914. Photo: Imperial War Museum*

**Lieutenant John Dickinson: King's Liverpool Regiment**

John Dickinson was the older brother of Robert Dickinson commemorated on Alsager War Memorial. He was born on 20th June 1894. He was an 'Apprentice Draper' to his father in the 1911 census. At the outbreak of war he joined the North Staffordshire Regiment as a private soldier, service number 40030 and was first posted abroad to France on 18th August 1915. He was promoted to Lance Corporal, service number 2935. In October 1915 John Dickinson was shot in the thigh and evacuated to hospital in Colchester where his parents visited him in hospital. He recovered, and re-joined his regiment and was selected in 1916 to return to England for officer training. He gained his commission on 6th January 1917 and was posted to the 1st Battalion, the King's Liverpool Regiment. He saw action in the Ypres sector including an offensive in September 1917 which brought about sixty one men killed, one hundred and sixty six wounded, twelve missing and three later died of wounds. Five officers died and four were wounded.

In January 1918 the Alsager Parish Magazine reported he was a prisoner of war. International Red Cross Records indicate Dickinson was captured unwounded when he was taken on 1st December 1917 during the battle of Cambrai. He was initially taken to Heidelberg then to Schweidnitz prisoner of war camp and transferred to Karlsruhe. He managed to get a telegraph message back to England *'Am well and prisoner of war, Karlsruhe, John Dickinson.'*

*Prisoner of war records: John Dickinson. From Red Cross Archives.*

After the war he was repatriated and settled in Alsager and married Mary Helen Christien in 1925. He lived in 'The Fields' and served as a Juror in the Assizes.

He was awarded the Victory Medal, the 1914/15 Star and the British War Medal

### Private John Rowland Ebsworth: South Lancashire Regiment

John Rowland Ebsworth was born in Norton in Hales, Shropshire on 19th June 1898 to John and Mary Ebsworth. His father was a gardener who originated from Alsager. Jack, as he preferred, had four sisters and was the only boy in the family. In 1911 the family lived in Sandy Lane, Alsager. He worked for the North and North Western Railway Company and left them to enlist on 20th December 1915. After being attested Jack joined the 1/5th South Lancashire Regiment, service number 50244. After embarking to France he was captured by the Germans on 30th November 1917 at Epeny, France, unwounded, and taken to Munster prisoner of war camp. He was repatriated on 22nd November 1918 and spent time in Ripon recovering from his ordeal. His prisoner of war records indicate his family were living in Wesley Street in 1918.

| | Lfd.<br>Nr. | a) Familienname<br>b) Vorname (nur<br>der Rufname)<br>c) nur bei Russen<br>Vorname des<br>Vaters | Dienst-<br>grad | a) Truppen-<br>b) teil<br>c) Komp. | a) Gefangennahme<br>(Ort und Tag)<br>b)<br>c) vorhergehender Auf-<br>enthaltsort | a) Geburtstag und -Ort<br>b) Adresse des<br>nächsten<br>c) Verwandten |
|---|---|---|---|---|---|---|
| a) | | EDSWORTH | Pte | 1/5th | Kpehy, 30,11,17 | 19,6,98. |
| b) | 164 | John R. | | S. L. | | Norton-in-lures |
| c) | | 50344 | | C. | Front | Worley 94,<br>Alsager |

After being discharged from the army Jack returned to work for the railway company he left in 1915. In 1939 he was living in Princes Road, Stoke-on-Trent with wife, Dorothy and son John. He was working as a chauffeur and gardener. He died in 1976 in Alsager.

### The Ellis Family

On 30th October 1915 the Sentinel newspaper reported on the four brothers serving in the British Army. Arthur Ellis, killed in 1915, has already been mentioned in the chapter *Deaths of Alsager Servicemen in 1915*. The Ellis family lived in Alsager between 1908 and 1924.

THE STAFFORDSHIRE WEEKLY SENTINEL, SATURDAY, OCTOBER 30, 1915

**FOUR SOLDIER BROTHERS FROM ALSAGER.**

Mr Hercules Arthur Ellis, the boy's father, was a solicitor and Town Clerk of Burslem. He was a personal friend of Rudyard Kipling's father. In 1908 he moved to a house in Alsager called 'Farfield' in Crewe Road. At the outbreak of war his four sons enlisted and his daughters Agnes and Frances joined the Voluntary Aid Detachment as nurses.

*Henry (called Hugh) Arthur and Robert photographed in 1902. Photo: Ellis Family collection*

## Lt. Henry Carthew Ellis: 40th Pathans.

Henry Carthew Ellis, usually called 'Hugh,' by his family, was born in 1891. A Solicitor, he first joined the Inns of Court Officer Training Corps and was commissioned 2nd Lieutenant on 10th December 1914 after progressing through Army Officer Cadet training. He served with the Cheshire Regiment from September 1915.He was promoted Lieutenant in September 1916. On 18th August 1916 the Nantwich Guardian reported Henry was seriously ill in hospital in Bombay after his health breaking down while he was fighting in Mesopotamia with the Cheshire's. The Indian Army list 1919 shows him as a serving officer. He joined the 40th Pathans having transferred to them in July 1918. He married Dagny Bergh, an American, in Bombay in 1920. He died in 1985 in Lancashire. He was awarded the 1914/15 Star, British War Medal and Victory Medal

*Henry Carthew Ellis called 'Hugh' by his family. Photo: Ellis Family collection*

## Captain Phillip Frederick Ellis: North Staffordshire Regiment

Phillip Ellis was born on 9th February 1884 in Burslem. He qualified as a Solicitor in 1907 and became Assistant Clerk to the Board of Justices. He served in the North Staffordshire Regiment and was responsible for the organisation of soldier training and other senior administrative duties at Butterton Hall, and in Grantham. He then became responsible for Regimental Transport for the 3rd /5th North Staffordshire Regiment. It served as a training battalion in England during the war. Phillip saw foreign service in 1916. In January 1917 he was discharged from the army on health grounds due to chest trouble after the Regiment had spent several days in blizzard conditions in Europe. His army record also states he may have contracted tuberculosis. He was awarded a Silver War Badge, number 3397 with the description *'Captain Phillip F. Ellis of Farfield, Alsager.'*

Phillip was presented with a rose bowl from his fellow officers engraved with the words:

*'Presented to Captain and Adjutant P.F. Ellis by Officers of the 3rd Battalion 5th North Staffordshire Regiment, as a token of their high regard and appreciation of his excellent services to the Regiment. January 1916.'*

In 1911 he married Catherine Bratt (whom he divorced in 1923.) In 1918 he moved to South Africa on health grounds and then to Northern Rhodesia working as a solicitor. In March 1923 Phillip married Dulcie Arton-Powell. He was awarded the OBE in the King's New Year Honours List 1938. *'Phillip Frederick Ellis. For public services in Northern Rhodesia.'* The award was for his work in drawing up the Mining Law for Northern Rhodesia. He was a prominent resident of Northern Rhodesia - a Member of the Legislative Council and Legal Advisor to the big mining companies (and also to a local African Paramount Chief, King Lewanika of Barotseland). He died in Ndola Northern Rhodesia (Zambia) in March 1942. He was to have been knighted but died prior to receiving the honour. For war service he was awarded the 1914/15 Star, British War Medal and Victory Medal.

## Major Robert Ellis M.C: Royal Army Medical Corps

Born in Wolstanton on 14$^{th}$ August 1889, Robert Ellis, RAMC, was commissioned 2$^{nd}$ Lieutenant on 4$^{th}$ May 1915.

*Major Robert Henry Ellis M.C. Photo: Ellis family collection.*

He was a qualified doctor and admitted to Membership of the Royal College of Surgeons in May 1914 having qualified at Birmingham University and St. Bartholomew's Hospital. He was in the Artists' Rifles Territorials before the Great War and trained with the Officer Cadets and was commissioned temporary Lieutenant on 5$^{th}$ August 1914. He embarked to France with the Royal Army Medical Corps on 23$^{rd}$ August 1914 joining the 5$^{th}$ Field Ambulance. On October 15$^{th}$ 1914 when with the 1$^{st}$ East Anglian Field Ambulance he was promoted to full Lieutenant. He was promoted to the rank of temporary Captain on January 1$^{st}$ 1917, becoming a full Captain on 16$^{th}$ February 1918. He later promoted to Acting Major.

He was awarded the Military Cross on 4th June 1917 for his work when commanding an advanced Field Dressing Station during the fighting in July 1916 on the Somme and for *'continuous good service since August 1914'*. In 1917 he was involved in the Battle of Arras. In 1918 he was given command of the 100th Field Ambulance in the Army of Occupation at Glessen. Robert was still a serving officer long after the Armistice and is on the Alsager Absent Voters list for 1919. He was Mentioned in Dispatches in the London Gazette in 1919 for his war service.

*Citation: Mentioned in Dispatches 1919*

In 1919 he was ordered to India, and saw service in Beluchistan and in 1920 in the Punjab. He retired in 1921 with the rank of Major, and was appointed to the Reserve of Officers. He gained a degree of Doctor of Medicine at London University in 1923. He married Marie Pedersen, also a doctor, in Edmonton, Middlesex in 1928 when he was 39. In the *1939 Register* Robert and Marie were recorded as living in Taunton, serving as a doctor and also manning an ARP First Aid facility. Robert continued to practice medicine in Taunton for many years. He died in 1978 in Taunton. Robert was awarded the Military Cross, 1914 Star with clasp, Victory Medal, and British War Medal. He was Mentioned in Dispatches.

*Medals Major Robert Ellis M.C. Photo: Ellis family*

## Nurse Agnes Jessie Ellis: Voluntary Aid Detachment

Agnes Jessie Ellis was born in 1886 in Burslem. In the Great War she first worked as a nurse in the Congleton area, Cheshire and then at the 1st Southern General Military Hospital, Birmingham. She then served as a Voluntary Aid Detachment (VAD) in Boulogne France for over 2 years until 1919.

*Agnes Ellis Red Cross VAD Card.*

She was awarded the British War Medal and Victory Medal. After the war she moved to Australia and married Alexander Mackenzie. She made one trip home to see her parents in 1938. She died in 1980 in Victoria, Australia.

# Frances Letitia Ellis: Voluntary Aid Detachment

Frances Leticia Ellis (France 1917)

*Photo: Ellis family collection.*

Frances Letitia Ellis was born on 22nd May 1881 in Porthill, Wolstanton. After her family moved to Alsager she played a supportive role in the household until the outbreak of the Great War. According to British Red Cross Volunteer records in September 1916 she worked 19 hours a week at Rode Hall, Scholar Green, as a nurse. In the following year she went to France to work with the French Red Cross in Caen. France's niece, Lucy Edward's (nee Ellis) says of her aunt: *'What I remember from my mother's conversations is that Aunt Fanny had been engaged to a son of the Goss family who was killed in the war. She never married, which was a shame, she'd have made a wonderful mother. She lived with her parents after the war and was a great favourite with us, the colonial children, making sand castles with us on that extraordinary beach at Weston-Super-Mare, or taking us to Eric Coates' Children's Concerts in the Winter Gardens. On cold English afternoons she helped us with my brother's 'model farm' on the hearth rug in front of an open fire. Over the years she kept all the family in touch with regular correspondence. My much younger sister is named Frances after her.'*

There are no records of an engagement between Frances and one of the Goss brothers, Raymond or Hubert. Francis was 9 years older than Hubert and 10 years older than Raymond, but the Ellis and Goss families knew each other and Alsager was a close community in the early 20th century.

Frances travelled to Java in May 1927 with the Nevitt family. She also arrived back to Southampton in 1929 from Las Palmas. Her occupation in 1927 is given as *'Bank Clerk'* on the ship's register. This may been an error. After the war she returned to Alsager, and later lived in Weston-Super-Mare with her parents who had retired to Somerset, but she returned to live her final years in Alsager with her brother Henry Carthew Ellis. She never married. She died in 1967 in Stoke-on-Trent.

**Private Ernest Fletcher M.M. : Machine Gun Corps**

Private Ernest Fletcher was born in Alsager in 1899 to William Henry and Francis Fletcher. The family lived in Wesley Street, Alsager. His father was a pottery worker. Edward was formerly a gardener in the employ of Mr Bailey of Green Bank. He served in the 19th Battalion, Machine Gun Corps, regimental number 90693 enlisting on 31st January 1917 from the Army Reserve. Ernest served in France from 28th March 1918 and was wounded in action on 1st June 1918. He was repatriated home and did not see active service again. On 21st June 1918 the Nantwich Guardian reported Ernest Fletcher had been wounded in the side and was in hospital in France. He was awarded a Military Medal for *'Holding his gun when overwhelmed by the enemy'*. On the 13th September 1918 the London Gazette confirmed he had been awarded The Military Medal for bravery in the field. He was also entitled to the Victory Medal and British War Medal.

He left the army on 17th February 1919 and was awarded a weekly pension of 5s 6d for a 10% disability. He married Bessy Perry in 1919.

**Gunner Frederick William Edwards: Royal Field Artillery**

*Fred Edwards at Alsager Armistice Day 1921 representing the B'hoys. Photo South Cheshire Archives.*

Frederick William Edwards was born in Alsager in 1896 to Lydia and Joseph Edwards. Jo was a building contractor in Alsager, and the family was one of the long standing families in the town. Fred was the youngest child, Ralph being the oldest born in 1885. Then came George, Florence, Francis and Tom (1894). The family lived at 'Woodbine', Crewe Road, and at the age of fifteen Fred became an apprentice joiner with Tom in his father's building firm. At the age of 19, on 24th

February 1916, Fred enlisted in **Stoke-on-Trent** in the Coldstream Guards, service number 18177. He was probably steered to join the guards because he was comparatively tall, 5 feet 10 inches. Fred was attested and commenced basic training. A letter amongst his service record is from his brother, Tom, to the Coldstream Guards asking if his brother can transfer to his own regiment, the Royal Field Artillery. Surprisingly, the army allowed Fred to transfer to the RFA after satisfactorily completing his probationary training in the Coldstream Guards. He was allocated service number 119913 and posted to the 49th Reserve Battery based in Surrey, and afterwards on 23rd November 1916 he was posted to the British Expeditionary Force in France and posted to 121 Brigade on 7th February 1917 as a Gunner. Fighting on the front line and undergoing strenuous work he suffered a hernia on 24th August 1917 and was invalided back to England aboard 'S.S Princesse'. He was hospitalised at Queen Mary's Hospital, formerly the Whalley Asylum, Whalley, Lancashire where he was treated between 6th September and 12th October 1917. On recovery he was transferred to Ripon, Yorkshire, before being posted back to France on 28th March 1918 to join 95 Brigade Royal Field Artillery, service number 101678. The Battery was made up of six gun teams, and Fred remained with them until he was demobilised in March 1919. Tom married Lillie Dale in 1921 and he returned to work in the building business until becoming a *'Hardware Dealer'*. He was President of Alsager B'hoys in 1928 when the B'hoys presented a new Standard to the British Legion. Fred died in 1965 in Alsager. Fred was awarded the British War Medal and Victory Medal.

### Gunner Thomas William Edwards: Royal Field Artillery

Older brother of Fred, Tom enlisted in the Royal Field Artillery, service number 101678 on 12th December 1915. He was only 5 feet 6 inches tall and could not be considered for the Guards because of his height. On 18th January 1917 he was posted to France in 55 Division, Ammunition Column, his job being a *'Wheeler'* on the artillery gun. He had received a certificate of competence as a Qualified Wheeler on 1st September 1916 in Woolwich. His unit was involved in the Battle of Pilkem Ridge, 31st July – 2nd August 1917, and the Battles of the Lys in April 1918. On 24th April 1918 he was taken to the field hospital with **wounds to** both legs but released back to duty on 22nd May 1918. He had been trying to ease a vehicle out of a ditch when his legs became stuck under a wheel when the animals in harness panicked. Tom was demobilised on 25th January 1919. Tom was awarded the British War Medal and Victory Medal.

## Lieutenant Commander Claud Herbert Godwin DSO: Royal Navy

*One of Alsager's most decorated serviceman.*

*Claud Herbert Godwin DSO from the Illustrated London News 1915.*

Claud was born in Alsager on 3rd December 1887, the son of the Rev. Herbert Godwin and his wife, Mary, who lived in The Wood, Mere Lane (Lodge Road). His brother George and sister, Erin, were born in 1885, and his sister Gertrude in 1893. Claud was baptised on 17th March 1888. He was the nephew of Mr Frank Rigby of Alsager. Claud went to school in Alderley Edge and joined the navy in 1903 on HMS training ship Britannia.

He qualified as Midshipman on 30th June 1904, and commissioned as Lieutenant on 28th February 1909. In 1911 he served on HMS Astrea in China as Lieutenant. He served in the Great War in the Dardanelles in 1914-15 and was Mentioned in Despatches by Vice-Admiral John de Robeck, and was created a Companion of the Distinguished Service Order (DSO) which was announced in the London Gazette on 16th Aug. 1915:

## THE SINKING OF THE "MAJESTIC": A SEVEN-MINUTES' SEA TRAGEDY.

*Page from the Illustrated London News 1915*

ONE OF THE BATTLE-SHIPS WHICH BEGAN THE ATTACK ON FORT DARDANUS,
FOUR MILES UP THE STRAITS; H.M.S. "MAJESTIC."

*Page from the Illustrated London News 1915*

The article in the *Illustrated London News* contained the following description; "Lieut. Godwin commanded H.M.S. Majestic's picket boat, and was responsible for the successful shot by which the enemy submarine E15 was destroyed after running aground ...On the morning of 18th April 1915 the British submarine B11 was unable to locate the German U Boat E15 because of fog. It had cleared by the afternoon, so the battleships *Majestic* and *Triumph* attempted to destroy it by gunfire. However, the shore batteries meant that they could not get closer than 12,000 yards, at which range they were unlikely to hit such a small target. The next plan was to send in two picket boats, one from each of the *Majestic* and *Triumph* on the night of 18-19th April. They were manned by volunteers and armed with a 14 inch torpedo each. Eric Gascoigne Robinson was given command. The boats were caught by searchlights as they approached the narrows. However, they were not hit and one of the beams accidentally showed the location of E15 for long enough for *Majestic's* boat, commanded by Lieutenant Claud Godwin, from Alsager, to fire its torpedo. A large explosion was heard and a flash seen. Godwin's boat was then hit by a shell, but the *Triumph* was able to rescue her crew, although one sailor died of wounds. Aircraft reported the next day that E15 was 'now a wreck.' All the men involved were awarded medals except Robinson, who was promoted to Commander. A diplomat in Istanbul was quoted as saying that a German officer said of the destruction of E15 that 'I take my hat off to the British Navy.'"

Godwin was invested with his DSO by King George V on 30th June 1917. Claud Godwin went on to serve on *HMS Duncan* in 1916 and *HMS New Zealand* between February 1917 and January 1919.

He was appointed a Lieutenant Commander in the Royal Navy on 28th February 1917. German minesweepers and escorting light cruisers were attempting to clear British-laid minefields in the Heligoland Bight in late 1917. The Admiralty planned a large operation for the 17th November to destroy the ships, and allocated two light cruiser squadrons and the 1st Cruiser Squadron covered by the reinforced 1st Battlecruiser Squadron and, more distantly, the 1st Battle Squadron of battleships. *New Zealand* was attached to the 1st BCS for this operation, which became known as the Second Battle of Heligoland Bight. New Zealand did not fire her guns during the battle.

On 31st December 1921 Godwin was appointed Commander and officially retired on 31st December 1933. However in 1937 he was recalled to the ranks and served in the Second World War. At 02.11 hours on 27th September 1941 the German submarine U-201 fired two torpedoes at *HMS Springbank* captained by Claud Godwin, which was part of convoy codename HG-73 north-northeast of the Azores. It received two hits. Most survivors were rescued by *HMS Jasmine,* commanded Lt.Cdr. C.D.B. Coventry, RNR, which went alongside to take off survivors and later scuttled *HMS Springbank* by gunfire after an attempt to sink her with depth charges failed. Other survivors were picked up by *HMS Hibiscus* (commanded by Lt. H. Roach, RNR), which landed them at Gibraltar and by *HMS Periwinkle* (Lt.Cdr. P.G. MacIver, RNR), which landed them at Milford Haven.

In 1942 Claud went on to be responsible for the *HMS Malabur,* a shore based command in the dockyard in Bermuda, reverting to the retired list in 1943.

He married Jean Hunter Godwin in 1918 and had one daughter. He died on the 16th November 1960 in Cattistock, Dorset.

Claud was awarded the following Great War Medals: DSO, 1914 Star, Victory Medal, British War Medal.

### Signaller Ernest Goodall: Royal Navy

Ernest Goodall was born in Monks Coppenhall, Crewe in 1898. In 1901 the family lived at 71 Talke Road Alsager. His father Joseph was an engine driver on the railway. Ernest joined the Royal Naval Voluntary Reserve, service number Z/1442. In the Alsager Absent Voters list he is described as serving aboard destroyer 'HMS Orlana. This was a misspelling of *HMS Oriana*, a dreadnought class vessel which came into service in September 1916. The *Oriana* went to the rescue of survivors from the torpedoed mail steamship *Galway Castle* in September 1918.

At 07.30 hours on 12th September 1918 when two days out from Plymouth, *Galway Castle* was torpedoed by the German submarine *U-82* and broke her back. At the time she was carrying 400 South African walking wounded, 346 passengers and 204 crew members. So severe was the damage that it was thought that she would sink immediately and it was apparent that *U-82* was lining up for another attack. In the rush to abandon ship several lifeboats were swamped by the heavy seas and many finished up in the sea. However, the U-boat did not mount a further attack and the *Galway Castle* continued to wallow for three days. Destroyers including *Oriana* were summoned by radio to rescue survivors who were taken back to Plymouth where it was ascertained that 143 persons had perished.

After the war Ernest returned to live in Talke Road until 1920, then he moved to Stoke-on-Trent. His brother, George, remained at 71 Talke Road. Ernest worked in the commercial vehicle industry in Tunstall and died on 11<sup>th</sup> May 1945 in Stoke-on-Trent.

### The Goss Family

Adolphus and Sarah Goss lost two sons in the Great War, Hubert and Raymond. Four other children who all served in the war survived. The contribution of the surviving four Goss children to the war effort was considerable. When the Goss brothers were photographed in the Weekly Sentinel in 1919 their sisters' stories were not covered in the paper.

*Picture: Weekly Sentinel 1919*

# Nurse Dorothy Goss: Voluntary Aid Detachment

*Dorothy Goss 1911 Photo: from the book, Willian Henry Goss, by Lynda & Nicholas Pyne*

Dorothy 'Dolly' Muriel Goss was born in 1894 in Alsager. She went to boarding school in St. Annes on Sea. After school her father refused her permission to go to Oxford University, a decision which bitterly disappointed her. After the onset of hostilities 'Dolly' served as a nurse at Rode Hall Hospital. She recorded in her memoirs that Queen Alexandra spoke to her when she visited the hospital. Dorothy's Voluntary Aid Detachment (VAD) registration card indicates that on 23rd June 1916 'Dolly' went to work at the First Southern Hospital, Birmingham until January 1918. She was awarded a scarlet stripe for service on 27th July 1917. Her VAD card does not record her later service when she went to France to nurse in Royaumont Abbey, 30 miles from Paris. The evidence for her foreign service comes from her Service Medal Card.

Between January 1915 and March 1919 Royaumont Abbey, France, was used as a military hospital by the Scottish Women's Hospitals, under the direction of the French Red Cross. After the war the Chief Medical Officer, Miss Frances Ivens CBE MS (Lond) ChM (Liverp) FRGOG (1870–1944), was awarded the *Légion d'honneur*.

Dolly returned to England to work at Queen Elizabeth Hospital, Millbank London, between January 1919 and June 1919. With her mother's failing health she returned to Alsager to nurse her. Dorothy Goss was awarded a long service chevron for her nursing work. She married Dr Percy Harpur MD in 1933 and later went on to become a member of Alsager Urban District Council. She was awarded the MBE for services to the community in 1968. She worked tirelessly for Royal British Legion, Alsager Branch, in the 1920s onwards becoming its Poppy Appeal Organiser. Harpur Crescent in Alsager is named after Dorothy. She was town Chairman of Alsager Urban District Council in 1943, 1949, and 1965. She died in May 1972. On the day of Dolly's funeral service at St Mary's Church a thief broke into her bungalow and stole her priceless collection of Goss ceramics. Her selfless duty and work for the public good was in marked comparison with the person who stole from her. The collection was never found. Dorothy Goss was awarded the British War Medal and the Victory Medal.

## Nurse Ethel Maud Goss: Voluntary Aid Detachment

*Photo: from the book, William Henry Goss, by Lynda & Nicholas Pyne*

Ethel Maud Goss was born in 1896. Ethel assisted her father, Adolphus, in many of his war projects including raising money for comforts for the Staffordshire Regiment and the Belgian Red Cross. Ethel Maud Goss joined the Red Cross in June 1915, and later worked with her sister at Rode Hall Hospital, First Southern General Hospital, Birmingham, and Queen Alexandra's London. She was awarded chevrons for her service. After the war, and the death of her mother in 1919, she became Dame Warden and Secretary of Junior Branch of the Primrose League in Alsager, and later the Poppy Appeal Organiser for the Royal British Legion. She opened up 'The Old Villa', her home, for the training of ex-servicemen. She married Harry Burne, a widowed clergyman, in 1936. She died in 1973.

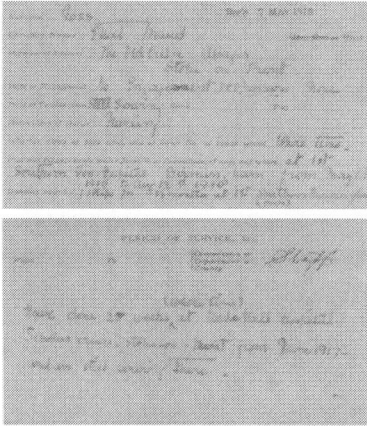

*Ethel Goss's VAD Registration Card.*

## Major Vernon Goss: Royal Field Artillery

*Photo: from the book, Willian Henry Goss, by Lynda & Nicholas Pyne*

Vernon William Goss was born in Alsager, Cheshire in 1887. Vernon was nicknamed 'Very.' He joined The North Staffordshire Railway in July 1905 beginning as an articled pupil in the electrical department, repairing and making telegraph and telephone and railway signalling equipment. A year later he spent 12 months in the drawing office estimating and surveying for telegraph lines. He progressed to maintenance and construction of electric train lighting in 1908. After gaining his City and Guilds qualification he joined the North Midland Divisional Telegraph Company of the Royal

Engineers as Subaltern. Within three years he had risen to the rank of Captain, a commission he resigned in 1914 to go to Ceylon to take up a position of Assistant Telegraph Engineer on the railways for the government. In 1914 Vernon Goss was working for the Government in Ceylon. When war was declared he was released from his duties and joined the Ceylon Tea Planters' Regiment as a rifleman and embarked to Egypt. He spent 5 months in Cairo at the time the Turks were attacking the Suez Canal and Goss wrote several letters to British newspapers.

In April 1915 Vernon was commissioned in the Royal Field Artillery as Second Lieutenant and transferred to the Western Front. The Guardian, 10th March 1916, recalled Vernon's encounters with the enemy. The article was reprinted the following day in the Crewe and Nantwich Observer. *'A patrol of three of us went out in front of our wire entanglements and had not got very far when we were fired upon by a point close to our wire., and about one hundred yards distant from us. Fortunately the Huns missed us despite, in fact, that we must have presented a very good target against the brightness of the moon behind us. We dropped flat and then opened fire against the flash and against a vague shadowy blotch which we could just see. Our shots told, and awful moans from the wounded Huns rent from the frosty air. A party of ours, thinking the groans were from us, went out, as they thought, to our rescue and brought in two wounded Huns, one of whom was so badly wounded in three or four places that he died almost immediately, and the other died within a few hours. The fellows had evidently come out to bomb our Saps, when we came along and spoiled their plans.'*

November 1917 saw Vernon Goss (Acting Captain) gazetted as acting Major and in May 1918 he was listed in a Roll of Honour in the Daily Mail. The Morning Post of 4th June reported Vernon had been awarded the Military Cross in the Birthday Honours. Although he had been wounded - not mentioned in his letters home, he recovered and returned to the Front. In December 1918 he was awarded the French *Croix de Guerre* with gold star after serving in the last great offensive in France.

Vernon Goss died in December 1968.

Vernon was awarded the 1914/15 Star, Victory Medal, British War Medal, Military Cross, and the Croix de Guerre with gold star.

## Major Clarence Richard "Dick" Goss: North Staffordshire Regiment

*Photo: from the book by Lynda & Nicholas Pyne. Willian Henry Goss early in the war before his commission.*

Clarence Richard 'Dick' Goss was born in Alsager in 1889 and worked with his uncle Huntly Goss at his Stoke Works before leaving home to work abroad before returning home to join up with the North Staffordshire Regiment, 5th Battalion in 1914, service number 2521.He initially refused a commission so he could fight at the front. He was posted to France on 5th March 1915 and was present when his brother, Raymond, was killed but Dick was wounded in the shoulder. He was evacuated to the Duchess of Westminster's Hospital at Etaples. Following his recovery he was promoted Corporal, then Sergeant, but accepting a commission as Second Lieutenant in June 1915. In 1917 he was promoted *'Acting Captain'*. On 23rd June he was appointed a full Lieutenant.

After the war he was a Lieutenant in the 1st Battalion Grenadier Guards and rose to the rank of Major. He was garrisoned at The Tower of London.

*Photo: 'Dick in the Grenadier Guards. Picture from Grenadier Guards Museum.*

Dick was awarded the 1914/15 Star, Victory Medal, and the British War Medal

His son, Richard John Victor Goss, a Captain in the Grenadier Guards, was killed on active service in North Africa in March 1943.

*C.R Goss's grave, Christ Church Alsager. He died on 14th September 1956. Photo: Author*

**Private Huntley Noel Goss: RAMC**

Another Goss survived the war. He was the Son of William Huntley Goss, Chairman of Alsager Urban District Council. Huntley was born in 1899. He was attested on 12th June 1917 as a pilot cadet with the Royal Flying Corps but did not qualify, and subsequently enlisted in the Royal Army Medical Corps, Service number 146662, and spent the war on home service. After the war he gained his pilot's licence.

# The 'Goss' Window St Mary Magdalene Church, Alsager

The window is an official war memorial registered with the Imperial War Museum (reference 42736). The inscription in gothic lettering on the bronze tablet beneath the window reads:

*'The window is a memorial to Sec. Lt Raymond Goss, 5th North Staffords killed near Ypres, August 13th 1915; Sec Lt. Hubert J Goss 10th Cheshire's killed at the Somme, July 13th 1916; their mother Sarah Ellen Goss, who died July 19th 1919, and all their gallant Friends and Neighbours who laid down their lives in the Great War.'*

*Photo: Author*

The official Imperial War Museum description of the window is as follows: *'Ornate stained glass window of two main lights with additional tracery lights above, Right light depicts St Michael. Left light depicts St Gabriel. Tracery lights at top of window; far left depicts M.C., (Military Cross.) Centre left depicts Regimental badge of Cheshire Regiment, centre right depicts Regimental badge of North Staffordshire Regiment. And far right shows 1914-15 Star Medal. At base of left light are unidentified arms with St George's Cross and crossed swords below.'*

The stained glass memorial window in St Mary Magdalene, Alsager, was designed by Karl Parsons of Norwood Middlesex and was executed in glass by the London Company of James Powell and Sons in 1926. The design included the Cheshire and North Staffordshire Regiments, the regiments of Hubert and Raymond Goss.

Karl Parsons' whole career was devoted to stained glass including the stained glass for the cathedral in Cape Town, South Africa. The window was the gift to the church of Adolphus Goss. The opening service was attended by members of the Goss family, the Royal British Legion, and the congregation of St Mary's Church. The church was full for the service.

The following description of the church comes from the Crewe and Nantwich Advertiser.

It is a lovely picture mostly in blues, violets and purples, very skilfully blended, pure and wonderfully rich in tone, and shewing great attention to detail; the product of a masterly and conscientious artist. The chief places are occupied by the figures of St. Michael, the Archangel of War and Justice, with his sword of flame, and his scales; and St. Gabriel, the Archangel of Peace and Purity, holding a lily, wreathed with roses, and with a diamond star on his breast. St. Michael stands on the blue firmament studded with stars; St. Gabriel is on a green earth be-sprinkled with flowers. Beneath are the arms of Cheshire and those of Mr. A. W. H. Goss (four swords interlaced, and two red crosses), with his motto, "For the King and Old England." In the tracery above, are the Military Cross, the badges of the Cheshire and the North Staffordshire Regiments, and the 1914-15 Star. The effect of the whole is very rich, beautiful and wonderful. The tablet is of cast bronze, with raised Gothic letters, and inscribed in the terms with which we commenced this report.

The newspaper report continues. *'In the window Raymond is depicted as St Gabriel and Hubert as St Michael. Gabriel is the messenger of the Annunciation and Michael is the champion of right against evil –a suggestion to us that, 'It is better to fight for the Good than to rail at the ill.'*

At the service the choir sang *'God shall wipe away all the tears'*. The Reverend Moir's address was based on the text,

*'Blessed are the dead which die in the Lord from henceforth; yea, saith the Spirit that they might rest from their labours and their works do follow them.'*

Rev. Moir, the Vicar of Alsager in 1926, said of Raymond and Hubert, *'Two brothers, a contrast in character but alike in this, in their reliability in all circumstances, in their fearless and unflinching sense of duty that caused them to volunteer instantly for active service. They were alike in not being ashamed of professing a manly type of religion, and to live up to it. The secret of their character seems to lie in the influence of their father and mother, brothers and sisters.'* He said the significance of the window was to, *'to depict in glass by sign and symbol the thoughts and memories of the mind and inscribe them on a tablet – more imperishable than the tablet of the mind - the names and rank of those commemorated. If the memories be sacred so was the memorial sacred.'*

The unveiling of the window was undertaken by Major Vernon Goss M.C. and the lessons were read by Sir Francis Joseph. Before leaving the church the British Legion and the greater part of the congregation, made up of family members, Scouts, the British Legion, and members of the Mother's Meeting, filed past the window.

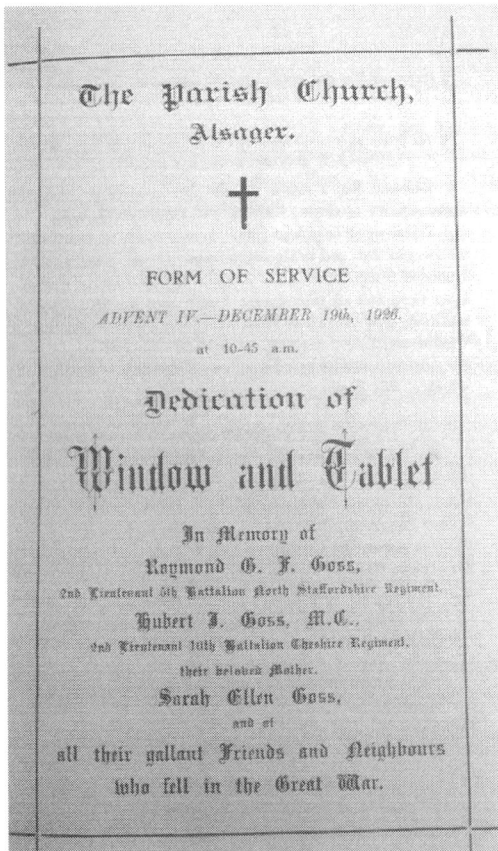

The Parish Church,
Alsager.

✝

FORM OF SERVICE
ADVENT IV.—DECEMBER 19th, 1926.
at 10-45 a.m.

Dedication of

Window and Tablet

In Memory of
Raymond G. F. Goss,
2nd Lieutenant 5th Battalion North Staffordshire Regiment.
Hubert J. Goss, M.C.,
2nd Lieutenant 10th Battalion Cheshire Regiment.
their beloved Mother.
Sarah Ellen Goss,
and of
all their gallant Friends and Neighbours
who fell in the Great War.

**A selection of some of the other Alsager servicemen and women who survived the Great War**

## The Greenwood family

In the Alsager Parish Magazine in December 1917 it was reported that five Greenwood brothers, whose parents lived in Wesley Street, and a grandson, were serving in the ranks. Frank Greenwood was the only family member to die in the war.

### Percy George Greenwood and Enoch Greenwood

*Both brothers had over eighteen years' service with the Royal Field Artillery and Percy further service in the Home Defence 1939-45*

On 16th August 1914 the brothers sailed to France and served in the Royal Field Artillery throughout the war. Percy was born in Betchton near Alsager in 1886. After school he became a wagoner on a farm in Barthomley. He enlisted in the Royal Field Artillery (RFA) in 1907 and served in India in Allahabad between 1908 and 1912 in the 39th Brigade RFA. He embarked to France on 14th August 1914 and served as a driver for the RFA, service number 50897, 18th D.A.C (Divisional Ammunition Column). He was promoted to Corporal in 1916 until 1919. In December 1917 the Alsager Parish Magazine reported Percy was missing but he managed to return to his unit.

After the war Percy re-enlisted with the RFA for a further period as a Gunner in the 15th Brigade. He was discharged on 27th February 1927 but enlisted in the 10th (Home Defence) Devon Regiment on 22nd September 1939. He married Louisa Aggett in Exeter in 1927. He died in Devon in 1967.

Enoch Greenwood was born in 1885 and like his brother Percy he joined the Royal Field Artillery and served in India before the Great War in the 39th Brigade. According to the 1901 census he was still living at home in Wesley Street with his parents and working as an 'Under Gardener.' In India he served in Fyzabad Oudh in the 28th Battery. Enoch married Annie Lewis in 1926 and settled in Shady Grove Alsager. He died in 1962.

## Driver Jess Grocott: Royal Field Artillery

*Photo: South Cheshire Archives*

Jesse John Grocott was the younger brother of James Edward Grocott commemorated on the Alsager War Memorial. Jesse was born in 1898 in Alsager, his family living in The Fields. Jess joined the Royal Field Artillery serving as a Driver, service number 911307 and on 15th October 1915 he disembarked in Egypt with the regiment and fought in Palestine. He was awarded the 1914/15 Star, The British War Medal and the Victory Medal. After the war he married Gladys Colclough in 1928, and in 1939 he was employed as a 'Drop Stamper' in a heavy engineering works and lived at 142 Crewe Road, Alsager. He was an active member of Alsager British Legion. In the year before his death he married Edith Bearpark in 1955. He died on 18th September 1956. In his will he left £940 to his wife of less than a year. His other brother, Arthur, served with the 5th Reserve North Staffordshire Regiment.

## Private Hugh Oswald Hancock: Cheshire Regiment

Hugh Hancock was born in Kidsgrove in 1897 and after his father's death in 1904 he moved to Shady Grove, Alsager with his mother, Mary Jane. After leaving school Hugh became a miner at Birchenwood Colliery, Kidsgrove. He enlisted in the 3rd Battalion, Cheshire Regiment, service number 45908, on 3rd September 1916 in Chester and was transferred to the 15th Battalion, Cheshire Regiment. Hugh was 5 feet 4 inches tall with a chest measurement of 33 inches. He may have actually been below 5 feet 3 inches tall because the 15th Battalion was a 'Bantam' regiment of men who were below 5 feet 3 inches tall. After basic training Hugh embarked to France with the 15th Battalion on 25th January 1917. The battalion underwent gruelling training and served in some of the most hard-fought battles of the war, such as the Battle of Arras in 1917. On 28th August 1917 Hugh was wounded in his left hand by accidental discharge of a weapon. It is not known if Hugh was to blame but he was not charged with committing a self-inflicted wound. He was taken to the 1st General Hospital, Rouen, and thereafter evacuated to England on September 9th 1917 to the 1st Southern Hospital, Small Heath, Birmingham. The wound did not get better and Hugh was forced to stay in the hospital for many months but as he recovered he was allowed out of the hospital until

5.45 p.m. daily. He overstayed the curfew on more than 10 occasions and had his pay stopped as a result. He was discharged from the army in September 1918 and transferred to the army reserve. He returned to Shady Grove to live with his mother. His service record implies he returned to work at Birchenwood Colliery but in what capacity is unknown. He was awarded 5s 6d weekly pension for a limited period. He was awarded the Victory and British War medal in 1922.

## The Harrison Family

### Petty Officer Diarmid Ian Harrison: Royal Navy

*Coriale, Gertrude, Diarmid, and Beryl Harrison*

*Photo: Harrison family collection*

Diarmid was born in Alsager on 13th June 1901. He enlisted in Devonport with the Royal Navy in May 1918 as a Boy Sailor on the training ship Impregnable. On 9th November 1918 he transferred to HMS Danae for patrol duties in the North Sea. He went on to serve in the Navy until 1928 on the ships *HMS Vivid* and *HMS Hood*, becoming a Petty Officer in 1922. He later re-joined the Navy serving on *HMS Drake* and received the Royal Navy Long Service medal in 1934. He died in Devon in 1984.

### Sergeant John Edward Harrison: North Staffordshire Regiment

Diarmid's father, John Edward Harrison, was born in Budbrooke, Warwickshire in 1871 and married Gertrude Ladbrooke in 1896. The family lived in Talke Road, Alsager. He was employed by Henry Pooley and Co., Kidsgrove, Staffordshire, as a fitter before he enlisted in the North Staffordshire Regiment. He had previously been a member of the Volunteers between 1908 and 1912, D Company 5th, Battalion North Staffordshire Regiment, service number 496. He completed annual training camps in Towyn, Abergavenny, Birmingham and Aberystwyth with the Volunteers prior to the Great War and reached the rank of Corporal.

Between 1914 and 1918, John served in D Company 5th BNS, 2nd 5th North Staffordshire Regiment Service number 2582, and later changed to Service Number 166378. The 2/5th Battalion TF was formed in 1914 and moved to Ireland in 1916 where it was involved in the Easter Rising. It served in France 1917–1918 and merged with 1/5th Battalion in February 1918. It is unlikely John joined them in France and he was transferred to the Labour Corps because of his age.

In 1918 he spent 13 days in hospital in Catterick, North Yorkshire, for 'debility', a problem with his right arm. With Unit 480, Labour Corps, Nottingham, he rose to the rank of Sergeant. He died in Alsager in 1952.

### Private Malcolm Brooke Harrison: North Staffordshire Regiment

*Photograph: Weekly Sentinel*

Malcolm Harrison was born in Butt Lane, Talke, Staffordshire, in 1899. He was John Edward Harrison's oldest son. Malcom's family moved to live in Talke Road, Alsager, when he was one year old. According to the 1911 Census, he was an 'Experimental Fitter' working on weighing machines. An article in the Weekly Sentinel, 1918, describes Malcolm's army service:

*'Private M.B. Harrison son of Sergeant Harrison, North Staffordshire Regiment, Talke Road, Alsager, enlisted in October 1914 when but 15 years of age. He has served in Gallipoli, Egypt and Palestine and was severely wounded in the right leg while serving in France on July 28th. His younger brother is serving in the navy.'*

Malcolm enlisted in the 7th Battalion, the Cheshire Regiment, service number 2554, on 28th October 1914. In 1916 his service number was changed to 290633. After basic training Malcolm embarked with the regiment to Turkey fighting in the Gallipoli landings. He sailed in July 1915 from Devonport, going via Alexandria to Gallipoli where it landed on 9 August 1915. He fought at Suvla Bay and Anzac Cove until the British Army was forced to withdraw to Egypt in December 1915. The battalion spent time in Palestine in the fight against the Turks, until on 31st May 1918 his Division moved to France. From 1st July 1918 his regiment was attached to the 102nd Brigade in 34th Division. Less than a month after joining the Division, Malcolm was wounded. He recovered from his wounds and re-joined his regiment serving out the remainder of the war in France.

In 1918 Malcolm wrote to the Vicar of Alsager, *'I have marched through Hebron, Bethlehem, and Jerusalem. Hebron is a very pretty place, Jonny Turk gave us a hot reception at Bethlehem, but when we had taken it and were marching through, the people lined the streets, shouting vive l'Angleterre, and one old lady caught hold of the Colonel's hand and kissed it. This was the same day as we entered Jerusalem. I had Christmas Communion in Jerusalem and the Padre gave me a card in commemoration.'*

Harrison was demobilised on 5th May 1919 and awarded a Silver War Badge, (number B198668.)

After the War, Malcom became a postman and moved to Winnipeg, Canada, stating he wished to become a farmer, but returned to live in Alsager in 1927. The documentation on his immigration papers from Canada give his occupation as 'Farmer'. He married Phyllis Ford in 1934 and had two children. He died in Alsager in March 1985.

*Malcolm and Phyllis Harrison with their children. Family photo.*

Malcolm received the 1914/15 Star, The British War Medal, and the Victory Medal

## Private James Henshaw: North Staffordshire Regiment

James Henshaw was born in Alsager in 1886 to Myra and John Henshaw. His father was a Colliery Manager. The family lived in Lawton Road in 1901 and moved to Station Road. James Henshaw was a chemist's assistant dispensing drugs in 1901. 1911 he became an Insurance Fire Inspector. James Henshaw was a batsman for Alsager Cricket Club before the Great War and was Secretary of the cricket and bowling club. At the outbreak of war, James joined the North Staffordshire Regiment, Service number 2928, and following training embarked to France on 5th March 1915 in 11 platoon, 'C' Company. He was slightly wounded in the attack on the Hohenzollern Redoubt in October 1915. He was transferred to 1/6th Battalion, North Staffordshire Regiment, service number 200459 and took part in the famous assault on the Riqueval Bridge over the San Quentin canal on 29th September 1918.

**SECRETARY OF ALSAGER CRICKET AND BOWLING CLUB.**

Private James Henshaw, of the First 5th North Staffs Regiment, who lives at Lawton-road, Alsager, and is the secretary of the Alsager Tennis and Bowling Club, has been wounded.

The following letter written by one of his chums, gives a vivid account of how he came by his wounds: "It happened yesterday (July 20th). He, along with two other chaps, named Blackstone and Kilgour, were acting as guides, their work being to take parties up to the different fire trenches. Yesterday at about four p.m. they started out themselves to deliver letters. It was on this journey that shelling started, and ended by them hitting Kilgour. Blackstone was attending to his wounds, while Henshaw went for the stretcher-bearers. Whilst on this journey he was hit in the shoulder by shrapnel. The doctor informs me it is only a flesh wound —no injury to bones. He had the best attention available, having one doctor in the trench. 'Jimmie' remained in the trench all night. I went up to see him this morning. He was quite cheery, smoking a cigarette. The doctor told me he was suffering from shock as much as anything. 'Jimmie' has just passed my dug-out along with the R.A.M.C. chaps on his way to the hospital. I wished him speedy recovery, and in return he wished us all 'Good luck.' I am sorry to say that Blackstone whilst dressing Kilgour's wounds was hit and received serious wounds. He passed away this morning. Kilgour has a broken leg."

Mrs. Henshaw has received sympathetic letters from the chaplain, and from the wife of the O.C., Colonel Knight.

*Nantwich Guardian 30th July 1915*

He was demobilised in February 1919. He was awarded the 1914/15 Star, the Victory Medal, and the British War Medal.

# Private Thomas Frederick Holland & Serjeant Walter James Hollinshead: Army Service Corps

*Walter Hollinshead (seated front left) and his friend Thomas Frederick Holland (centre rear) with whom he established Holland & Hollinshead Motors in Alsager after the war. Photo: Sentinel*

Thomas Frederick Holland was born in Alsager in 1891 to Henry and Elizabeth Holland. His father was a gardener. T.F Holland was a chauffeur in 1911. His brother Isaac Bernard Holland was a motor mechanic. They enlisted together on 23rd August 1914 and both served in France. After demobilisation he formed a business partnership with William Hollinshead. He married Daisy Hannah Rowland in 1919 and died in 1941.

Walter James Hollinshead was born in Pattingham, Staffordshire, United Kingdom in 1890 to Eliza and James Hollinshead. His sister Ada was born in 1882, Beatrice (1896), and Gladys Maude (1897). Walter's step sister, Clara Smith was born in 1887. In 1901 the family were living in Shady Grove, Alsager. Walter's father was an agricultural labourer. By 1911 the family were living in Crewe Road and Walter was working as a motor mechanic. He joined the Army Service Corps on 9th November 1914, service number MI/1668, and was posted to 75 Company Mechanised Motor Transport working as a motor engineer at the ammunition park for the 8th Division. This later became the base for the 1st Army. Walter was responsible for vehicle repairs. The Army Service Corps vehicles transported ammunition to the front line. Walter served in France before Christmas 1914 and was later promoted Serjeant. In 1915 Walter married Alice Hodgkinson in St Mary's Church, Alsager. He was demobilised in 1919 and returned to live in Alsager as a motor engineer. He opened a garage, Holland & Hollinshead, with his friend F. Holland. His son, Walter Raymond, was born in 1924. Walter James died in 1985. He was awarded the 1914 Star, The Victory Medal, and the British War Medal.

# Private Arnold Victor Hopwood: North Staffordshire Regiment.

*Photo: Sentinel.*

Arnold Victor Hopwood (known as Vic) was born in Talke, Staffordshire, in 1892 to Mary and Thomas Hopwood. His sister Eva Hopwood was born in 1884, and his brother Lawrence Hopwood was born in 1889. By 1901 the family was living at 57 Crewe Road, Alsager. In 1911 Vic was working as an 'iron erector'. He enlisted with the North Staffordshire Regiment, 1/5th Battalion as a private, service number 2581 on 5th August 1914. He served in 'B Company'. He arrived in France with the regiment on 5th March 1915 and was soon in the firing line. Vic wrote a letter to his mother, re-printed in the Sentinel newspaper in April 1915.

The Sentinel reported he was slightly wounded in the attack on the Hohenzollern Redoubt on October 13th 1915: *'2589 Pte Hopwood A.V Lilac House, Crewe Rd. Alsager. No.8 Plt. B. Coy wounded slightly.'*

On 4th September 1916 Vic was invalided out of the army due to wounds

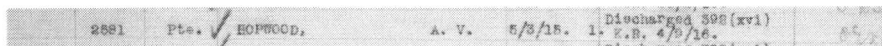

His silver war badge no. 25,204, was awarded on 17th February 1917. He was awarded the 1914/15 Star, the British War Medal, and Victory Medal.

### Gunner Jack Howarth: Royal Field Artillery.

*One of Alsager's Youngest Army recruits*

John Thomas Howarth (known as Jack) was born in Alsager on 13th May 1899 to John and Alice Howarth. In 1901 they were living in Station Road, Alsager. His father was a gardener. Jack was confirmed into the Anglican Church at St Mary's. On 4th January 1916 Jack travelled to Preston and enlisted in the Royal Field Artillery. He gave his age as 19 and 7 months, occupation as labourer, and his home address as Crewe Road, Alsager. He was given service number 116436. He was under 5 feet 5 inches tall with a 25 inch waist, a very underdeveloped physique. He had blue eyes and a fresh complexion. On 9th February 1916 he was invested as a gunner with the 4th Reserve Brigade. It is uncertain his parents knew he had enlisted. He trained as a gunner until it was discovered after 126 days service that he was underage and he was discharged from the army. On 9th May 1916, Gunner Jack Howarth was brought home to Alsager by his parents from Woolwich barracks. The Royal Field Artillery Service record states his given age was a 'mistake'. His forwarding address after discharge was given as Crewe Road, Alsager. He was 16 years 11 months when he was discharged. His service record stated he was of 'good character', And states, 'conduct satisfactory'. It is known that Jack re-enlisted in the army when he was old enough to do so. He joined the 9th Cheshire Regiment, service number 60294, transferring to the 2nd Manchester Regiment. The Parish Magazine reported in June that he was 'missing' in France but a month later said he was in a prisoner of war camp. Jack returned to Alsager after the Armistice and in 1920 was living with his parents in Station Road. He married and went to live in Nantwich and worked as a 'Railway Shunter'. He died in 1965.

### Able Seaman Charles Howells: Royal Navy

Born in Stoke-on-Trent on 22nd December 1882, Charles lived in Audley Road, Alsager, and worked as a railway clerk at Alsager Station. He enlisted on 6th August 1914 at Chatham, Kent, service number M9675. He was 5 feet 7 inches tall with blue eyes and light hair. He worked on *HMS Thalia*, a shore based facility for minesweepers and patrol boats based at Invergordon, Scotland between 1916 -1919. *Thalia* was an old cruiser built in 1870 and was used for storing equipment, relaxation, crew dining, and berthing. Charles' rank was 'Able Seaman, Residential Attendant.' After the war Charles returned to live in Alsager. In 1922 he lived at Coton House, Audley Road.

## Signaller George Henry Johnson: Manchester Regiment

George Henry Johnson was born in Alsager in 1895 to Mary and George Johnson. His brother John W. Johnson was born 1893, his sisters Amy Johnson in 1896 and Mabel in 1899. George lived in Sandy Lane, Alsager. In the 1911 census George was working as an errand boy in Alsager. In April 1918 the Sentinel reported George was in hospital wounded and was in the Manchester Regiment. It stated prior to enlistment George worked for Messrs Liptons in Tunstall, Stoke-on-Trent. George served as a signaller in the Manchester Regiment, service number 277601. He was posted to the 2/7th Battalion, Manchester Regiment and later transferred to the 1/7th Battalion. He is recorded in the 'Absent Voters' list for Alsager 1918, and in 1919 indicating he was still in active service in 1919. In 1923 after being demobilised he is recorded on the electoral register. He was awarded the British War Medal and the Victory Medal. His brother, Private John. Johnson, who worked for Boyce Adams, grocers, before the war, fought with the Black Watch. John was wounded in 1917 and spent time in hospital.

## Lt Colonel Harry Johnson DSO: North Staffordshire Regiment

*Photograph Sentinel 1918*

Lt. Colonel Harry Johnson was the highest ranked member of the armed services from Alsager. During 1917 he was Commanding Officer of the fifth battalion of the North Staffordshire Regiment. Harry Johnson's home address was 'Hayleigh', Sandbach Road, Alsager.

Lt. Colonel Johnson served in the North Staffordshire Regiment for over seventeen years, and had seen action in South Africa, receiving the Queen's Medal, before serving in the Great War. He was commissioned 2nd Lieutenant in the North Staffs Regiment on 3rd July 1897. On 1st April 1908 he was promoted Captain. On 8th December 1914 Captain Johnson was promoted Major in the 5th North Staffordshire Regiment.

In September 1914 he had been selected to lead the 2nd/5th Battalion in their battle training at Butterton Hall, Staffordshire. In April 1916 his battalion was sent to Ireland during the 'Easter Rebellion'. He was posted to France with the battalion in February 1917 and promoted Lt. Colonel. In 1918 he was awarded the DSO but on 21st March 1918 as part of the great German Spring Offensive he was wounded by a bullet and captured at Bullecourt. Nineteen officers from the Battalion were captured or killed in the same offensive.

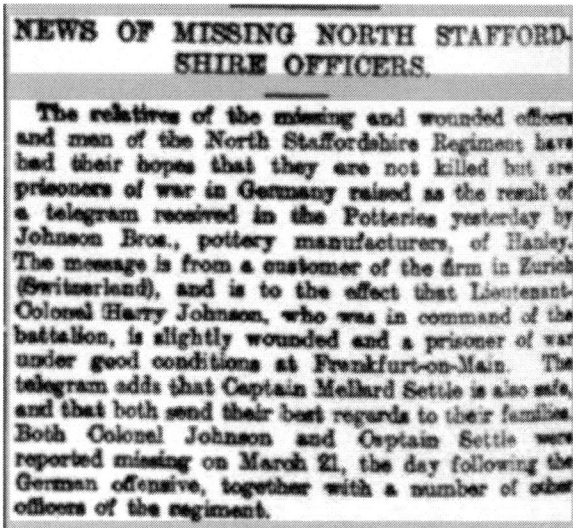

## NEWS OF MISSING NORTH STAFFORD-SHIRE OFFICERS.

The relatives of the missing and wounded officers and men of the North Staffordshire Regiment have had their hopes that they are not killed but are prisoners of war in Germany raised as the result of a telegram received in the Potteries yesterday by Johnson Bros., pottery manufacturers, of Hanley. The message is from a customer of the firm in Zurich (Switzerland), and is to the effect that Lieutenant-Colonel Harry Johnson, who was in command of the battalion, is slightly wounded and a prisoner of war under good conditions at Frankfurt-on-Main. The telegram adds that Captain Mellard Settle is also safe, and that both send their best regards to their families. Both Colonel Johnson and Captain Settle were reported missing on March 21, the day following the German offensive, together with a number of other officers of the regiment.

*Report from the Birmingham Post April 1918*

German records gave his date of birth, as 27th January 1878, and his place of birth as Stafford, and his British address as Hayesleigh, Alsager. He was imprisoned in Frankfurt and then Karlsruhe. On arriving at Karlsruhe the International Red Cross records show Johnson managed to wire a message to Britain to inform his family he was a prisoner. On 21st May Johnson managed to send a message back to Britain regarding the receipt of Red Cross Parcels.

On his return to Britain his medals were withheld pending an enquiry to why as Officer Commanding the 5th Battalion he had allowed himself and a large number of his regiment to be taken as prisoners of war. He was found to be blameless.

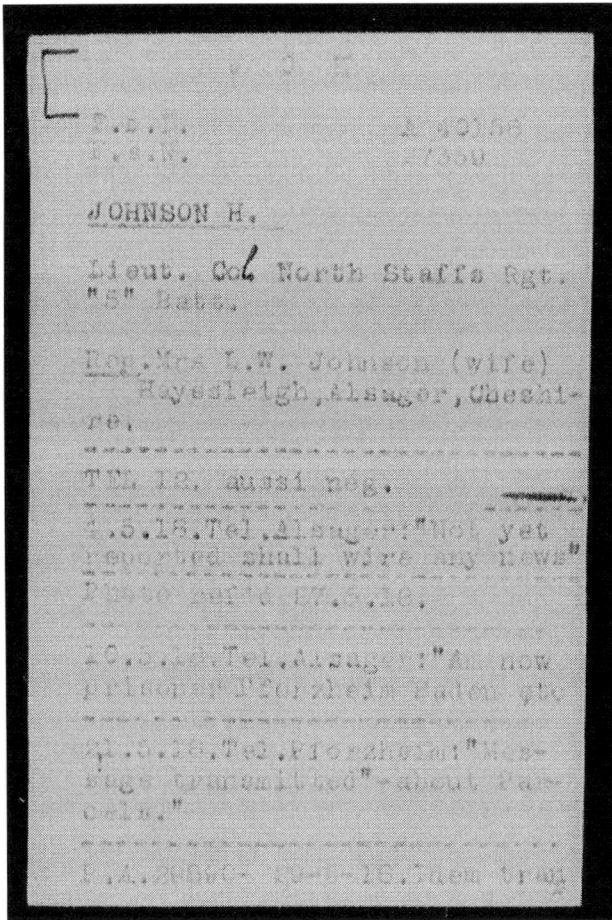

*Johnson's International Red Cross Information card*

On 18th December 1918 Johnson's family managed to transmit a message to him in Germany. Soon afterwards Johnson returned to Britain and freedom. His 'Medal Card' states he was on the 'Exonerated Officers' List' and no blame was given to him for his and his battalion's action on 21st March 1918. The date on the medal card for this decision was 13th October 1922. He was awarded the 1914/15 Star with emblems, the Victory Medal, and the British Medal. He later claimed the Territorial Force War Medal. He was also awarded the DSO in 1918. After the war he became Chairman of H & R Johnson Tiles Ltd. Who's Who 1935 gives a synopsis of part of his career. His telephone number was 'Alsager 32.'

JOHNSON, Colonel Harry, D.S.O. 1918; T.D.; D.L.; J.P.; Chairman of Directors H. & R. Johnson, Ltd.; Vice-Chairman, Potters Insurance Co. Ltd.; b. 27 Jan. 1878; s. of late R. L. Johnson of Butterton Hall, Newcastle, Staffs.; m. 1914, Lucy Winifred Twyman, Abergavenny; one s. one d. Educ.: Newcastle High School; Bath College. Served South African War with 1st V.B. North Staff. Regt. (Queen's medal and four clasps); European War, 1914-19 (D.S.O., Despatches); in command of 5th N. Staff. Regt. 1917-23; wounded and taken prisoner 21 March 1918; founded the firm of H. & R. Johnson, Ltd., 1901; absorbed the businesses of Alf. Meakin, Ltd., 1908, Sherwin & Cotton, 1911; W. Sherwin & Co., 1912; and A. Johnson (Tiles) Ltd., 1920; all of which are glazed tile works; Past President of English Ceramic Society; National Science and Arts Bronze Medallist for Pottery; Freedom of County Borough of Hanley conferred in 1901. Recreations: tennis, shooting, squash-racquet. Address: Boden Hall, Scholar Green, Cheshire. T.: Alsager 32. Club: Carlton.
JOHNSON, Engineer Rear-Adm.

## Major George Spencer Jacobs:  Cheshire Regiment

*German Prisoner of War for over four years*

George Spencer Jacobs was born in 1885 in Burslem to Elizabeth and George Jacobs. His father was a Brewer's Foreman Cooper. His sister Evelyn was born in 1890. Before 1901 the family moved to Alsager and lived in a house in 'The Fields'. In the 1901 census George Spencer Jacobs is described as a 'pupil teacher', presumably at Alsager National School adjacent to Christ Church. In 1904 the staff log book at the National School included George S. Jacobs as an Assistant Teacher. George went on to study at Chester Training College. In the 1911 census George was identified as working in Bishop Stortford, Hertfordshire as a school teacher. He became a part-time soldier, a 'Teacher-Soldier' and was commissioned on 10th February 1912 and put on the Reserve of Officers. Before war broke out George was recalled into the army when he was working as a teacher in Southport. He was drafted to the 1st Cheshire Regiment in Derry. According to the Liverpool Echo he was part of the contingent who brought the regimental colours to Chester Castle before being dispatched to France on 10th August 1914. George was captured at Andregertes on 24th August in the retreat from Mons and sent to Crefeld (spelled Krefeld after 1930) prisoner of war camp. In 1914 Parr's Bank, Crewe received a piece of paper from Germany in the form of a cheque and a half sheet of paper dated 23rd September asking the Bank to inform his next of kin that he was a prisoner of war. Jacobs' father informed the Sentinel newspaper who reported the story saying he was grateful his son was well enough to write in a legible hand.

There were at this time some five or six hundred officer prisoners in Crefeld camp – British (including Empire and Dominions), French (and colonials), Russian and Belgian, and each day the numbers were swelled by more prisoners till eventually there was a total of about one thousand. The various nationalities fed separately but were all mixed up in the various living rooms throughout the camp – a former German Cavalry Barracks specially converted. George was later moved to Ströhen Prisoner of War camp near Hanover. On 20th September 1918 the Nantwich Guardian announced.

*"The Gazette de Holland," of August 30th contained the following announcement. "We learn that Lieutenant G. Spencer Jacobs, Cheshire Regiment, has lately become engaged to Mlle Marie Monnier, daughter of Colonel and Madame Monnier of Brussels. Colonel Monnier, who was in command of one of the Belgian Lancer Regiments, is interned in this country. (Lieutenant G Spencer Jacobs is the older son of Lieutenant G.H Jacobs and Mrs Jacobs of Alsager. He was taken prisoner at Andriegnies, near Mons, August 24th 1914, spent 10 months as a prisoner of war in Germany, and has been interned in Holland at Scheveningham since December 25th 1917.)"*

Jacobs was an exchanged prisoner. Exchanged prisoners in Holland were still prisoners of war, merely housed in a neutral country by mutual agreement between the combatant nations. Their status was slightly different from those combatants who strayed across the border and were interned. The difference being that the Dutch government had absolute control of the internees and would not allow them to leave. Jacobs was repatriated to England on 12th December 1918. After the war he was too ill to go with his regiment to India in 1921.

In the Second World War Captain George Jacobs (Retired) was commissioned Lieutenant on 27th April 1940 and took part in the Expeditionary Force and was amongst the men who successfully returned from Dunkirk. He then took up a position managing British Prisoner of War Camps using his knowledge and experience to good effect. After the war he joined Dover Staff College in the rank of Major until forced to retire through ill health in June 1947. The Dover Express reported in 16th July 1948 that George had died suddenly in Dover. He left a widow Marie G. Jacobs, with whom he had fallen in love with in Holland in 1918.

Jacobs was Mentioned in Despatches for his gallantry in the retreat from Mons. He also earned the 1914 Star, Victory Medal and the British War Medal.

## 2nd Lieutenant Arthur John Jenkinson: North Staffordshire Regiment

Arthur John Jenkinson came from Church Lawton and had worked as a clerk in an iron foundry before enlisting in 1914 in the North Staffordshire Regiment. He was an intelligent man and was to excel as a soldier gaining rapid promotion to Corporal. After basic training he embarked for Gallipoli in July 1915, service number 11235, with the 7th Battalion, North Staffordshire Regiment. The Battalion alighted at Anzac Cove on 9th July. They struggled along the beach to Rest Gully trench positions. Fifty nine men were killed. During August the men moved into trenches with the Worcester Regiment. In October 1915 Rev. Waller wrote in the parish magazine that Arthur Jenkinson, a former chorister and member of H.A. Thomas's bible class, had been wounded in action. After he recovered he recommenced duties and was promoted Sergeant. The Battalion was evacuated from their positions in late December to Cape Helles and in late January to Egypt. Arthur was accepted for a commission in 1917 and on 14th December 1917 he was gazetted 2nd Lieutenant and transferred to the 1/5th Battalion, later absorbed into the 2/5th Battalion. He took part in the Battle of St. Quentin Canal in late September 1918. After the war he moved to Pear Tree Cottage, Church Lawton before taking up employment with the civil service in Ealing, London. He married Susannah and lived in London until his death in 1948.

## Lieutenant Dyfrig Gwyn Jarvis-Jones: North Staffordshire Regiment

*Photo: National Archives*

Son of Thomas Robert and Mary Jarvis, Dyfrig was born in Hanley in 1896. His parents originated from Caernarvonshire, his father being a draper's manager. In 1901 the family were living in Moss Side Manchester before moving back to Stoke-on-Trent. The family then lived in Bath Street, Hanley. Dyfrig was sent to Dolgellau Grammar School in Mid Wales where he was in 1914 a sergeant in the Officer Training Corps. He joined the North Staffordshire Regiment straight from school as a private soldier and was quickly promoted sergeant.

He was commissioned 2nd Lieutenant on 7th August 1915 to the 5th North Staffordshire Regiment. He embarked to France soon afterwards.

The London Gazette record: '*5th Battalion, The Prince of Wales's (North Staffordshire Regiment); the undermentioned to be Second Lieutenants. Dated 7th August, 1915: —Serjeant Dyfrig Gwyn Jarvis Jones*'

On 30<sup>th</sup> June before the battle of the Somme in 1916, Lt. Jarvis Jones crept out of the British trenches at midnight with a soldier across No Man's Land towards the German positions. His function was to report on the state of the German wire to the left of Folly Trench. He found there was a gap of 30 yards and another gap of 15 yards where the British Guns had destroyed it. There were great tangles of wire close by. In his report he said the British if supplied with mats would be able to access the German parapet and enter the German trenches. He also identified small gaps near Oundle trench for the artillery to weaken the German defences. His report however emphasized large parts of the German wire was uncut. After ninety minutes he returned to the British lines to report to his Adjutant.

Jarvis-Jones had made previous trips across No Man's Land and identified German wire defences. Unfortunately his reports that only small parts of the wire had been cut did not stop the Generals ordering the attack on July 1<sup>st</sup>, with disastrous consequences.

Jarvis-Jones was wounded by a gunshot to the jaw in the attack on 1<sup>st</sup> July during the battle of the Somme at Gommecourt. He was evacuated from Le Havre on the *Lanfranc* on 2<sup>nd</sup> July to Southampton. A machine gun bullet had hit his jaw, deflected down his neck exiting through and smashing his right shoulder blade. He was sent to the Cambridge Hospital Aldershot and returned to duty with the 3/5<sup>th</sup> North Staffordshire Regiment on 2<sup>nd</sup> January 1918 at the No. 1 School for Instruction for Infantry Officers ( Middlesex Regiment) but was discharged medically unfit on 1<sup>st</sup> May 1918. In 1918 his address on the Absent Voters list was given as 93 Crewe Road Alsager, in the 8<sup>th</sup> Battalion North Staffordshire Regiment. He was still living at the address until 1924. He married Marjorie Moss in Nottingham in 1924. Jarvis Jones moved to Surrey. In 1940 he was recalled into the army. The London Gazette, 5<sup>th</sup> January 1940: *'Lt. Dyfrig Gwyn JARVIS-JONES (107704), late N. Stafford R. to be lieutenant in the Ordnance Corps from 27<sup>th</sup> November 1939'.* He was promoted to Major. Major Jarvis-Jones died on 16<sup>th</sup> May 1942 in Northumberland. It was likely it was a munitions accident. His probate states his home address was Hampton on Thames and his widow was Marjorie Jarvis-Jones.

He is buried in a Commonwealth War Grave in the tiny village of Well in the graveyard of St Michael's Church, near Bedale, Yorkshire.

## Fireman Francis Jepson: Royal Navy

*Picture of Francis Jepson: Southampton Archives.*

Francis was born in Alsager on 14th November 1892. He lived in Chancery Lane. His father was the sexton of the parish church. He joined the Royal Navy and served five years before the war on the Victory 11, the Renown, and the Hindustan. He was 5 feet 3 inches tall with grey eyes, brown hair and a fair complexion. He was discharged from the Royal Navy with *'re-entry not appropriate'*, but after commencement of the war he served in the merchant navy. In September 1917 it was reported in the Alsager parish magazine that Francis Jepson from Alsager had been awarded a medal for gallantry (Médaille Militaire) by the French Minister for Marine. Francis helped to rescue passengers from a French steamer which had gone ashore on a reef. His rank was 2nd Mate. His gallantry enabled him to re-join the Royal Navy. He served again with on *HMS Wildfire*, service number 935089 with the rank of Fireman. He was demobilised in 1919 and awarded a Silver War Badge. He went on to be awarded the British War Medal and Victory medals.

## Private John Kennerley: Tank Corps

John was born in 1881 in Alsager to John and Emily Kennerley. By profession he was a house painter and employed men. In 1906 he married Constance Parkes in 1906 and they lived in 'The Fields' Alsager. He enlisted as a Sapper in the Royal Engineers, service number 231443, and was attested on 11th December 1915 and was placed on the reserve and was not mobilised until February 1917. He had been confirmed medically fit for duty in June 1916. He was initially based on home duties. He was 5 feet 9 inches tall with a 38 inch chest. On 12th June 1918 he was transferred to the Tank Corps, service number 306084, and served in the 8th Battalion, (Industrial Group 30). He served abroad in France from 18th June1918. On 30th August he was hospitalised in Trouville,

France. He recovered and was finally discharged on 19<sup>th</sup> March 1919. John returned to live in Alsager. He died in Stoke-on-Trent in 1946.

## Lt. Charles Roy Lynam: Royal Field Artillery

Charles Roy Lynam was born in Tittensor, Staffordshire, on 20<sup>th</sup> November 1892 to Henry Middlemore Lynam, who died shortly after his son's birth, and Harriet Lynam. The family moved to Alsager in 1913 when Charles was working as a 'Pupil Architect and Surveyor.' They lived in Chancery Lane. Charles' brother, Harry Valentine Lynam, living at the same address, was Surveyor to Alsager Urban District Council. Charles Lynam enlisted in December 1914 in the Royal Field Artillery, service number 100. He embarked to France with the Regiment on 28<sup>th</sup> February 1915. On 21<sup>st</sup> December 1917 he gained a commission as Second Lieutenant. He was still serving in late 1919, a year after the Armistice. He later moved to Sevenoaks in Kent working as a Civil Engineer and Chartered Surveyor. He was awarded the 14/15 Star, British War Medal and Victory Medal. He died in 1970.

His bother Harry Valentine Lynam was an important member of the Alsager community in the Great War. As well as being Council Surveyor, he was chairman of the Belgian Refugees Committee, and chairman of The Prince of Wales Relief Fund, in the town. The Council fought to stop him being conscripted in 1916 seeing his job as surveyor as indispensable. Harry was also Recorder and Vice President of the B'hoys of Alsager, and as surveyor worked tirelessly to improve Alsager's poor sewage and water supply. He married Blanche Parkes, daughter of the landlord of the Alsager Arms Hotel.

## The McMahon Family

ALSAGER FAMILY WHICH IS HELPING TO "CARRY ON."

*Left to right: Norman, Catherine, Hilda, Frank, Minnie, Willie McMahon from the Sentinel.*

In 1918 the Weekly Sentinel reported the plight of an Alsager family in Shady Grove struggling to *'keep going'* during the war. With both their parents dead and two brothers serving in the army, Minnie McMahon, aged 16, was left looking after her younger siblings; Doris 14, Hilda, 12, Catherine 13, and Norman 8. Her eldest brother, Frank was serving in London on anti-aircraft defences and her next brother, Willie, was serving with the East Lancs. Regiment. Their mother, Emily McMahon was buried on 17th August 1918 aged 42. The soldiers survived the war. Both Frank and William are shown in the Electoral Register for Alsager in 1920. Frank McMahon became a porter on Alsager railway station after being demobilised in 1919. He retired on 4th September 1959 and died in Alsager in the same year.

*Arthur was a war hero and played a prominent part in the opening ceremony of the War Memorial. He commanded the group of ex-servicemen who marched in the procession at the unveiling in 1920.*

*Arthur Maddock. Picture: Sentinel.*

Arthur Victor Maddock was born in Wolstanton, Staffordshire, United Kingdom in 1898 to Dora and Arthur Henry Maddock. He came to live in Alsager before 1901 and the family lived in Church Road. They moved to 'The Cedars' before 1911. His father was a prominent member of Alsager Urban District Council. 'Victor', as he preferred to be called, was an only child. His father and grandfather were both earthenware manufacturers in the pottery industry. His uncle and family lived in Sandbach Road, Alsager. Maddock studied at Malvern College where he was a member of the Officer Training Corps.

Victor enlisted early in the war with the Royal Field Artillery and was commissioned 2nd Lieutenant in 1915. He was posted to France on 19th November 1915. On 1st June 1916 he was promoted Lieutenant. In October 1917 he was awarded the Military Cross for gallantry in the field. The citation: *'For gallantry and disregard for danger during an important attack. Because of an enemy barrage his telephone wire to his headquarters was broken and Maddock went through the barrage six times with his linesmen to repair the wire, afterwards sending back valuable information to headquarters.'* He was only 19 when he won the Military Cross. After the war Victor was awarded the Croix de Guerre by the French Government. The citation for the Croix de Guerre: *'Lieutenant Arthur Victor Maddock M.C 'A' Battery, 231 Brigade R.F.A. On 27th and 28th Sept 1918 before Bellinglise this officer shewed great courage and great perseverance in taking up ammunition to the advanced guns both day and night under very violent fire. During all the operations of Sept. 27th to October 18th Lt. Maddock shewed great personal bravery and untiring energy and his services were of inestimable value.'*

> Lt. Arthur Victor Maddock, R.F.A.
> For conspicuous gallantry and devotion to duty as F.O.O. during an attack. Owing to the heavy enemy barrage his telephone wire was constantly broken. He went six times through the barrage with his linesmen repairing the wire, and was enabled eventually to send some valuable information back.

*Citation for the Military Cross*

In 1922 Victor was living at 'Greenlands' Alsager. Victor served as Captain with the Royal Field Artillery after the war in the Territorial Force He married Ethel Edith Whiskerd in 1934 in Norfolk. He died in Truro, Cornwall, in 1958.

### Basil Mayer: 3rd Corps of Hussars and Tom Mayer: Scots Guards

*Brothers of Lieutenant F. Bert Mayer, killed in action 1915*

Tom Mayer, born in Alsager, was living with his widowed mother in Poulton, North Cheshire at the outbreak of war. Born in 1889 he was an electrical engineer. He enlisted with the Scots Guards, army number 11001 and embarked to France on 25th February 1915. He was promoted to Lance Corporal. He was wounded in action in Flanders in 1915 and was evacuated to England where he convalesced in Halifax, Yorkshire. The Nantwich Guardian reported on 5th January 1917 that Private Tom Mayer, Scots Guards, was awarded the Military Medal for running fifty yards over open ground when encountering heavy fire to tend to an officer who was wounded. He helped to carry the officer 300 yards back to safety. On 27th November 1917 he was commissioned 2nd Lieutenant. Tom Mayer died in 1953 in Glasgow.

His brother, Basil Mayer, was born in Alsager in 1890 and was a Chartered Accountant. He was a private in the 3rd Corps of Hussars, Service number 265203. He embarked to Egypt with his regiment on 28th April 1915, and then was posted to Turkey. He was dangerously wounded in the Dardanelles and was in hospital in Cairo in October 1915. He recovered and was demobilised from the army on 23rd March 1919. He married Margery Doggett and lived in Croydon, Surrey. He died in 1955. Both brothers earned the 1914/15 Star, the British War Medal and the British War Medal as well as Tom winning the Military Medal.

## Sergeant Reginald Harry Mayer: Tropical Force, Australian Imperial Force

Reginald was an Alsager-born man who fought for the Australian Imperial Force in the Great War. He was unrelated to other men of the same surname in this book (Basil, Bert or Tom Mayer.) Having served in the British Army in South Africa and India Reg was dismissed from the army for fraud. Having spent a year in a military prison in 1911 in Karachi he left India and moved to Australia with his wife and child. Whether the Australian recruiting sergeant was informed of Reg's convictions is uncertain, but he did state on his application form his 13 years' service with the 1st & 2nd South Wales Borderers. Born to Adelaide and Edward Mayer in Alsager in 1880, Reg was brought up in Field House, now part of Fields Road. He joined the British army in 1899 and fought in South Africa gaining service medals during the Boer War. During his service in India he was seconded to the Ceylon Volunteer Force and it was during this time he was convicted for fraud. His wife Gladys, whom he married in 1907, was left with a young child, Gladys Madeline Mayer, born in 1911, to look after in difficult circumstances. Reg had all his military medals taken from him by the British Army. Once in Australia Reg became a farmer and enlisted in the Australian Imperial Force

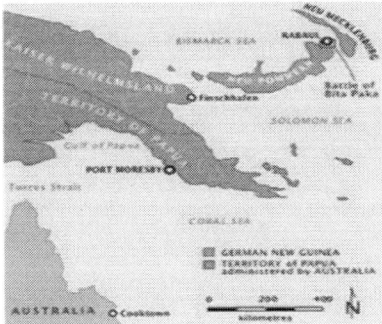

on 17th July 1915. He enlisted in the Tropical Force, a part of the Australian Naval and Military Expeditionary Force which specialised in fighting in tropical climates. In September 1914 the Australian Tropical Force had managed to win a small but significant battle in German New Guinea taking control of Rabaul at the battle of Bita Paka, destroying German wireless systems. The Australians suffered six dead and four wounded. Reg was later part of the force which garrisoned Rabaul.

*German New Guinea 1914*

Reginald was first promoted Lance Corporal, then to Sergeant on 1st August 1916. While the garrison of 600 men was not attacked, the difficult climate in New Guinea caused many deaths due to disease. Reg was discharged from the army in July 1918 and returned to live in Western Australia. He was presented with his British War Medal and Victory Medals in 1925. Despite losing his Boer War medals he would have gained some consolation of receiving his Great War Medals. Reg's son, Rex, was killed in action in Crete in 1941. Reg died in Perth, Australia, in 1941.

# The Mitchell Brothers

Three out of the four Mitchell Brothers who joined the army in September 1914. Private William Herbert Mitchell, 4<sup>th</sup> North Staffordshire Regiment; Corporal George Ashley Mitchell, of the same regiment; Lance Corporal Samuel Mitchell, 9<sup>th</sup> North Staffordshire Regiment. George later transferred to the 7<sup>th</sup> East Yorks. Regiment and William to the Machine Gun Corps. Picture: Sentinel.

## Private William Herbert Mitchell:  Machine Gun Corps

William Herbert Mitchell was born in Alsager in 1891 to Rhoda and William Mitchell. His father was a labourer who died in 1916. His brother Samuel Mitchell was born 1892, George Ashley in 1895, Arthur in 1896, a sister Ailsa in 1904, and a brother Harry, in 1907. In 1911 William was recorded as a house painter on the census but on joining the army on 2<sup>nd</sup> September 1914 in Burslem he gave his occupation as plumber working for Jas. Edwards having worked an apprenticeship for him. Although William enlisted with the North Staffordshire Regiment on 5<sup>th</sup> September 1914 he soon transferred to the East Yorkshire Regiment, service number 18323, in the 4<sup>th</sup> Battalion. William was 5 feet 7 inches tall and had blue eyes and light brown hair. Records state he had a 40 inch chest. He transferred to the 4<sup>th</sup> Battalion on 8<sup>th</sup> May 1915 and was included in the draft to France on the same day returning from duty on 22<sup>nd</sup> October 1915. On 25<sup>th</sup> October 1915 William embarked for Alexandria arriving on 28<sup>th</sup> and then transferred to Salonika, Greece arriving on 3<sup>rd</sup> November 1915. On 22<sup>nd</sup> May 1916 William was posted to the Machine Gun Corps, 83rd Company, and promoted Lance Corporal on 12<sup>th</sup> December 1916. In 1916 he suffered several bouts of illness; scabies in August, and malaria in September and October. He was evacuated to England in December 1916 but returned again to Salonika in 1917.

William was promoted Serjeant on 10th August 1917. He returned home to England and married Ellen Moores in Mow Cop on 28th August 1918. Returning to the Mediterranean he underwent a short spell in the 79th General Hospital Tarranto, Italy in late September 1918 before returning to Greece. William received a long service award emblem in Salonika on 3rd March 1919 just before returning home. He was discharged from the army on 21st March 1919 in Grantham. William remained in Alsager working as a house painter. He was a longstanding member of Alsager British Legion. He died in 1959.

William received the Victory Medal, the British War Medal, the 1914/15 Star and the long service emblem.

The Mitchell family lived in Shady Grove, Alsager. They were not related to Private Benjamin Mitchell of Crewe Road, Alsager, killed in action, May 1918.

### Private John Munslow:  North Staffordshire Regiment

*Picture: Sentinel*

John Munslow was born near Llandudno on 23rd March 1896. The family lived at 2 Fields Terrace, Alsager. He was an electrical engineer and enlisted with the North Staffordshire Regiment in Hanley on 28th August 1914 with the 1st /5th Battalion, service number 3469. He served in No.8 Plt. B. Coy. John was 5 feet 9 inches tall with grey eyes and brown hair. The service record says he had a 34 inch chest with 2 inch expansion. He embarked to France on 5th March 1915 and was wounded on 21st August 1915. According to the Nantwich Guardian, 17th September 1915, John was injured when noise from bombardment perforated his ear drum. He was evacuated to Cheltenham Racecourse Hospital, England for an operation. His mother visited him there. He was in hospital and on home service until December 1916. He was discharged from the army on 1st December 1916 because of his wounds after 2 years 65 days service. On 16th February 1917 he was awarded a Silver War Badge number LB5438 with the instructions—'*to be worn on right breast and not on a military uniform*'.

**Air Flight Mechanic Robert Ivor Munslow: Royal Flying Corps/ Royal Air Force**

*Picture Sentinel*

Robert, born in 1896, was John Munslow's brother. Before the war according to the 1911 census his job was 'Motor Driver'. He joined the Royal Flying Corps, service number 22825, on 16th February 1916 after being transferred from the army and saw service in France as an Air Flight Mechanic before suffering from deafness and being hospitalised in England in June 1916. After a few weeks he re-joined the Corps and was posted to Salonika on 16th December 1916 where he was based until 18th September 1918. In 1919 he was promoted Flight Corporal before moving to Prees Heath, Shropshire, on 1st July 1919. He was demobilised to the RAF Reserve on 3rd August 1919. He was awarded the British War Medal and Victory Medal.

## Worker Kathleen O'Brien: Women's Auxiliary Army Corps

Kathleen was born in Alsager on 19th February 1897. She is an example of a women who managed to improve her life opportunities because of the war. At the age of 12 she suffered from diphtheria and by 14 was working as a domestic servant in the Potteries. In 1911 she was living with her father in Blake Street Burslem. A Roman Catholic, she developed close links with the Dominican Convent in Hartshill. When she was 20 she took employment as a housemaid in Southport and in January 1918 applied to join the Women's Auxiliary Army Corps. She passed the interviews and obtained references from her employer, her former parish priest in Stoke-on-Trent, and Sister Luce Bertrand, at the Dominican Convent. She enlisted on 30th January 1918 and underwent training in the north of England and then on the south coast lodging at the Kimmell Hostel, Folkestone to where she moved on 25th March. She arrived in France on 3rd June 1918 to take up her position as a storekeeper. She was issued with 1 greatcoat, 1 coat, 1 frock, 2 pairs of overalls, 1 pair of shoes, 2 pairs stockings and she was paid £0.3s.6d ( £0.15p) per week. She was 5 feet 2 inches tall, with dark brown hair, 'average build', 8st 4 lbs, and worked at Wimereux, General Headquarters of the British Army in France. She gave her home address as the Dominican Convent Stoke-on-Trent and her next of kin as Sister Luce Bertrand. She was allowed very little leave from the service, a week in 1918 and 2 weeks from 5th to 19th June 1919. On 3rd September 1919 she agreed to extend her employment in the WAAC but was demobilised on 28th November 1919 from Unit 11 WAAC, France. After demobilisation she gave her address as the Connaught Club Hostel, London, and later an address in Highgate, London, and her occupation was as a clerk. In 1920 she was still unmarried and living in Kent. She was awarded the Victory Medal and British War Medal. It is doubtful she would have been able to gain training and employment as a storekeeper and then a clerk without the opportunities which came during the Great War.

*QMAAC storekeeper Workers at Vendraux 1918 with male staff. Photo by Olive Edis*

## Lt. James Hough Palin: Yorkshire Regiment

*He rose from being a labourer to become a commissioned officer.*

James Hough Palin was born in Kidsgrove on 1st January 1884. His father was a master joiner originating from Wheelock, and his mother Harriet, came from Kidsgrove. James had two older sisters, one of whom became a headmistress in an Alsager school, and one older brother. In 1911 James was working as a warehouseman in a pottery factory but he decided to join the army and enlisted in the 1st Battalion Royal Scots Fusiliers, service number 6846, as a professional soldier before the commencement of the Great War. In August 1912 he married Ada Shaw and they came to live in Alsager in Audley Road. On 28th November 1914 Corporal James Palin embarked to France with the British Expeditionary Force. He fought in the first battle of Ypres. By 11th May 1915 he is recorded as being wounded and placed in 13th Stationary Hospital which was in Boulogne. He was already promoted to Sergeant at this date. After recovering he transferred to the 1st Battalion North Staffordshire Regiment, service number, 23978. The Battalion fought in northern France and in April and June 1916 it suffered casualties of well over 500 in two serious gas attacks; on both occasions when in trenches north of Wulverghem. James was selected for training for a commission and completed his training on 23rd February 1917. On 5th March he was transferred to the Yorkshire Regiment, the Green Howards, 7th Battalion. In the Nantwich Guardian of 4th May he was reported as being wounded and his wife as living in Audley Road, Alsager. In the 1919 Absent Voters list for Alsager, James Hough Palin is recorded at on active service and attached to the 53rd West Yorkshire Regiment, the young soldier battalion. After service in the army James came back to live in Alsager. James and Ada had two daughters. In the Second World War he served as an Air Raid Warden. He died in 1957.

*James Hough Palin (ARP Warden 1939) Photo from South Cheshire Archives*

## Nurse Dorothy Palfreyman; Voluntary Aid Detachment

*Dorothy Palfreyman. Picture; the Sentinel*

Dorothy Palfreyman was born in Leicester in 1890, the daughter of J.J. Palfreyman. The family moved to live in 'Heathfields' Alsager. Dorothy nursed with her sister, Ethel, at Rode Hall Red Cross Hospital from its opening. She became engaged to Captain H. Collier M.C. from Manchester whom she married in St Mary's Church, Alsager in 1920. The reception in the grounds of Heathfields was for one hundred guests amongst *'profusely flowering rhododendrons'*.

## 2nd Lieutenant Gerald Wylly Palfreyman M.C. : Royal Fusiliers

The youngest son of J.J. Palfreyman, Gerald was born in Leicester in 1891. After school he returned to Leicester and worked as a 'shoemaker' lodging in the city and working at his brother Frederick's shoe manufacturing business. He moved to the United States but returned on *S.S Arabic* on 13th April 1913 at the beginning of the war to enlist and joined the public school battalion of The Royal Fusiliers, service number 6118. He went to France as a Private and served through the winter of 1915 being quickly promoted to Lance Corporal. In April he returned to Britain to train for a commission; he was posted to the OTC in Oxford for part of the time. Following his training he was gazetted 2nd Lieutenant on 16th July 1916 and posted to the Leicester Regiment

and entrained to Mesopotamia. He saw much service including the push towards Baghdad. He was wounded two days before the city was reached and evacuated to Bombay in India to hospital. Although suffering from a gunshot wound in the chest his condition rapidly improved. He was awarded the Military Cross for conspicuous gallantry for his action in Mesopotamia and Mentioned in Despatches in the Gazette on 15th August 1917. His Military Cross was confirmed on 23rd August 1917. He retired from the army in 1920 and lived in Leicester becoming a shoe manufacturer. He married Norah Watters in Leicester in 1928. Gerald died in November 1964. Gerald was also awarded the 1914/15 Star, the British War Medal and the Victory Medal.

## Private Percy John Palfreyman: Army Service Corps

*Photo Sentinel*

Percy John Palfreyman was born in Leicestershire in 1880. In 1911 Percy was living at his father's house, 'Heathfields' and assisted in his father's pawnbroking business before enlisting in the Army Service Corps in 1915, aged forty. He was awarded the British War Medal and Victory Medal. He married Olive Muriel Long in 1916. He lived in 'Glenhorne', The Fairway, Alsager, and died in 1955.

## Cranmer Thomas Parkes: Army Service Corps

Tom Parkes lived for several years in the Alsager Arms where his father was the 'Hotel Keeper.' He followed in the family business working as 'Assistant Brewer' catering at meetings of the B'hoys of Alsager. He moved to Bowness, Windermere for a short while before returning to marry Winifred Maud Bloore in Audley in 1915. He enlisted in Chester in December 1915 but was not mobilised until 15th May 1917 when he joined the Army Service Corps at Grove Park, service number M/32198. He transferred to the Motorized Transport Section 717 Company and embarked to France on 19th June 1917. He was based in St Omer.

Tom was 5 feet 10 inches tall and had a 37 inch chest. He remained in the M.T. Company until after the end of the war. He was discharged to the army reserve in January 1919. After the war Tom remained in Alsager and became a manager in a pottery factory. His son, Flying Officer Cranmer Kenneth Parkes, Royal Air Force, was killed in the Second World War and is commemorated on Alsager War Memorial.

## Sergeant Thomas Staley Pidduck: Royal Garrison Artillery

Thomas, born in 1886 in Wolstanton, Staffordshire, was the cousin of Norman Pidduck whose name appears on Alsager War Memorial. He was the son of Ellen and Thomas Pidduck. His father died before 1911. He studied at Repton School, Derbyshire. Before the Great War he was the manager of Fitton and Pidduck's Flour Mill, Burslem, Stoke-on-Trent. He married Gwendoline Settle on 19th June 1912 at St Mary's Church, Alsager. Gwendoline was the sister of Mellard and Reginald Settle both killed in the Great War. His daughter, Margaret Joan was born in 1914 and daughter Gwendoline Joyce in October 1916. They lived at the 'Woodlands', Crewe Road, Alsager.

He enlisted in the Royal Garrison Artillery service number 151385 on 28th March 1917 and served at home in England until August 1917. He was promoted Sergeant on 22nd August 1917 in 132 Battery Royal Garrison Artillery. On 26th August 1918 the Sentinel reported Thomas Pidduck was in hospital. He was hospitalised in the General Hospital Rouen on 7th August 1918. He was suffering from *'trench nephritis, severe inflammation of the kidneys'*. Thomas was transferred to the Borough Hospital, Birkenhead, on 18th August 1918. He was medically discharged from the service on 28th January 1919 and awarded a Silver War Badge on 21st February 1919. He received a £0. 13s. 0d. a week pension for his two children. He was awarded the Victory and British War Medals. Thomas Pidduck died in 1969.

### William James Pincher: Royal Fusiliers

*One of the first men to enlist in 1914.*

William James Pincher was born in Linley near Alsager in 1886 to Charles and Mary Pincher. Sometimes he gave his name as *Pinches* and several records are in that surname. Aged 14 he was working in a coal mine as a 'driver' pushing trucks. By 1911 he was living with his widowed mother and uncle and working as a coal hewer. He married Frances Ellen Tomlinson in the same year and they lived in Linley Lane. William enlisted on 9th November 1914 in the Royal Fusiliers in Burslem. He is recorded as being 5 feet 7 inches tall, 144 pounds and with brown hair. Following basic training he embarked to France on 27th July 1915 and fought with the 5th Battalion, A Company, service number 8975. After a year of service he was hospitalised with nephritis first at the 38th casualty clearing station and afterwards at the 10th District Hospital, Rouen, on 27th July 1916 before being evacuated to England on 20th August 1916. He recovered and was to be transferred to the Royal Engineers, 'Train Troops', but it appears this did not happen. On 14th May 1917 he was discharged from the army on medical grounds and awarded a silver war badge on 21st May 1917. In the same month he was awarded a pension of 8s 3d for 29 weeks. William was awarded the British War Medal and Victory medal. William and his family of three boys, Reginald, William, and Frank, remained in the Alsager area. William James died in 1929.

### Private George Bertram Pyatt: Royal Marines Light Infantry

George Pyatt was born in Harecastle, Kidsgrove on 12th February 1897. His parents were Mary and George Pyatt. His father was a blacksmith and later innkeeper at the Lodge Inn, Alsager. George's brother Clarence Pyatt was born in 1898, Eric in 1906, and his sister Edith in 1900. Edith Pyatt was to work at Rode Hall Hospital during the war doing ironing duties. George left school at thirteen and went to work in the collieries near Kidsgrove. At the outbreak of war George went to Liverpool on 3rd September 1914 and enlisted in the Royal Navy and was transferred to Deal, Kent to a training depot. As he was under age he was not allowed to go on active service until he reached the age of eighteen in February 1915. George was assigned to the Royal Marines Light Infantry at Plymouth and between 1st January 1916 and 8th September 1917 he served aboard MHS Columbella, marine number 17118. The Columbella was mainly engaged in inshore waters patrolling and on convoy duty. In 1917 George returned to duty in Plymouth in the Royal Marine then in 1918 he served on *HMS Roxburgh* which was one of six Devonshire-class armoured cruisers built for the Royal Navy. During his service on the ship the *Roxburgh* rammed a German submarine while escorting a convoy. In 1919 George joined the Royal Navy Reserve and continued to re-enlist every five years until the start of the Second World War. In 1940 he joined *HMS Valiant* in the spring of that year. Valiant was part of a fleet which included the HMS Ark Royal. It was engaged in firing near Scapa Flow and in patrols off the Norwegian coast. On 9th June from 23.45 hours to early the next morning the convoy was under German air attack by six aircraft but avoided damage. On 26th June Valiant departed Scapa Flow for Gibraltar as the French Fleet had surrendered to the enemy and the Italians had declared war on the allies. In late July 1940 George was deemed too old to continue in the ranks and was discharged. In 1942 he returned to Crewe Road Alsager and obtained a job as postman in Stoke-on-Trent. He was one of the few Alsager men who served in both World Wars. George Pyatt died in 1961.

### Sergeant Fred Roberts: Royal Field Artillery

*Photograph: The Sentinel.*

Frederick John Roberts was born in Fenton, Stoke on Trent, in 1883. His father John was a chemist. His family moved to live in Talke Road, Alsager in the 1890s and on leaving school Fred became a storekeeper. In 1905 Fred joined the Royal Field Artillery, service number 43836, having already spent some time in the Militia. His service record describes him as 5 feet 8 inches tall, with dark brown hair and eyes. Fred joined the 16th Battalion and embarked to India with his regiment. He transferred to the 28th Field Battery RFA remaining in India for several years. His regiment returned to Europe following the outbreak of the war. He was promoted Corporal on 22nd December 1914 and embarked to France on 17th January 1915. He was promoted Sergeant on 11th June 1915. On 6th

215

September 1915 a shell landed by him and his gun crew, blowing one man to pieces and blowing Roberts several yards. Comrades did not expect to find him alive. The army report says the wounds were *'accidental'* which implies the shell was from a British gun. According to the Nantwich Guardian, 15th September 1915, his left hand was blown off by the shell. The newspaper gave his home address as Talke Road, Alsager. He was discharged from the army on 21st January 1916. He applied to the army in 1916 for *'an artificial limb'* so he could re-join the war effort but he was not readmitted to the ranks. In 1916 Fred was living in Station Road, Alsager. He wore an official armlet to show he was unable to fight because of his injuries. He was awarded a Silver Award Badge on 25th June 1918 and was awarded the 1914/15 Star, Victory Medal, and British War Medal in 1922.

### Gunner Samuel Malkin Shaw: Royal Garrison Artillery

Samuel Malkin Shaw was the son of William and Eva Shaw, Mona Terrace, Crewe Road, Alsager. Sam left school and worked as a joiner. He served with the Royal Garrison Artillery, being attested 29th December 1915. He was posted to Athlone, Ireland in the 25th Reserve Battery in 1916. On 1st February 1917 he was posted to 327 Heavy Siege Battery after qualifying as a *Skilled Wheeler* at Ordnance College, Woolwich Barracks. Posted to France and Belgium with 327th Siege Battery he sailed from Southampton on the 12th May 1917 and disembarked Le Havre on the 13th .The Battery fought at Messines in 1917 and Cambrai in 1918. The battery became part of the Australian forces. The battery was eventually merged with other heavy artillery groups. Sam was wounded (gassed) in 1917 from the effects of a gas shell but recovered to serve until 1919. Sam Shaw was the landlord of the Lodge Inn for many years. Sam died in 1992 aged 97; the last Great War soldier from Alsager to

die.

*Sam Malkin Shaw, in St Mary's Choir. Photo Alec Shaw.*

Sam Shaw was awarded the Victory Medal and the British War Medal

*Sam Shaw. Taken at Alsager carnival in fancy dress the 1920s) Photograph: South Cheshire Archives Crewe.*

## Gunner James Sherratt: Royal Field Artillery

James Sherratt was born in 1898. He worked as a carter before the war and enlisted in the Royal Field Artillery on 24th June 1915, service number 100124. He initially worked as a driver with the 5th Reserve Brigade until being posted to France on 26th June 1915 with 379 Battery RFA. On 3rd October 1916 he suffered a gunshot wound to his left eye and was evacuated to a field hospital and afterwards to the Colonial Red Cross Hospital, Poole, Dorset. Following treatment and recovery he was posted to home duties before returning to France on 16th May 1917 to 379 Battery. In August 1917 he was gassed but did not suffer permanent injury but complained of having to vomit periodically (Medical Record). In August 1918 he suffered injury to his feet from shelling and was evacuated to England after treatment at the 8th General Hospital, Rouen, France. Following rehabilitation he worked as a driver at Ripon Depot, Yorkshire until being posted to the Army Reserve in March 1919. John married Ethel Irene Daysh in 1918 in Hampshire and returned to live in Well Lane, Alsager, after the war. In 1919 he was became a porter with the North Staffordshire Railway Company based in Harecastle, Kidsgrove. He joined the National Union of Railwaymen in 1919. James was a member of the Alsager War Memorial Committee in 1919. He was awarded the 1914/15 Star, the Victory Medal, and the British War Medal.

## Corporal John Sherratt: Machine Gun Corps, previously 1/5th North Staffs Regt.

John Sherratt, brother of James Sherratt, was born in Alsager in 1894 to Betsy and Joseph Sherratt. His sister was named Minnie. The family lived in Station Road. John's father was a platelayer with the North Staffordshire Railway Company. John worked for George Edwards (Alsager) as a *'carter'*. He was five feet six inches tall with a chest measurement of thirty three inches. John initially joined the 5th Battalion North Staffordshire Regiment Territorial Force in 1910. He gave his age as seventeen years four months. He underwent annual camp training at Buxton, Abergavenny and

Aberystwyth for three consecutive years. He embarked to France with the North Staffordshire Regiment on 5th March 1915, service number 2580 in 8 Platoon B Company, and was promoted Corporal. He was transferred to the Machine Gun Corps later that year, service number 21863. He was demobbed on 19th February 1919. He was awarded the 1914/15 Star, the Victory Medal, and the British War Medal.

### Sick Berth Attdt. Joseph Simcox: Royal Navy

*Served at the battle of Jutland*

Joseph Simcox was born in Hartshill, Stoke-on-Trent on 2nd August 1888. His father, Arthur, was a gardener. His mother's name was Louise. The family moved to Talke Road, Alsager after 1901. He was an *'Under Brakeman'* on the railway. He enlisted in the Royal Navy in on 17th August 1912, service number M4920 and trained at Victory 1 base in Portsmouth. He was 5 feet 5 inches tall with a 37 inch chest, dark brown hair and blue eyes. He served on HMS Hospital Ship *Plassy* between 1914 to May 9th 1918. *Plassy* was involved in major evacuations from France. In late 1914 the 3rd Engineer Morgan wrote

*'On October 25th 1914 the Plassy was sent to Calais, where horrible sights met the eyes of the ship's company. There had been tremendous fighting on the previous days, resulting in 5000 Belgian casualties, and the sufferers had been brought to Calais in readiness for transportation to England. The unfortunate men were in a terrible condition. Apart from their ghastly wounds they were mud-stained and dirty, not having had their boots or clothes off for about four weeks. The Plassy, was fitted up exactly like a hospital, with two operating theatres, doctors, nurses, attendants, etc. As quickly as possible the wounded were taken on board and surgically treated, the ghastly consignments periodically made to the furnaces speaking eloquently of the severity of the operations. Public print is not a place in which to describe the fearful sights and odours provided by the shattered and decaying members of the gallant Belgians, who bore their sufferings with fortitude. On the trip to Southampton the Plassy carried 620 wounded, 400 in cots and 200 of the less seriously hurt on deck. On arrival the wounded were put ashore as quickly as possible, and the vessel raced back to Calais, where another contingent waited. They were homeless and foodless, having been driven before the Germans. The next trip was to Dunkirk, where there was greater excitement than at Calais, owing to the proximity of the Germans, the guns being distinctly heard. While the Plassy was in port two Taubes tried to bomb the town, but four Allied airmen drove off the raiders. The Entente Cordiale was unmistakably evident, for French and British submarines and destroyers were lying side by side in the harbour, virtually "rubbing noses". Monitors, something like big armoured punts, left Dunkirk in the morning, peppered the Germans on the sand dunes during the day, and returned to the port at night.*

*During the Plassy's visit a torpedo boat captured two vessels laden with 65,000 bags of flour for the Germans at Ostend and brought them into Dunkirk. Immediately this haul was secured, the French erected ovens in all the cargo sheds on the water front, and turned out bread at a great rate. So, that instead of the 65,000 bags of flour feeding the Germans, they were transformed into bread for the Allies fighting at Dixmude and that locality.*

*It was at this time that a French ship laden with refugees bound for England was torpedoed and sunk, though its human freight was fortunately saved. The Plassy had to lie at anchor while this French ship was loading, and took her berth when she sailed.*

*By this time French wounded had arrived in Dunkirk, and they were in an even worse plight than the Belgians at Calais. They were in a truly horrible state. As they were taken from the trains they were laid on the quay. Then the stretchers were carried to the ship's side, put in a cradle and lowered into the hold. Apart from wounded, the refugees who had crowded into the port made a heartrending picture.'*

In 1916 the *Plassy* was involved in helping the wounded from the battle of Jutland including survivors from HMS Tiger on 31st May 1916. One officer and nineteen ratings died on board HMS Tiger at the Battle of Jutland.

*Jutland survivors aboard HMS HS Plassy 1916. Picture: Wikipedia*

In May 1918 Symcox joined *HMS Hospital Ship Karapara* as a Sick Berth Steward. The Karapara had 300 beds and 240 medical staff. After the war Joseph remained in the navy serving in Malta and on *HMS Calipso* until 1927 earning a long service and good conduct medal. In 1922 he qualified as a Sick Berth Principal Officer. After the navy Joseph lived in Portsmouth with his wife Winifred and died in March 1967. He was awarded the 1914/15 Star, Victory Medal and British War Medal.

### Lt. Joseph Frederic Lacy Spite: Royal Field Artillery

Joseph Spite was born in Tunstall on 18th January 1893 and moved to Alsager before 1911 and lived in 'Sunnyside'. He worked as an insurance clerk. His father, Robert, was a carriage builder. In 1914 Joseph married Kathleen Burgess and they moved to a house in Sandbach Road, Alsager. He enlisted in the Royal Field Artillery, service number 805810, in late 1914 and quickly gained promotion to Acting Sergeant. He fought in France from February 1915. He applied for a commission and gained it on 23rd November 1917, the notice appearing in the London Gazette on 4th December 1917. He returned to his regiment as 2nd Lieutenant but on 21st March 1918 he was captured at Bullecourt during the German spring offensive and taken to Germany as a prisoner of war to the officer's camp at Karlsruhe. Karlsruhe was described as a distribution camp for officers. He was then sent to Pforzheim, Baden. He was repatriated on 11th December 1918. After an enquiry he was exonerated from blame for being captured by the enemy and is on the *'exonerated officers list'*. Being exonerated was a condition of being entitled to his campaign medals. Joseph was awarded the 1914/15 Star, the British War Medal and Victory Medal. After the war Joseph returned to insurance work. In the Second World War he was an ARP 'Contract Officer' He died in 1968. His brother, Norman Spite, born 1896, served with the King's Liverpool Regiment and Labour Corps.

219

# Rev. Harold Augustine Thomas

*Photo St Mary Magdalene Church.*

Harold Thomas was the Assistant Curate in Alsager between 1912 and 1915 and kept close links with the parish after enlisting in the Army as a private soldier. He was an outgoing and personable man who enjoyed taking part in community events. Harold was of the few men who served in all three services, army, navy, and RAF in the Great War. He worked as a Naval Chaplain between 1916 and 1919.

Harold Augustine Thomas was born in Tonge Moor Lancashire in 1883. His father Francis Thomas was a Church of England clergyman originally from Caernarvonshire. His mother, Frances, was from Lincolnshire. Harold had three siblings, Norah born in 1885, Wilfred born in 1886, and Madge born in 1895.

In the 1901 Census the family was shown as living in the vicarage, Chorlton Cum Hardy, Lancashire. After school Harold gained a B.A. at Jesus College Oxford, the *Welsh College* as it was known in Oxford. He was awarded a Meyricke Scholarship at Jesus College for academic performance in 1905. To qualify the Scholarship or Exhibition is based on the recommendation of the students tutor to the July meeting of Governing Body. He passed his Classical Moderations examination in 1905 and gained a B.A in English Language and Literature in 1907, and was awarded an M.A in 1913.

After university Harold followed his father into the church and in 1909 was appointed Curate in Runcorn, Cheshire where he served until 1912.

*The Manchester Courier and Lancashire General Advertiser on 20 December 1909 announced Harold's appointment of Deacon at All Saint's Runcorn.*

DEACONS.

George Anderson, B.A., of Trinity College, Dublin, licensed to St. George's, Stockport; Bertram Harold Pemberton, L.Th., of the University of Durham, of St. Paul's Missionary College, Burgh, and of St. Stephen's House, Oxford, licensed to St. Peter's, Stockport; Harold Augustine Thomas, B.A., of Jesus College, Oxford, licensed to All Saints', Runcorn; John Robert Towers, L.Th., of the University of

Three years later, in 1912, Harold became Assistant Curate to Rev. Waller in Alsager being inducted by the Bishop of Chester on 14th March 1912. Later that year the Staffordshire Sentinel said he organized church garden parties, and children's church activities in the parish. Harold was also the opening batsman for Alsager Cricket Club in 1912.

ALSAGER v. WOLSTANTON AMATEURS.

Alsager.—Rev H A Thomas c Hammond b Pemberton 32, G Clarke c Cooper b Pemberton 10, R Bloore c Brosd b Pemberton 4, W Jenkinsne b Roberts 3, F Ehrill c Lloyd b Roberts 3, F Bailer b Pemberton 0, V Edwards c Wilkinson b Pemberton 1, J Henshaw not out 16, R Alcock not out 2, extras 5; total (for seven wickets) 76.

Thomas soon became a popular and active member of the church community helping to organise parish garden parties. During his time as a curate Harold lived in a house in 'The Fields' Alsager

After war was declared Harold was unsure whether to enlist or remain in Alsager as Curate because the vicar was *'incapacitated with blindness from carrying on alone ... It was my duty to stop'*. In the end he decided to go but there were *'moments of strain'* when he discussed the proposal with his fiancée. In his memoirs he said the vicar was distressed when he told him he has going to join the army but *'helpful'*. He fought with his conscience and joined the Royal Army Medical Corps, service number 2549. He gave his farewell sermon at St Mary's on Sunday 29th May 1915 to a packed congregation and special Whitsuntide music was sung by the choir. Without medical qualifications Harold could only join the RAMC as a private soldier working as an orderly. He did his basic training in Norfolk in a camp containing thirty thousand troops. Harold wrote letters back to Alsager detailing the difficulties he encountered such as having to sleep in rat infested barns with twenty one other soldiers but he still found life *'phenomenally lazy'* compared with being a Curate. He also encountered hostility when he tried to pray but it only strengthened his Christian faith. He said tea and dry bread was the staple diet for the troops. On July he moved to Thetford and lived under canvas, twelve to a tent. On 29th July 1915 Thomas left Devonport for Suvla Bay, Turkey, and arrived on 15th August with the 2/3 East Anglian Field Ambulance (54th Division). He worked in field hospitals close to the front line in Suvla Bay and Anzac Cove and wrote letters to Alsager describing stretcher bearers struggling to bring the wounded back from casualty clearing stations.

LETTERS FROM THE FRONT.

Copy of letter received by the Vicar on Sept. 3rd, 1915.

Private H. A. Thomas, No. 2549.
1/3 East Anglian F. H. Amb. B. Section.
Mediterranean Exp. Force.

Dear Vicar,

Our voyage out was safely accomplished. We passed the usual ports, and had a march through an . . . . town. Then to an island base, and then in torpedo boats here last Sunday. We were moved up to the trenches that night, and began work at once. The fighting had been very fierce for 48 hours. Have been under all sorts of fire, rifle, shrapnel and big shells. Our camp receives attention by the latter twice a day. Yesterday I had 30 hours duty at a dressing station, and spent the night out on the hills. It was very cold and raining. The life here is of the roughest description, and we are mostly an unpresentable crew and quite unrecognisable. However we are all very cheerful, and I am quite well and standing it all in first class form. We have had losses already in our ambulance, and of course we never know our fortune from hour to hour, but have ceased to worry about that. I can not say anything about the operations in a military line, except that we are optimistic. It is boiling hot here in the day time, but very cold at night. I was very grieved to hear of young Robinson's death, and of Mrs. Serjeantson's accident. Please remember me to both families, and let this letter go to the Institute.

In great haste Yours ever,

H. A. THOMAS

*Alsager Parish Magazine, November 1915.*

He also wrote about the appalling blizzards encountered by the troops in November 1915.

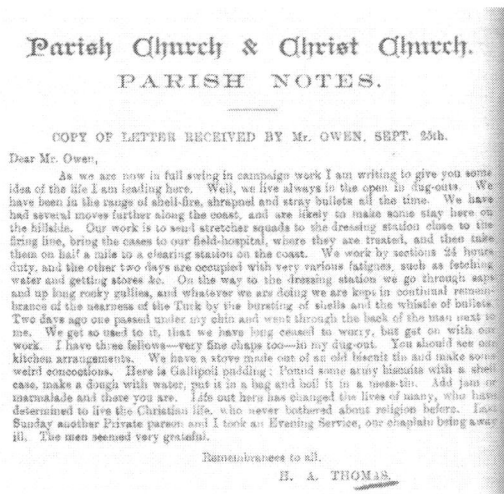

## Parish Church & Christ Church.

### PARISH NOTES.

COPY OF LETTER RECEIVED BY Mr. OWEN, SEPT. 25th.

Dear Mr. Owen,

As we are now in full swing in campaign work I am writing to give you some idea of the life I am leading here. Well, we live always in the open in dug-outs. We have been in the range of shell-fire, shrapnel and stray bullets all the time. We have had several moves further along the coast, and are likely to make some stay here on the hillside. Our work is to send stretcher squads to the dressing station close to the firing line, bring the cases to our field-hospital, where they are treated, and then take them on half a mile to a clearing station on the coast. We work by sections 24 hours duty, and the other two days are occupied with very various fatigues, such as fetching water and getting stores &c. On the way to the dressing station we go through saps and up long rocky gullies, and whatever we are doing we are kept in continual remembrance of the nearness of the Turk by the bursting of shells and the whistle of bullets. Two days ago one passed under my chin and went through the back of the man next to me. We get so used to it, that we have long ceased to worry, but get on with our work. I have three fellows—very fine chaps too—in my dug-out. You should see our kitchen arrangements. We have a stove made out of an old biscuit tin and make some weird concoctions. Here is Gallipoli pudding: Pound some army biscuits with a shell case, make a dough with water, put it in a bag and boil it in a mess-tin. Add jam or marmalade and there you are. Life out here has changed the lives of many, who have determined to live the Christian life, who never bothered about religion before. Last Sunday another Private parson and I took an Evening Service, our chaplain being away ill. The men seemed very grateful.

Remembrances to all.

H. A. THOMAS.

On 14th December his unit was evacuated from the front line. He was too ill to board ship to go to Alexandria by ship and was instead invalided to the Canadian Hospital Mudros where he remained until Christmas Eve. He then took the hospital ship Aquitania to England back from the Dardanelles arriving home on 2nd January 1916. He spent until 10th March in Southern General Hospital. Despite his experiences Harold applied to join the Army Chaplain Service but was rejected after being interviewed in February 1916, the interviewer commenting on his notes that Thomas was *'worn'*.

Not daunted, Harold applied for and gained a commission as a chaplain in the Royal Navy on 18th March. On March 19th Thomas returned to Alsager for a brief visit and addressed parishioners from the pulpit about his work with the Royal Army Medical Corps.

He gained his commission on 13th May 1916. On the same day he visited Alsager again. That same month, 18th May, he married Dorothy Lake in Runcorn, but had no time to settle down being appointed Acting Chaplain to HMS Lowestoft, a light cruiser working with the Mediterranean Fleet on 20th May. She was flagship of the 8th Light Cruiser Squadron in the Mediterranean. He served in the ship until May 1917 looking after the spiritual needs of the crew. The ship was involved in supplying troops in North Africa and Palestine, blockading enemy ships around the eastern Mediterranean and looking for German Submarine bases. He later served on HMS Devonshire in the Atlantic protecting convoys between Scotland and New York.

*HMS Lowestoft, 1917, in Lesbos, Greece. Photo Wikipedia*

In 1918 Harold Augustine Thomas was attached to the Royal Air Force as Chaplain/ Captain first at RAF Manston, Kent, at the School of Observers, becoming later responsible at RAF Uxbridge for the South East Area of England. He was Deputy Chaplain in Chief. He was demobilised on 19th December 1919. After the war he was awarded the title Honorary Chaplain to the R.A.F.

After the war Harold and Dorothy Thomas raised two children, Mark and Monica, and Harold returned to full time parish work. For his war service Harold was granted the 1914/5 Star, the Victory Medal, and the British War Medal.

*Harold's cigarette case, (Thomas family photograph.)*

In 1920 Harold became Curate of Melksham, Wiltshire until 1924, and became Vicar of St. Minver, Cornwall, then Vicar of Hove, 1945-53. He ended his career in Bexhill on Sea and died on 21st January 1960 aged 83. *The private papers of Rev H.A Thomas are held at the Imperial War Museum in London.*

### Staff Sergeant Richard Harold Timmis: Royal Army Medical Corps

Richard was born in 1880 in Barthomley. His sister Emma, was born in 1881, sister Florence Timmis was born in 1882, his brother Herbert was born in 1883, Peter in 1884, and his sister Violet in 1900. Richard's father was a farmer of Woodside House. The farm was situated adjacent to Crewe Road between the *Plough Inn* and Radway Green. Richard's mother, Emma, nee Thornhill, originated from Barthomley. After school Richard became a cashier on the railway with the North Staffordshire Railway Company. He married in 1911, Carrie Booth, of Alrewas, Staffordshire, and they came to live in Alsager. Richard enlisted in the Royal Army Medical Corps and rose to the rank of Staff Sergeant, service number 25213, during the war. He was awarded the British War Medal and Victory Medal, indicating he saw active Foreign Service after 1916. Richard lived in Alsager after the armistice and died in 1970 aged ninety. He was a member of the B'hoys Club of Alsager.

### Sapper Herbert Edward Timmis: Royal Engineers

Herbert Timmis was born in Alsager in 1883. After school in Alsager Herbert took employment with a pottery firm as a clerk. Herbert enlisted in the Royal Engineers, service number T 2366 with the rank of Sapper. Herbert survived the war and continued to live in Alsager until his death in 1957.

*Edwardian photograph of the Timmis Family. South Cheshire Archives*

**Lieutenant Reginald Tivey: M.C North Staffordshire Regiment**

*Photo: Tivey family archive*

Reginald Tivey was born 1888 in Birmingham, Warwickshire to printing clerk and commercial traveller Tom Brown Tivey and his wife Louisa Teresa Prince. He was the second of three sons (Harold and Tom Brown) and also had two sisters (Ida Eveline and Gladys). In May 1915 the Alsager Parish Magazine announced Reginald was serving with the North Staffordshire Regiment. He had served previous time in the Army when he attested for service in 1914. He enlisted in the 1/5th North Staffordshire Regiment, service number 3076, as a private soldier, and served in France and Belgium from 5th March 1915. He was commissioned 2nd Lieutenant on 29th May 1917. He earned the Military Cross for bravery on 6th June 1918. He was injured several times and spent time at the Military Hospital situated in Radcliffe on Trent in 1918. In 1919 he married Military Nurse Elizabeth 'Katie' Birks. After the war ended, despite suffering greatly with disability caused by war injuries, he worked as a clerk at the Customs and Excise office retiring with the distinguished rank of senior clerical officer in 1949. Reginald died in 1950 in Stafford. His medals and memorabilia along with his brother's medals were auctioned in 2012 realizing over £2,000.

*Tivey brothers' medals. Sale catalogue*

*Reginald Tivey (standing rear, second from right) Amcote Auxiliary Hospital, Radcliffe on Trent 1918*

Reginald was awarded the Military Cross, the 1914/15 Star, British War Medal, Victory Medal and Silver War Badge (no.176875/3 in 1919)

## Sergeant Tom Brown Tivey M.M: Northumberland Fusiliers

*War hero, novelist, explorer*

Born 1892 in Burslem, Wolstanton, Staffordshire, Tom was the fourth of the five children born to Louisa Teresa Tivey, and his father Tom Brown Tivey, with whom he shared an identical name. In 1911 the family were living close to St Mary's church, in The Avenue, Alsager, and Tom was working as a bank clerk with Lloyds. Wanting to travel Tom went to Canada and was working as a telephone switchboard operator at the Toronto Lunatic Asylum when war was declared. He returned home and joined the Leicestershire Regiment, Service number 16436, on 14th December 1914. Alsager Parish Magazine recorded him enlisting in early January 1915. He was promoted to Acting Corporal and then full Corporal on 21st January 1916 when embarking with the 2nd Battalion, Leicestershire Regiment to Mesopotamia (Modern Iraq). Suffering from malaria he recovered to see action against the Turks. He took part in the battle to recapture Baghdad, and after this was wounded on 24th April 1917 suffering a gunshot wound to his leg, the bullet passing right through it. Recovering in Baghdad and then in Basra Hospitals, he was injured again on 17th August 1917 with a severe gunshot wound to the chest. He was awarded the Military Medal on 21st December 1917 for gallantry. He transferred to the Northumberland Fusiliers, 2nd Garrison Battalion in Basrah, as he was no longer fit for the front line again. In 1918 he worked as a clerk for the Regiment still classified as a Sergeant. In late 1918 he suffered from influenza and was again in hospital in Basrah. He was discharged from the army in April 1919. After the war he returned to Canada and earned money as a fur trapper, explorer and writer. Later in life he returned home and married the sister of his brother's wife, Lilian Madge Birks. He took up writing fiction and successfully published several novels, becoming a crime novelist writing such works as *Marenka of Monteney, Trapline, A tale of the North, When Daylight Dies* and *Riddle of the Snows*. He died in Whitchurch, Shropshire in 1966 aged 73

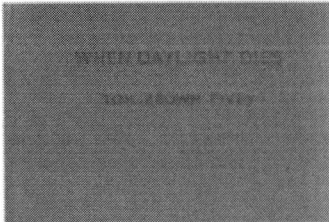

*Original cover: When daylight comes*

## Sick Berth Attendant Francis Rupert Walker: Royal Navy

Frank Walker was born 17th May 1887 in Alsager. The family lived in Crewe Road in 1901. He had four sisters and one brother. His father John was a 'Coal Dealer' and later worked at the Alsager waterworks. In 1911 when Frank was 23 he was working as a joiner but also volunteered with the local Ambulance Unit. His service record describes him as 5 feet 10 inches tall, 37 inch chest, hazel eyes, and brown hair. Alsager Parish Magazine describes him with the men who were serving in 1914.

In 1914 he was part of the incredible action to bring injured soldiers out of Belgium. His story, printed in the Nantwich Guardian in October 1914 conveys all the drama of the incident. The detail about spies is not exaggerated. Francis was part of the Naval Brigade sent into Belgium to assist the faltering Belgian army. After nearly a month of journeying from place to place by battleship, cattle truck and other vehicles he finally reached Lierre, Belgium on 4$^{th}$ October 1914. That night fighting commenced. The Germans used aeroplanes to identify the British troops who were dug in in trenches but the German artillery were able to target them easily. Within fifteen minutes Frank and his colleagues had more than thirty casualties to deal with. They established a base hospital at a public house and the surgeon came in and asked for six volunteers to go to the trenches. Frank's friend Billy went and was hit in the eye. The Brigade began to retreat and were forced to defend themselves in a village about five miles from Antwerp. They developed another base hospital in a public house and dug trenches in the garden. A dispatch rider arrived and said they were almost surrounded so they decided to make a dash for it. They filled the motor ambulance with the wounded and they managed to get through to safety. The unit could not understand how their positions had been given away. They had been accompanied for a couple of days by 2 female Belgian nurses. No one suspected them but a piece of paper fell out of one of the nurse's pockets when she was attending to a wounded soldier it was clear that she was writing down all British troop movements with the intention of passing the information to the enemy. The two women were immediately taken away and shot.

Writing to Mr E. Rushworth, Superintendent of Alsager Royal Corps of Ambulance, First Sergeant Smith spoke of the bravery of Walker, Bevan, and the others men who worked under *'galling fire'* for five days at Lierre and Oude God near Antwerp.

Frank returned home and then resumed his duties on *HMS Pembroke*, service number, M9788 as Royal Naval Auxiliary Sick Berth Reserve Attendant (R.N.A.S.B.R.). *HMS Pembroke* was a training establishment. In December 1915 Frank was working on the hospital trains bringing the injured back to the French Ports. According to the Nantwich Guardian he was unable to attend the marriage of his sister, Sarah, in St Mary's Church, Alsager. He served throughout the war until demobilisation in 1919. In 1939 he was the licensee of an inn in Salford. He was awarded the 1914 Star with clasp, The Victory Medal and the British War Medal. His Great War medals were sold at Auction in 2007. F.R Walker died in Salford in 1947.

## Percy Walker: Royal Garrison Artillery

:

*Percy Walker, sitting centre. Photo: Sentinel Newspaper.*

Percy Walker was born in 1896. He was one of three brothers who all fought in the war. John William and Alfred Walker all served in the artillery like Percy. Although they were all born in Worcestershire they came to live in Audley Road. Percy lived most of his life at 79 Audley Road. When he enlisted he was working as a shop assistant but soon took to army life and was promoted Corporal and then Sergeant. In later years Percy worked as a sales representative for a mail order firm.

## Private Robert Ashley Watson: Royal Marines Light Infantry.

Robert was born in Barthomley on 1894. His father, Ephraim, was a schoolmaster at the National School Alsager. In 1911 he worked as a 'Lamp Man' for the North Staffordshire Railway Company but the following year joined the merchant navy and became a waiter working aboard SS Franconia. On 12th June 1912 he joined the Royal Navy and trained in Deal, Kent, joining the Royal Marine Light Infantry, service number 17437. In 1913 he served on *HMS Implacable* and in 1914 *HMS Antrim*. On 10th July 1915 he joined *HMS Duncan* based at Taranto to reinforce the Italian Fleet in the Adriatic. This force had been formed in May 1915 to reinforce the Italian Navy in bottling up the navy of Austro-Hungary. The formation of the force had been part of the agreement in which Italy joined the allies in the war. Robert was invalided from Italy on 22nd November 1915 arriving home on 6th December 1915. He remained at Chatham Kent until 3rd March 1916 when he was discharged from the navy. He went to live with his sister Hilda Oulton in Shrewsbury and not to remaining family in Cheshire. He died from his war injuries in 1923 in Shrewsbury.

### Private Arthur Wood: Northumberland Fusiliers

The brother of William Wood killed in action in 1915, Arthur was born in September 1892. He grew up in Crewe Road where his father ran a grocery business. After school he trained to be a bricklayer with George Edwards's builders, of Crewe Road. Arthur was one of the first to enlist in August 1914 joining the 7th Battalion of the North Staffordshire Regiment, service number 15819. He trained in Britain before embarking to Gallipoli in October 1915 with the 7th Battalion. After the British army withdrawal from Turkey, Arthur was taken to Egypt where he served for three years on the Mesopotamia front in Asmara and Baghdad. From January 1916 he served as a Private in the Northumberland Fusiliers, service number 76990. In 1916 he suffered his first bout of malaria and spent time in the Base Hospital Asmara, and later in Baghdad. He also suffered from sandfly. After the Armistice Arthur was transferred to India where he served until March 1919. After discharge Arthur returned to Alsager but soon moved to the USA to make a home in New York. He married Grace, from Ireland, and they raised a family. Arthur worked as a stone mason in New York. He died in 1975 and is buried in Broome, New York. Arthur was awarded the 1914/15 Star, the British War Medal and the Victory Medal.

### Myrtle Annie Wood: Queen Mary's Army Auxiliary Corps

*Photo Sentinel*

Myrtle Annie Wood, sister of Arthur and William, was born in Alsager in 1894 and lived with her family in Crewe Road. Her father was a grocer. She was an *'assistant home worker'*, a domestic servant, before the Great War. She then qualified as a librarian to *'A1 standard'*, and at the outbreak of war went to work in a munitions factory in Aintree, Liverpool for two and a half years. In May 1918 she joined the Queen Mary's Army Auxiliary Corps as a VAD, service number 40164, and moved to the south of England for training. In July 1918 she was posted to serve in France and Belgium, and remained in the service until leaving the Corps on 20th December 1920. She married John Carley in 1923 and died in 1976.

Myrtle was awarded the British War Medal, and the Victory Medal.

*Her brother, William Wood, on the Alsager War Memorial, was killed in action in April 1916.*

*Wood's Grocers, Crewe Road, Alsager, Myrtle Wood, right. Photo: South Cheshire Archives, Crewe.*

### Charlie Young: King's Shropshire Light Infantry

Charlie Young was born in Alsager, in 1898 to Alice and William Young. His father was a domestic gardener. The family lived in Lawton Road and moved to Shady Grove during the Great War. He was employed as a blacksmith's apprentice. Charlie enlisted in Crewe on 19th August 1916 but was placed in the Army Reserve because of his occupation. He was mobilised on 16th April 1917 in the King's Shropshire Light Infantry as a Private soldier, service number 204194. He enlisted in the 2nd Battalion but was transferred in October 1917 to the 1st Battalion which served on the Western Front and took part in the great Passchendaele Offensive (3rd Battle of Ypres). In January 1918, the battalion was serving with 5th Army and met the brunt of the great German Spring Offensive on 21st March, being just about annihilated at Lagnicourt; not one combatant officer was left and only 53 other ranks came out of the action alive. The battalion was completely re-formed under Lt. Col. Meynell and within ten days of being all but destroyed, was back in the line at Ypres. Charlie went missing on 22nd March 1918 and on 19th April was designated a prisoner of war. He was in Munster and Friedricksfeld prisoner of war camps and was repatriated to England in December 1918. He was transferred to the 4th Battalion and served at home until 16th September 1919 when he was discharged. He married Beatrice Dakin in 1920.

# Military Awards gained by people with Alsager connections in the Great War

**Military Cross. 7 awards:** Captain Robert Ellis M.B; 2nd Lt. Hubert John Goss; Major Vernon Goss; 2nd Lt. William R.G Holland; 2nd Lt. Victor Maddock; 2nd Lt. Gerald Wylly Palfreyman; Lt. Reginald Tivey

**Military Medal. 7 awards:** Private William Affleck; Private James Henry Baylis; Private Ernest Fletcher; Private Tom Mayer; Corporal Albert Edward Riley; Sergeant Tom Brown Tivey

**Distinguished Service Order (D.S.O.). 2 awards:** Lt. Col Harry Johnson; Lt. Claud Herbert Godwin

**Mentioned in Despatches.6 awards:** Captain Robert Ellis; Private Frank Glover; Lt. Claud Herbert Godwin; Major George Spencer Jacobs; 2nd Lt. Gerald Wylly Palfreyman; 2nd Lt. Norman Andrews Pidduck

**Croix de Guerre (France). 2 awards:** Major Vernon Goss; Lt. Arthur Victor Maddock

**Médaille Militaire (France). 1 award:** Fireman Francis Jepson.

**The 1914 Star, the 1914/15 Star, Victory Medal, British War Medal: Numerous awards. Individual details are provided in biographies**

# The 'Roll of Honor'

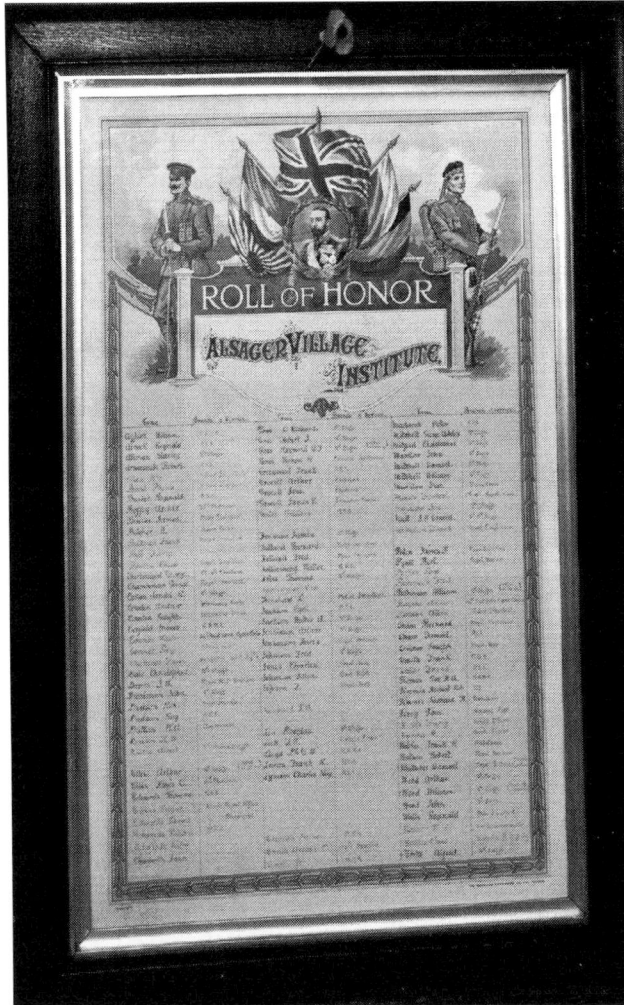

A Roll of Honour hangs in Alsager Town Council offices listing servicemen in the Great War. It does not include all the servicemen who enlisted. In some cases men changed regiment and only their first regiment is listed on the roll. It is unknown why the Roll has the American spelling of 'Honor.' The template for the document was printed in Birmingham. The Nantwich Guardian of 10th March 1916 stated it refers to men who were members of Alsager Institute. It records at the end of August 1917 one hundred and two members of the Institute were on the Roll of Honor. The Roll pictured has one hundred and ten Members of Alsager Institute who served in the war. It demonstrates the importance of Alsager Institute in the life of the town.

# Alsager in 1919. Celebration and Remembrance

## The British Red Cross Alsager War Working Party

In April 1919 The British Red Cross Alsager War Working Party concluded its meetings after four and a half years. They started work on 10th August 1914 and since had collected £688.3s.3d and made 5443 garments for servicemen. They had a balance in hand of £70 6s.8d which was distributed as follows: Alsager Club Room, £2; Alsager War Memorial £10; Lord Robert's Memorial, £10; Sailor's Society, £10; St Dunstan's Hostel £38.6s.8d.

On 27th March 1919 the last patients at Rode Hall Hospital were transferred to Stoke hospital. 5050 men were cared for there between 1917 and 1919. In the London Gazette, Supplement 31840, Page 3830, the Officer in Charge of the hospital, Katharine Ffoulkes was awarded the O.B.E.

## The Peace Celebrations 1919

Victory and peace celebrations were postponed until summer and were combined with the annual Alsager Carnival held on 19th July 1919. The following description comes from the Sentinel. A *'Grand spectacular parade'* led by Kidsgrove Town Band paraded through the town to the Parsonage Field. (Now Alsager School playing fields behind Christ Church.) The rejoicing began with the ringing of the bells from 9am until noon. Prizes were awarded for various sections: *Tableaux on Wheeled Vehicles; Decorated Cycle and Costume; Fancy Costume; Decorated Perambulators with child.*

Special prizes for Character Costume were restricted to Service and ex-Servicemen. The winners were Messrs. Henshaw and Lea, second were Messrs. Parkes and Fletcher, and third Mr Sherratt. Others taking part were the Fire Brigade, the Chairman and Members of the District Council, and a large contingent of commissioned officers and NCOs, Service and Ex Servicemen, who were loudly cheered all along the route. On the Parsonage Field (Alsager School) sports were held through the afternoon and at 4pm all the children between the ages of four and sixteen were entertained to tea. At 5.30pm the committee entertained to tea the Service and ex-Servicemen, with their wives, and the dependents of those who had fallen in the war. The Chairman of the Council, Mr T. Owen extended to them a hearty welcome on behalf of the people of Alsager, remarking it was the day they had been looking forward to for the past four or five years. He sincerely hoped that *'we should soon be enjoying peace in the industrial world'*. He also invited the participants to a *'whist drive and dance'*. Those who had fallen had not been forgotten, a temporary monument having been fixed, with a Union Flag flying at half-mast and a laurel wreath attached to it.

 It bore the words *'Ye that live on, mid England's pastures green, Remember us and think what might have been'*

After the prize-giving for the sports the proceedings concluded at 10.30 pm with a display of fireworks and the National Anthem.

*A blurred but important photo from the Sentinel, 1919, of the carnival and peace celebrations moving past St Mary's Church. Children are riding on a hay wain in the procession. (Note Milton House in the background and the high wall that once surrounded the garden.)*

*Peace celebration in August 1919 at Rode Hall. Young ladies representing the allies*

In October 1919 the parish magazine announced fundraising for a memorial window for those former pupils of St Mary's (Sunday) School killed in the Great War. £90 had been raised and Messrs Heaton, Butler and Baines designed the two light window, to be situated on the south side of the church. The window represented St Alban and St George. No names are given for those the window commemorates, but we know the following former pupils were killed in the Great War: *Henry Jenkinson, Norman Pidduck, Frank Lucas, Reg and Mellard Settle, Cyril Jackson, Robert Dickinson, and the Goss brothers, Hubert and Raymond, Frank Glover, and William Robinson. Frank Marfleet and Christopher Mitford.*

*The window constitutes a registered war memorial with the Imperial War Museum (reference 42743). The official description: Stained glass window of two main lights with additional tracery lights above. Left light depicts St George. Right light depicts St Alban. Photo: Author*

## The Planning and Building of the Alsager War Memorial

The word cenotaph means *'empty tomb'*. War memorials and cenotaph have a special emotional importance. Why did so many towns and in Britain raise considerable amounts of money to build them? The reason must be that most people could not afford to visit military cemeteries overseas and many of the fallen had no known grave so British cenotaphs and memorials became places where people could grieve and pay their respects. In 1921 King George V participated in a remembrance service at the cenotaph in London for the first time. The form of that service, with minor changes, has remained and been used throughout the country since then.

The First Official Armistice Day was held in the grounds of Buckingham Palace on the morning of 11th November 1919. The first Two Minute Silence in London (11th November 1919) was reported in the *Manchester Guardian* on 12th November 1919. *'The first stroke of eleven produced a magical effect. The tram cars glided into stillness, motors ceased to cough and fume, and stopped dead, and the mighty-limbed dray horses hunched back upon their loads and stopped also, seeming to do it of their own volition. Someone took off his hat, and with a nervous hesitancy the rest of the men bowed their heads also. Here and there an old soldier could be detected slipping unconsciously into the posture of 'attention'. An elderly woman, not far away, wiped her eyes, and the man beside her looked white and stern. Everyone stood very still ... The hush deepened. It had spread over the whole city and become so pronounced as to impress one with a sense of audibility. It was a silence which was almost pain ... And the spirit of memory brooded over it all...'*

In 1918 a collection was held in St Mary's towards a war memorial but nothing of significance happened until 11th July 1919 when Alsager Urban District Council, Cheshire, resolved to form a committee of the whole of the council, *'with powers to add to their number ...celebrating peace by providing a memorial.'* *'The Druids, and Foresters, to be asked to send one representative each. Two representatives of discharged, demobilised soldiers or sailors be appointed.'* Also, *'two ladies to be appointed from Alsager Ladies Bowling Society.'*

The Druids and Foresters were Friendly Societies which provided life insurance. The war memorial committee was formed and later joined by the following clergymen: Rev. S.P. Hadley, Rev. A.H. Waller, and Rev. A. Burgoine. The demobilised servicemen who joined the committee were former soldiers: J. Sherratt, W. Hollinshead, and J. Henshaw. Two ladies from Alsager Bowling Society were invited to join. Miss J. Horsley was nominated to participate. The council surveyor was tasked with commissioning a monument and the committee set about raising funds for its construction.

**Other prominent members of the War Memorial Committee:**

**Councillor Arthur Henry Maddock**

*Photo: Cheshire Archives*

**Arthur Henry Maddock,** father of Lt V. Maddock, was a prominent Alsager councillor and by profession an earthenware manufacturer in the Potteries. He lived at *'The Cedars'*, Alsager. His son won the Military Cross in the war.

### Rev. Alfred Waller, Vicar of Alsager 1913-24

Alfred Hamilton Waller was the son of the Rev. Charles Henry (University College, Oxford, 1859) [sometime Principal of the London College of Divinity]. He was born on 25th October 1867, in Islington London. He gained a B.A. 1889 and an M.A. in 1902. He was ordained a deacon in Canterbury in 1890; and as a priest in 1891. He was the Curate of Tonbridge, 1890-3; Curate of St John's, Waterloo, Liverpool, 1893-1902; Curate of Hoole, Cheshire, 1902-5. He died suddenly in 1924. His nephew, C.R. Waller, is commemorated on the Alsager War Memorial.

### Dr Henry Crutchley M.D.

Henry Crutchley was born in Shropshire in 1840. He served as Alsager's medical practitioner for many years. He donated the land, adjacent to Sandbach Road and Ashmore's Lane, for the Alsager War Memorial to be built. In retirement he lived in *Holmcroft* next to the memorial. Henry Crutchley died in 1923.

**Thomas Frederick Owen: Chairman of Alsager Urban District Council**

*Photo: Cheshire Archives*

Thomas Frederick Owen was born in Chorlton, Manchester in 1858 but grew up in Eccleshall and later in Stoke-on-Trent. He opened a grocery business in Alsager after 1901 and served as Chairman of the District Council in 1921. During the war he worked as a driver for Rode Hall Hospital giving lifts to patients. He lived at the 'Wood' Alsager. He worked hard to make the war memorial project successful. He unveiled the Alsager War Memorial in 1920. He died in March 1924.

**William Huntley Goss: Councillor and prominent ceramic manufacturer in Stoke-on-Trent.**

He lost two nephews in the Great War. He worked tirelessly for the War Memorial project.

*Photo: Cheshire Archives*

## Adolphus Goss

One of Alsager's greatest men, Adolphus Henry William Goss was born in Marylebone, London in 1854. He was a ceramic designer and creator of many of the 'Goss' ceramic miniatures of the 'Heraldic' design in the family firm, W.H. Goss & Sons, in the Potteries. Adolphus was responsible for the introduction of the heraldic design and many of the verses which accompanied them. He lived in several houses in Alsager during his life principally 'The Old Villa', in Sandbach Road. He was one of the founders and first President of the B'hoys, organisation which did so much for the fundraising for the Alsager British Legion. He gave the B'hoys a two handled shillelagh which is to be seen on the President's table at each meeting. Adolphus Goss lost two sons in the war and became the first President of Alsager British Legion after its formation in 1925. During the Great War he served as Chairman of the Alsager Military Appeals Tribunal from January 1916 hearing the cases of men who wished to be exempted from conscription. He was also Chairman of the War Savings Committee and was also Vice Chairman of the Congleton Division, Cheshire Red Cross Financial Committee, during the Great War. He was instrumental in sponsoring the 'Goss' stained glass window in St Mary Magdalene Church commemorating his sons. Adolphus was also a member of the Meteorological Society and The Field Club, and was a sidesman at St Mary's Church and was responsible for much of the fundraising to build the church in 1898. He was a good amateur photographer and gardener. He presented his collection of photographs to St Mary's Church. He was a lifelong Conservative and Unionist and councillor in Alsager. He died in February 1934.

Goss wrote for one of his heraldic designs: *'Seeke out the good / in every man/ And speake of all/ the best that you can/Then will all men speake well of thee/ And say how kind of harte you be'*

## The work of the War Memorial Committee

The war memorial committee began its work in 1918 and several proposals were submitted for consideration:

Endowment of a bed in the North Staffordshire Infirmary

Provision of a Recreation Ground

Provision of an open air swimming bath

Erection of a monument: one half of funds for the monument and the remainder for the dependents of the fallen

A memorial window in the Parish Church

A building of a Tower for the Parish Church with a chiming clock and a Memorial Tablet

Over the following months fundraising commenced and the various proposals were debated and altered by the committee. It was decided to hold a democratic election to choose the winning proposal. The Staffordshire Sentinel announced the results:

*'477 voting 30 papers being spoiled. The following is the result:*

*Monument at the corner of Dr Crutchley's house and surplus money given to widows etc. 290 votes*

*Monument at corner of Dr Crutchley's House, 83 votes*

*Recreation Ground and monument erected therein, 16 votes*

*Monument in St Mary's churchyard, 9 votes*

*Monument at corner of Lodge Road and Crewe Road with surplus money to widows etc. 3 votes*

*Monument at corner of Church Road and Crewe Road, 0 votes'*

The proposals for the church tower and memorial window were abandoned before the vote was taken. The Monument was finally opened eleven months after the formation of the committee on 19th June 1920, Dr Crutchley having given the land at the rear of his garden at the junction of Sandbach Road and Ashmore's Lane for the memorial. On 13th July 1920 Alsager Urban District Council agreed to maintain the monument and bear the cost of the footpath.

*Site of War Memorial before construction. Photo South Cheshire Archives*

**'The Unveiling and Dedication Service for the Alsager War Memorial'**

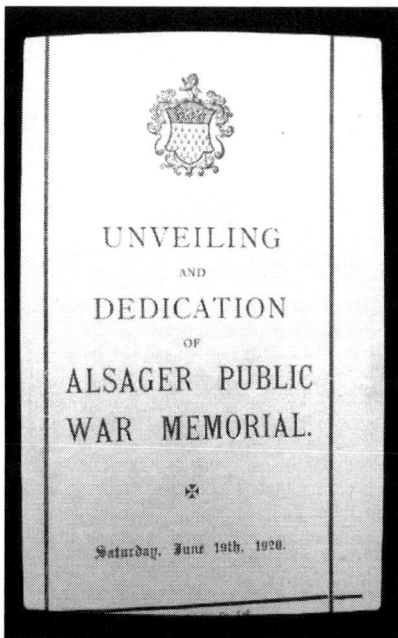

*Front Page of the Unveiling and Dedication Service. Cheshire Archives*

*The unveiling and dedication ceremony and the work of the committee was reported in the Staffordshire Sentinel on June 21st 1920. It is reproduced below.*

**Alsager War Memorial: The Unveiling by the Chairman of the Council. (Sentinel Report)**

*'It is generally admitted that Alsager has not been behind in the desire to perpetuate the memory of those who served and made the supreme sacrifice in the Great War. When the form of the memorial was decided, subscriptions towards the funds flowed in freely with the result Mr Thomas Frederick Owen, Chairman of the Urban District Council and the Memorial Committee, was in a position, before he had completed his first year in office, to announce that the necessary amount had been realised. Mr Owen has been a moving spirit in the scheme from the commencement, and he has been wholeheartedly supported by Members of the Council, Members of the Memorial Committee and the residents in general. The secretarial work was readily undertaken by Mr H.V. Lynham, the council's surveyor, whose organising abilities have been of great service to Alsager during and since the war in connection with various prominent objects. This occasion of the unveiling of the Memorial on Saturday will always stand out as a red letter day in the history of Alsager.*

*By the courtesy of Dr Crutchley the Memorial Committee were able to erect the monument in a prominent position, which has gone by the name of "Dr Crutchley's corner". The Memorial, which has cost over £1000, is composed of three granite bases, the bottom one being 9 ft. square. On the pedestal is statue of a soldier, carved in Windway stone. The figure is perfect in every detail, with full fit, and stands at the "ready" with a rifle and a bayonet. The total height is 17 feet. The monument is protected by wrought iron railings, and presents a noble appearance.'*

On three sides of the monument are carved the names of the following soldiers who fell in the Great War.

Captain M. Settle, Lieuts F.B Mayer, M.F Leek, and J.W Davies, Sec. Lieuts R.G.F Goss, M.J Goss M.C., A.G Hammersley, N.A Pidduck, R.W Settle, W.R.G Holland M.C, and C.R. Waller. Sergt. F. Greenwood, Corpls. S Whittaker and W.A Jackson, Lance Corpls J. Grocott and A. Ellis, Gunner J Higgins, Rifleman F. Riley, Sec Air Mechanics A.T Davies and R. Dickinson, Engineer S.P Jones, Privates F. Glover, R.F.G Hall, W. Wood, S.M Allman, C. Mitford, H.C Dale, W Robinson, F.K Lucas, W. Higgins, R.J Sant, C.H R Savory, T. Cartwright, H. Morris, F.C Challinor, G.H Whipp, W Bostock, P. Nutt, C.S Jackson, H.F Marfleet, and B Mitchell.

The following is also inscribed on the monument:

*"In grateful memory of the Alsager men who fell in the Great War 1914 -1919"*

*"They loved not their lives more unto the death.' -Revelation. Xii, 11"*

(A modern version from the Study Bible of this verse is 'and they did not love their lives so as to shy away from death').

At the rear of the monument is a representation of the Alsager Arms.


**The Service in the Church**

'A procession which was assembled at the council offices was composed of the police, Kidsgrove band, ex-servicemen (in command of Capt. Victor Maddock M.C), VAD nurses, ambulance men, fire brigade, Chairman and Members of the council, Druids, Shepherds, Foresters and the buglers of the Batt. North Staffs Territorial Forces (in command of Sergt. Yates).

Headed by the Kidsgrove band the procession proceeded to the church, part of which had been reserved for the relatives of the fallen. The church was quite full and the service, which was conducted by ministers from the various denominations was exceedingly impressive. After the hymn, *"O God our help in ages past"* and prayers by the Reverend J. P. Davies (Curate of Alsager) the first lesson was read by Mr T. Paxton Barrett. The Hymn, *"Ten thousand times ten thousand"* was rendered, and the second lesson was read by the Vicar (the Rev. A. H. Waller). With great fervour the hymn *"Lead kindly light"* was sung. This was followed by an address by the Rev. A. Farrar,

(President of the local Wesleyan Community from Sandbach) who said he was grateful of the opportunity to associate himself with those of the parish and others in paying tribute to the great services which the fallen heroes had rendered in the Great War. They were ever indebted to those heroes who had fought and had laid down their lives for the British nation and the Allied Powers. He had taken part in such services on several occasions and they had always been visibly impressive. Those fallen soldiers of the parish had now passed into the invisible world and *"Death comes not informal to him who is fit to die"*. These heroes had been fit to die, and they had bartered their lives willingly in the interest of civilisation, humanity and religion. He sympathised very deeply with the relatives of the fallen.

The hymn *"Through the night of doubt and sorrow"* proceeded the prayers and grace by the Vicar, and the procession including the choir, church wardens and clergy slowly and reverently moved out of the church, the hymn *"Onward, Christian Soldiers"* was rendered.'

**The Unveiling Ceremony.**

'On arrival at the memorial a large crowd had gathered and everyone sang the hymn, *"Fight the Good Fight"*.

Alsager Parish Magazine reported Mr Noble, Primitive Methodist Minister, formerly of Alsager and latterly of Audley made the address at the monument. Mr T.F. Owen was unanimously chosen by the Memorial Committee to perform the unveiling ceremony, *'a graceful tribute to the untiring energy and tactfulness displayed by him in the months of strenuous work that had passed since the scheme was launched. A large number of wreaths were placed at the foot of the monument after the sounding of the Last Post.'*

Mr Thomas Frederick Owen, (Chairman of the Council) who then unveiled the memorial, said there were one or two things he would like to mention. It might be out of place, but he would not have another opportunity. It had just been mentioned to him that it was not generally known that after paying for the memorial, the balance would be given to the soldiers' widows and dependents in Alsager. One gentleman had told him that he gave a subscription which was intended for the memorial, not knowing anything about the second object. That gentleman, however, was sending on another cheque for the second deserving object. He did not want anyone to be left out or feel offended because they did not understand this, and the committee were willing to receive further contributions to the second project. It must however be done as quickly as possible as the subscription list would soon close. He would like to thank all those who have assisted in all the numerous ways in providing the memorial so quickly and successfully. Their thanks were also due to the Hon. Secretary, the sculptor, contractor, and last but not least, Dr Crutchley for giving the beautiful site on which they have erected their monument.

Mr Owen said that a singular coincidence had happened with regard to the memorial. The man who had carved the names on the stone was born next door to him and his father had been three times Mayor of Hanley. The man who had carved the figure was also born a few doors away from him (Mr Owen.) Both men were in Mr Owen's class at Sunday school. They had both been in the Army. The Sentinel Report gives the name of the Contractors as Mellors Ltd.

{W & R Mellor Ltd, Masons and Sculptors, were based in Moorland Road, Burslem. They were incorporated in 1894 and dissolved in 1956. The firm also constructed the war memorials in Burslem and Fenton.}

{*By a process of careful elimination it is considered that the sculptor of the soldier on the Alsager War Memorial is Clifford Wallett born in Shelton, Stoke-on-Trent, in 1885.*

*Mr Owen was not technically correct when he had said the man who carved the figure was 'born a few doors away.' The man who lived a few doors away from Owen was Oswald Clifford Wallet born in 1857. His son, Clifford, carved the Alsager War Memorial. Thomas Frederick Owen, a grocer, lived at 96 Quay Street, Manchester with his uncle in 1881 and the Walletts lived at 24 Brunswick Street in Chorlton in 1881. The Wallets moved to Hanley in 1884. Thomas Frederick Owen moved to Hanley in 1888. By coincidence they lived close to each other in Stoke Road, Hanley in 1901. The Owens lived at 51 Stoke Road and the Walletts at 31 Stoke Road. Oswald Henry Clifford Wallett was the manager of Mellors in Burslem. Oswald, who usually called himself Henry died in 1910. His son, Clifford, joined Mellors as a carver. On the 1901 census Clifford is described as a 'stone carver.' In 1911 he was living in Well Street, Hanley, Stoke on Trent, and is described as a 'Stone Carver' in the census. He married Marie Spooner in 1906 and they had two children before his wife died in 1918. Clifford Wallett died in 1943.*

*Clifford Wallet also carved the war memorial in Burslem, Stoke-on-Trent (unveiled in 1921). C. Wallet's name is associated with the Burslem monument and it shares many artistic similarities to the Alsager memorial. Clifford's brother, Harry Wallett, was also part of the business working as a monumental mason.*}

*Clifford Wallett, carver of the war memorials in Alsager and Burslem*

**The Sentinel report continued**. 'Mr Owen said he would proceed to unveil the memorial in grateful memory of the men of Alsager who had given their lived for their country, and had helped to thwart the German in his ambition to rule the world. He recalled the gallant deeds of *"that contemptible little Army"* and how the Allied Powers had crushed the nailed fist of the Huns. He (Mr Owen) thought that the enemy were so beaten that the German Nation would rise no more to terrorize any other nation. He hoped that on all occasions when the inhabitants of Alsager saw that memorial it would remind them of what the Alsager boys had sacrificed for them. Might the inhabitants of Alsager never forget their duty to those who had returned? To those who had lost sons, husbands or relatives he hoped that each time they saw the memorial it would remind those

246

mourning them they, at least in Alsager, appreciated the supreme sacrifice of the fallen. He felt honoured in being asked to unveil the memorial. Many of the heroes were known to him personally and he treasured some beautiful letters he had received from them in France.

Amid deep silence Mr Owen then unveiled the memorial.

*The Betterment of Humanity (sermon by Rev R.C Noble)*

The Rev. R.C. Noble said that during those impressive moments their thoughts were with those who made the supreme sacrifice, and their souls stood still in deep reverence. On occasions like these they found it difficult verbally to express their feelings and their sincere gratitude to those departed souls. They had gathered at that spot to understand the meaning of all the symbols of that monument. When they looked upon that place of sanctuary they understood that the symbols were based on sacrifice. Those who had made that sacrifice stood in the front line of all human history; they had died for truth, freedom, and the upholding of righteousness. Those men had died so that the light of the world should not go out. They had gone forward and died, so that the light should not be extinguished, but should burn ever brighter ..."

The unveiling and service had similarities with current Remembrance Day Services. It included a procession and a speech, but some of the tradition of the Armistice Day service, had yet to be established such as the laying of wreaths of poppies. The poppy emblem was adopted by The Royal British Legion as the symbol for their Poppy Appeal, in aid of those serving in the British Armed Forces, after its formation in 1921. The photograph of the opening service in Alsager shows how displays of lilies were used as a tribute to the fallen. In 1921 laurel wreaths were placed by the memorial. It is noticeable in the 1920 and 1921 photographs there were no men wearing uniforms at the services. After the official speeches relatives and friends of the fallen were invited to come forward to lay wreaths against the monument. The Reveille was played, and the hymn, *'For All the Saints'* sung. After a benediction the procession returned to the Council offices where proceedings ended with the singing of the National Anthem.

*The opening ceremony June 1920. Thomas Frederick Owen, Chairman of the Council, (left of memorial - glasses and white beard.) Crowds gather round the memorial. Photo South Cheshire Archives.*

*Opening Ceremony Saturday June 19th June 1920. Photo: Mr Reg Boffey.*

*The first Armistice Day service was held on November 11th 1921. Photo: South Cheshire Archives*

Alsager War Memorial is registered with the Imperial War Museum (IWM) as an official war memorial (reference 42742)

The official IWM description is as follows: *'Figure of First World War Serviceman in full uniform and puttees carrying rifle and bayonet. Figure surmounts stone column. Column bears names and inscriptions in incised black lettering. Stepped stone base. Metal plaque of town arms on Second World War tablet.'*

## The Wesley Place Methodist Church Great War Memorial

Wesley Place Methodist Church contains a memorial plaque to five church and Sunday School members who were killed in the Great War. The plaque constitutes an official war memorial registered with the Imperial War Museum (IWM reference 42730). It is a wall-mounted brass plaque with a wooden mount. It has black and red incised lettering with an etched border of leaves.

*Photo: Author.*

The inscription reads:

*'Erected to the Glory of God and in grateful memory of the men of this Church and Sunday School who served in the Great War 1914-1918. The following men laid down their lives:*

*Challinor, Frederick Charles*

*Davies, John Wesley*

*Greenwood, Frank*

*Jackson, Walter Amos*

*Savory, Charles Henry Reginald'*

# The War Memorial through the years

Alsager British Legion and the community has honoured the names of the fallen since 1925. It is not the purpose of this book to deal with the Second World War and the names added after that conflict.

A new Standard for the Legion was sponsored by the B'hoys of Alsager in 1928. Alsager British Legion. Its Chairman, Captain Maddox, sought the new standard so it could compete for 'The Haig Trophy,' and to *'cement the existing friendship between the two Societies'*. A very large congregation assembled at St Mary's Church on 6th May 1928 when a dedication for the New Standard was held. The Reveille was played by R. Crinean from Alsager Boy Scouts. The standard was placed in front of the memorial until sunset with a formal guard by the British Legion.

*Mr F. Edwards, Alsager B'hoys Society and Mr Adolphus Goss, President of Alsager British Legion at the 1928 dedication to the new British Legion Standard. Photo: South Cheshire Archives*

The memorial has changed little over the last century, the railings being removed before the Second World War. The names of the dead from the Second World War were added to the monument in

1947 by Mellors Ltd, the same firm who constructed it in 1920. The plaque was dedicated on Armistice Day 11th November 1947.

Also in grateful memory of the Alsager men who gave their lives for their country in the world war 1939 - 1945.
G W BULLOCK
L J HARRIS
P HART
A E MOSELEY
R B MOULTON
C K PARKES
H PIERPOINT
R RIGBY
B SHORTLAND
S C WEDGWOOD
R S WOODCOCK

*The memorial on an old post card.*

## The Remembrance Garden and Henry Harpur

*Henry Percy Harpur and Memorial Garden Plaque*

Dr Crutchley's successor as medical practitioner in Alsager, Dr Henry Percy Harpur, formerly a Captain in the Royal Army Medical Corps, left land for a small remembrance garden adjacent to the war memorial. Harpur was Adolphus Goss' son in law. A plaque next to the garden has the following inscription:

*The memorial has the following inscription: 'This land was given in honoured memory of Henry Percy HARPUR, M.D. Capt. RAMC. There was healing in his hands and humanity in his heart.'* The Gardens are registered with the Imperial War Museum (reference 42741) as a war memorial.

Henry Percy Harpur was born in Strabane, Ireland in 1888 to Mary Ann and William Harpur. His brother William Harpur was born in 1869. James Harpur was born in 1874, and his sister, Frances Marion Harpur was born in 1881. Henry's father was a timber merchant. Henry studied medicine at Dublin University and is recorded on the medical register 1913 as a 'Doctor and Surgeon'. At the outbreak of war Henry enlisted in the Royal Army Medical Corps and gained a commission as 2nd Lieutenant. He was based in France at the 13th General Hospital, Boulogne, and later served on the front line being wounded at the battle of the Somme in July 1916. Henry was promoted to Captain and posted to Jubbulpore, India, where he eventually became Commanding Officer. He was demobilised from the Army in 1919 and took the position as doctor in Alsager following the death of Dr Crutchley. In 1922 Henry married Dorothy Goss and they took up residence in Dr Crutchley's former home, Holmcroft. Henry and Dorothy had one daughter, Doreen. Henry Percy Harpur died in 1956. In the Great War he was awarded the 1914/15 Star, the Victory Medal, and the British War Medal.

# Repair and re-dedication of the Alsager War Memorial

With the hundredth anniversary of the beginning of the Great War approaching, The Alsager War Memorial Trust was formed on 5th September 2011 with the intention of refurbishing the monument to its original condition. It was decided to appeal to individuals, groups, societies and businesses in Alsager for help in raising the funds to restore the Memorial. £3,485 was donated locally through this appeal. In addition a grant of £2,500 was made available from Alsager Town Council. The effort and support by local individuals, organisations, and Town Council was considerable and very much appreciated. This meant that nearly £6,000 was available to go towards the first stage of the restoration. The firm of Conservation Building Services of Oswestry were selected to carry out the refurbishment which they did with considerable skill. In addition The War Memorials Trust agreed the project was eligible for a grant from their Small Grants Scheme. £2,130 was awarded to the project. Part of their description of the conservation work follows:

*'In the past a temporary wooden bayonet had been attached to the rifle using a cement mortar, and was later strapped for support using metal wire, which had subsequently begun to rust. Rust can stain and cause damage to stone so it is important that any ferrous metals which are exposed to the elements are either appropriately maintained and treated or are removed, where appropriate. In this case, as the strapping was a temporary solution it was removed and the bayonet was carefully taken down. All traces of cement were stripped from the surrounding stone and a new, historically accurate bayonet was carved using a stone to match the soldier.'*

A new stainless steel armature was let into the hand and secured using an epoxy resin, then the rifle end was formed around that and the bayonet was attached to the rifle using a screw thread. Finally, the memorial was cleaned using a low pressure steam cleaning system and the sky-facing joints were re-pointed using a lime mortar.

Steam cleaning using a low pressure setting is a gentle yet effective method of cleaning and sterilising stonework. It removes organic growth from the stone without the use of harsh chemicals or abrasive methods. Over-cleaning of stone is one of the most common causes of irreversible damage to war memorials as it involves the incremental erosion of the surface of the stone and wears away detailing and carving and it can cause stones to become friable or crumbly, particularly softer stones such as sandstone. By only cleaning historic stone where absolutely necessary (i.e. if deposits are causing damage to the stone or obscuring the inscriptions), it is possible to preserve the fabric of the memorial and prolong its lifespan so that the war memorials existing today can continue to serve their commemorative purpose for future generations."

*The refurbished War Memorial. Photo: Conservation Building Services Ltd 2014*

On Sunday 3rd August 2014 the War Memorial at Alsager was rededicated at a special service coordinated by The Royal British Legion, Alsager Branch; Alsager Town Council; and The Alsager War Memorial Restoration Trust. There was a short parade at 2.30 pm from Civic Centre Car Park across Lawton Road and along Ashmore's Lane to the memorial. The parade to the memorial was headed by the Parade Commander, Mr Trevor Coleman RBL Alsager, and the Band of 2493 Squadron, Air Training Corps, commanded by Flt. Sgt. Phillip Johnson The ceremony was attended by over 250 people and began with an introduction by Cllr. Mrs Shirley Jones, who explained the contribution and support the town had made to the restoration. She also commended the efforts of many people in Alsager who had contributed so readily to the restoration of the War Memorial. The Rededication and prayers were performed by Rev. Bryan Halson of St Mary's and centenary wreaths were then laid by:

Mrs Joelle Warren, Vice Lord Lieutenant of Cheshire; Cllr Mrs Shirley Jones, Chairman, Alsager Town Council; Cllr Wesley Fitzgerald, Mayor, Cheshire East Council; Cllr Colin Burgess, Chairman, Alsager War Memorial Restoration Trust; and the Chairman, Royal British Legion, Alsager Branch. Relatives and friends of the 'Fallen' and members of community groups in Alsager then placed white Remembrance Crosses in the lawns, each showing the name and service details of the sailor, soldier, or airman listed. The lawns had been earlier transformed into a miniature 'Flanders Field' echoing the famous lines of "...the fields where the poppies blow, between the crosses, row on row, that mark our place". The Last Post was sounded by Jacquie Kilsby of Roberts Bakery Band, followed by 'Silence and Reveille'. A Benediction was given by Rev. Bill Anderson, of Wesley Place Methodist Church in Alsager, followed by the National Anthem. Following the service the parade returned to the Alsager Civic Centre. The rededication was considered 'A most fitting and memorable ceremony' to the Fallen and their sacrifice.

*The refurbished memorial by candlelight, August 2014. Photograph Muriel Dale*

# Conclusion

Over three hundred Alsager men fought in the war. Over 200 joined up from the Alsager district over one weekend in December 1915. By 1918 there were 185 servicemen on the Absent Voters list and 38 in the supplemental list making 223 men. In 1919 this reduced to 208 men. By 1920 only 19 men were in the services. But all these figures do not include the number of men born in the town who had moved away and were no longer on the electoral roll.

The Great War caused many personal tragedies. 42 men from the Great War are named on the War Memorial. Another 13 with a significant connection with Alsager were also killed. Many lives were prematurely cut short by the wounds they received. Some recorded in this book suffered mental illness. Women served at home and in France, and many took over men's work but lost their jobs in 1918. Some women won the right to vote, but when many women left the farms, factories, nursing and military service they could not find comparable work. Women were displaced from jobs they had filled when men went off to fight. The war brought great dislocation to families with many families moving away so they could make a new start. Some parents of dead servicemen such as William Robinson and Sarah Ellen Goss died prematurely and Ellen Pidduck never recovered from the loss of her son.

Farms took a long time to recover from the war. Many of the leading families lost sons and to some extent the end of the war lessened the class distinctions in the town. Despite this, the Alsager War Memorial Committee dedicated the names on the War Memorial in order of military rank. In many towns and villages names on the war memorials were given in alphabetical order. (After the Second World War the dead were not recorded in order of military rank on the Alsager memorial.)

Most significantly the war drained vast quantities of wealth out of the town. Alsager families bought £75,000 in war bonds. (Value in 2015 = £3,844,221. Source: Bank of England inflation calculator) A post Great War Labour politician wrote of the 1917 War Loan *"No foreign conqueror could have devised a more complete robbery and enslavement of the British Nation"*. Interest was initially paid at 5% but was slashed to 3.5%. High post war inflation reduced the value of the interest paid on the bonds. In the 1930s the government stopped paying back the capital amount of the loan, re-paying only interest of 3.5%. The value of war bonds was significantly reduced by inflation. Broadberry and Howlett estimate that between 11% (including human capital) and 14.9% of wealth (excluding human capital) was lost in Britain during the Great War. In Britain unemployment was a major problem after the war due to the large loss of life and wounded soldiers, who were now unable to work due to their extensive injuries or psychological disorders such as shell shock or insomnia. In June 1921 a crisis figure was reached as 2 million people were now unemployed, this now effected the British people dramatically, the pressure on the British people increased with the depression in 1920, resulting in unemployment remaining at 10 percent or more of the workforce for two decades. The British Government finally repaid its war bond loans in 2015.

Looking at the 1939 Register (the census substitute of that year) many of the servicemen who originated from Alsager moved away, mostly to the Potteries but some further afield. Some families remained in the town, but many soldiers continued to serve in the army, such as the Goss brothers, Vernon and Dick, who moved away, as did Lieutenant Maddock and the Ellis brothers.

Administratively the Great War did not change Alsager. The powers used by central government during the Great War - rent control, food rationing, nationalization of strategic industries - were discontinued after it. The Alsager Urban District Council did not lose its administrative responsibilities until 1973. It carried on in much the same way as before after 1918. The *'land fit for heroes'* as Lloyd George promised Britain in 1918, didn't materialise nationally except the large-scale building of council houses with the Housing Act of 1919 and unemployment insurance in 1920. Alsager did not build any council houses which may be one reason why some returning soldiers moved to towns where new council houses were being provided. There were no new schools in Alsager for another twenty years after the Great War. At the eve of the Second World War very little had changed in the town. Its organisations; the Institute, its social clubs, and its churches continued to flourish. Some citizens such as Dorothy and Ethel Goss recognised the needs of ex-servicemen and began to help them through their charitable work. The Alsager Royal British Legion was one of the first branches to form in Cheshire in 1925 with Adolphus Goss becoming its first President.

It was only with the Second World War and the building of Radway Green munitions factory that Alsager was forced to adapt to a rapidly rising population and changing circumstances.

The people of Alsager worked hard and gave a great deal for the Great War effort. They did not forget the sacrifice. In 1938 the parish magazine records there were up to 1000 people in St Mary's church for the Armistice service. The preacher was the Vicar of Tunstall, Rev. S.S. Linsley. The vicar, Rev. C. Potts wrote of Linsley. He is *'a man with a definite and fearless message, which compels attention and makes people think'*. Linsley's message was one the congregation would have endorsed, **'Most of us believe that our soldiers saved our honour and independence, and their memory lives with us for what they did and the spirit in which they served.'**

Little did Rev. Linsley know that within a year Britain would be at war again and the people would be called on to make personal and financial sacrifices once more.

*Alsager War Memorial. A dramatic picture by Steve Wallace 2015*

# The Royal British Legion, Alsager Branch

The Alsager Branch has commemorated its war dead and served its members, ex-service personnel, and raised funds for the Poppy Appeal since 1922.

*Royal British Legion Dinner, St Mary's Church Hall c.1950. The guests were veterans from both World Wars. Picture: South Cheshire Archives*

*1955. George Cummings retiring Standard Bearer Royal British Legion, Alsager Branch. He served from 1927 to 1955. Picture: South Cheshire Archives.*

The Alsager Branch of the British Legion continues to serve Alsager and its servicemen and women past, present, and future.

It has commemorated the hundredth anniversary of the death of every man on the Alsager War Memorial

Four commemorations one hundred years to the day of their deaths for Alsager Servicemen at Alsager War Memorial by the Alsager Branch of the Royal British Legion, Civic representatives, and citizens.

Photos: Alison Blaney

# Index

Index of names, publications, map, and organisations

# Medals awarded in the Great War 1914-19 awarded to Men and Women whose biographies appear in this book

## 1914 Star (or Mons Star)

This bronze medal award was authorized by King George V in April 1917 for those who had served in France or Belgium between 5th August 1914 to midnight on 22nd November 1914 inclusive.

## 1914/1915 Star

This bronze medal was authorized in 1918. It is very similar to the 1914 Star but it was issued to a much wider range of recipients. Broadly speaking it was awarded to all who served in any theatre of war against Germany between 5th August 1914 and 31st December 1915, except those eligible for the 1914 Star. Similarly, those who received the Africa General Service Medal or the Sudan 1910 Medal were not eligible for the award.

Like the 1914 Star, the 1914-15 Star was not awarded alone. The recipient had to have received the British War Medal and the Victory Medal. The reverse is plain with the recipient's service number, rank, name and unit impressed on it.

## British War Medal

The silver or bronze medal was awarded to officers and men of the British and Imperial Forces who either entered a theatre of war or entered service overseas between 5th August 1914 and 11th November 1918 inclusive. This was later extended to services in Russia, Siberia and some other areas in 1919 and 1920.

## Victory Medal

It was decided that each of the allies should each issue their own bronze victory medal with a similar design, similar equivalent wording and identical ribbon. The British medal was designed by W. McMillan. The front depicts a winged classical figure representing victory.

Territorial Force                                    War Medal

Only members of the Territorial Force and Territorial Force Nursing Service were only eligible for this medal. They had to have been a member of the Territorial Force on or before 30th September 1914 and to have served in an operational theatre of war outside the United Kingdom between 5th August 1914 and 11th November 1918. An individual who was eligible to receive the 1914 Star or 1914/15 Star could not receive the Territorial War Medal.

## The Silver War Badge

The badge was issued on 12th September 1916. The badge was originally issued to officers and men who were discharged or retired from the military forces as a result of sickness or injury caused by their war service. After April 1918 the eligibility as amended to include civilians serving with the Royal Army Medical Corps, female nurses, and staff and aid workers.

Around the rim of the badge was inscribed *"For King and Empire; Services Rendered"*. It became known for this reason also as the *"Services Rendered Badge"*. Each badge was also engraved with a unique number on the reverse, although this number is not related to the recipient's Service Number.

The recipient would also receive a certificate with the badge. The badge was made of Sterling silver and was intended to be worn on the right breast of a recipient's civilian clothing. It could not be worn on a military uniform.

The Mercantile Marine War Medal established 1919

The Board of Trade awarded this campaign medal, the Mercantile Marine War Medal, to people who had served in the Merchant Navy and who had made a voyage through a war zone or danger zone during the 1914-1918 war.

# Gallantry Awards

### The Military Cross

The Military Cross was a decoration for gallantry during active operations in the presence of the enemy for **individuals in the British Army, the Indian Army or the Colonial Forces.** Commissioned officers with the rank of Captain or below or Warrant Officer were eligible for the award. From June 1917 officers of the rank of captain but who had a temporary rank of major could receive the award. From August 1916 an individual could receive one or more Bars to the Military Cross. Recipients of the medal are entitled to use the letters M.C. after their name.

### The Military Medal

Instituted on 25$^{th}$ March 1916 (and backdated to 1914). The Military Medal was awarded to other ranks of the British Army and Commonwealth Forces. It was an award for gallantry and devotion to duty when under fire in battle on land. On the reverse of the medal is inscribed *'For Bravery in the Field'*. Recipients of the medal are entitled to use the letters M.M. after their name.

### Distinguished Service Order (D.S.O.)

The D.S.O. was

The D.S.O. was Army and was, however, The D.S.O. distinguished presence of the equivalent rank Force.

instituted by Royal Warrant on 6$^{th}$ September 1886.

originally instituted as an award for officers of the British Commonwealth Forces, usually at the rank of Major. It also awarded to officers at a rank above or below Major. could be awarded for an act of meritorious or service in wartime and usually when under fire or in the enemy. It was also made available for officers at the in the Royal Navy and, from 1$^{st}$ April 1918, the Royal Air

## Mentioned in Despatches (M.I.D)

*"Mentioned in Despatches"* is not an award of a medal, but as a commendation of an act of gallantry it is included in this listing. To be *"Mentioned in Despatches"* is when individuals are mentioned by name and commended for having carried out noteworthy act of gallantry or service. A Despatch is an official report written by the senior commander of an army in the field. It would give details of the conduct of the military operations being carried out. A bronze oak leaf was issued and could be worn on the ribbon of the British Victory Medal.

Croix de Guerre (France)

The Croix de Guerre may either be awarded as an individual or unit award to those soldiers who distinguish themselves by acts of heroism involving combat with the enemy. The medal is awarded to those who have been *"Mentioned in Despatches"*, meaning a heroic deed or deeds were performed meriting a citation from an individual's headquarters unit. The unit award of the Croix de Guerre with palm was issued to military units whose members performed heroic deeds in combat and were subsequently recognized by headquarters.

Médaille Militaire (France)

Awarded for bravery. The Médaille Militaire was awarded in reasonably large numbers to allied forces including British service men and women in the 1914-18 War.

The Memorial Plaque - to those who died in the war

It was issued to next of kin. The relative named as the *"next of kin"* in a serviceman's Service Record was sent a form to complete as a statement to confirm all the living next of kin of that serviceman and the person to whom the plaque and scroll should be sent. From 1919 and for several years after the end of the Great War there were over 1,000,000 plaques and scrolls sent to next of kin in commemoration of their soldiers, sailors, airmen and 600 women who died as a direct consequence attributable to service in the Great War. All those who died between 4th August 1914 and 30th April 1919 whilst in military service in the battlegrounds of the theatres of war and in the Dominions. It included death as a result of sickness, suicide or accidents in the Home Establishments, or as a result of wounds incurred during their time in military. (This plaque commemorates William Fletcher Portsmore, Worcestershire Rgt. Great Uncle of the author.)

HE whom this scroll commemorates was numbered among those who, at the call of King and Country, left all that was dear to them, endured hardness, faced danger, and finally passed out of the sight of men by the path of duty and self-sacrifice, giving up their own lives that others might live in freedom. Let those who come after see to it that his name be not forgotten.

The Memorial Scroll (which was sent to next of kin with the bronze plaque.)

In October 1917 it was announced in *The Times* newspaper that it had decided also to issue a commemorative scroll to the next of kin in addition to the bronze plaque. The scroll would be printed on high quality paper, size 11 x 7 inches (27cm x 17cm). The name of the person commemorated was inscribed at the bottom of the scroll.

# Acknowledgements

The following were principal sources for this book to which the author acknowledges:

*Alsager Parish Magazine* 1888-1928

*Alsager, its Place and its People*, Alsager History Research Group, 1999, ISBN 0953636305

Cheshire Archives, Chester.

*The Alsager Collection*: South Cheshire Family History Centre, Crewe.

Stoke-on-Trent Archives -*Staffordshire Sentinel* and *Weekly Sentinel*

Commonwealth War Graves Commission.

British Electoral Registers, the National Archives.

The British Library: National Newspaper Collection, Boston Spa

The Imperial War Museum, *War Papers of Harold Augustine Thomas and photographic collection*

England & Wales, National Probate Calendar (Index of Wills and Administrations), 1858-1966.

National Archives: for British Army Service Records, Women's Army Auxiliary Corps Index, 1917-1920, British Army WWI Medal

Rolls Index Cards, 1914-1920. British Army Regimental Archives.

UK, De Ruvigny's Roll of Honour, 1914-1919

*Police Gazette*

National Army Museum: UK, *Army Registers of Soldiers' Effects, 1901-1929*

*William Henry Goss* by Lynda & Nicholas Pyne

British Census 1881, 1891, 1901, 1911.

*London Gazette 1914-21*

Mr Mark Mills- Lt Norman Pidduck's Great Nephew

Susan Webb, Jesus College Cambridge, re. Charles Raymond Waller.

Mr Alec Shaw

*London Illustrated News* 1915

'*A Lack of Offensive Spirit?': The 46th (North Midland) Division at Gommecourt 1st July 1916* Alan MacDonald. Iona Books 2008

Brown and Hopkins 1955: *Seven Centuries of Building Wages, Economica, Vol 22*

Mike Turnock & Elaine Heathcote re: Lance Sergeant Charles William Yorke

Mrs Lucy Edwards re The Ellis family.

*Weekly Sentinel,* 1912-1921

The Census, 1880, 1891, 1901, 1911.

International Red Cross Archives, internet.

*The Economics of World War I* Cambridge University Press 2005 edited by Stephen Broadberry, Mark Harrison. ISBN 978-0-521-8512-8

*Jottings of Alsager, by* Mabel Wilson, self-published 1973

23307396R00151

Printed in Great Britain
by Amazon